Papers on Indian Writing In English

Papers on Indian Writing In English

Second Revised and Enlarged Edition

VOLUME 1 : POETRY

A.N. DWIVEDI

ATLANTIC

PUBLISHERS & DISTRIBUTORS (P) LTD

Published by
ATLANTIC
PUBLISHERS & DISTRIBUTORS (P) LTD
7/22, Ansari Road, Darya Ganj, New Delhi-110002
Phones : +91-11-40775252, 40775214, 23273880, 23275880
Fax: +91-11-23285873
Web: www.atlanticbooks.com
E-mail: orders@atlanticbooks.com

First Edition: 1991
Second Edition: 2001

Printed & bound in India by Atlantic Print Services

PREFACE TO THE SECOND EDITION

I feel immense pleasure in bringing out the second revised edition of this book for the benefit of readers and researchers. The book has been out of print/circulation for quite some time. The affectionate persuasion of the present publishers compelled me to re-issue the book. I thank Dr. K.R. Gupta for this.

A.N. DWIVEDI

PREFACE TO THE FIRST EDITION

I have been keenly interested in Indian Writing in English for the last two decades, and the present volume on Indian-English Poetry is a direct offshoot of this unflagging interest of mine. I have collected and put together here some twenty papers of mine which were earlier published in various Indian and foreign journals or in different books and anthologies. These various sources of original publication of my papers have been acknowledged at the very beginning of each published paper (in footnotes), and wherever such acknowledgements do not occur it should be presumed that the papers were not published earlier and that they are now being published for the first time. In fact, I have written a few more papers on Indian-English Poetry, but they have been deliberately left out and only those papers have been included in this volume which are supposed to be representative and worthwhile.

A.N. DWIVEDI

CONTENTS

1

Indian Poetry in English

I

A BACKWARD GLANCE

Indian-English poetry (call it 'Indo-Anglian' or 'Indo-English' poetry) made its beginnings under adverse circumstances and passed through a chequered career. It came into being at a time when Britishers ruled supreme in India, and initially thrived in the hands of such poets as Henry Derozio (half-Indian and half-Portuguese), Kasiprasad Ghose, the distinguished members of the Dutt family, Toru Dutt and her elder sister Aru Dutt. Derozio, who is rightly called 'the National Bard of Modern India' gave us *The Fakir of Jungheera and Other Poems* (1823), which describes the fluctuating fate of the Brahmin widow named Naleeni and is full of Byronic echoes. Fortunately, the Oxford University Press of New Delhi has recently brought out a beautiful edition of Derozio's selected poems, paying thereby a befitting tribute to this master of poetic craft. After Derozio, Kasiprasad Ghose kept the torch of Indo-Anglian poetry burning by publishing *The Shair, or Minstrel* of about 200 pages in 1830. Although Ghose wrote a number of poems on Indian festivals, he seems to have largely worked under the impact of Sir Walter Scott. That's why Prof. Dunn has branded his verse as "agreeably imitative and everywhere pleasing."[1] In the second quarter of the 19th century, the talented members of the Dutt family — Gooroo Churn Dutt, Raj Narain Dutt, Michael Madhusudan Dutt, and Shoshee Chunder Dutt — composed verses of varying length and quality. But for Madhusudan Dutt (born 1824) who produced a long metrical romance in English, *The Captive Ladie* (1849), recounting the love-adventures of Prithvi Raj Chauhan and Sanyogita, others in the Dutt family as mentioned above are not so notable. Even Madhusudan is remembered today more for his Bengali epic entitled *Meghnad-Badh Kavya* than for his English romance. Besides, Hur Chunder Dutt with his two volumes of verse — *Fugitive Pieces* and *Lotus Leaves* — made a notable contribution, though he can't be rated very high amongst the Indo-English poets.

The Dutt family once again impressed the poetry — reading public by bringing out *The Dutt Family Album* in London (1870), which contained 66 poems by Govin Chunder Dutt, 73 poems by Omesh Chunder Dutt, 47 poems by Greece Chunder Dutt, and barely 11 poems by Hur Chunder Dutt. Due credit must be given to Govin Chunder Dutt, the illustrious father of Toru Dutt, to have introduced an introspective vein and style in poetry, as may be seen in his poems "Romance" and "Wordsworth." Most of Govin's poems tend to be didactic in tone and religious (specifically Christian) in temper. The *Album* should be valued as a remarkable reflection on the ideal situation prevailing in the Dutt family for literary exercises, — the kind of situation that impelled Toru Dutt and Aru Dutt to indulge in a feverish literary activity of a certain standard (considered in the light of what had been written till then). Govin was a renowned poet and linguist, having produced two volumes of poetry entitled *The Loyal Hours* (1876) and *Cherry Stones* (1881); and Toru's mother had ably translated *The Blood of Jesus* into Bengali.

Of the two daughters, the elder one — Aru Dutt — has given us very little, just eight poems in all collected in Toru's *A Sheaf Gleaned in French Fields* (1876), but whatever little she has produced is full of pathos and taste. The noted English critic, Sir Edmund Gosse, felt a sense of "surprise and almost rapture"[2] when he first read her rendering of Victor Hugo's poem "Morning Serenade," For a novice in poetry, Aru may serve as a stepping-stone to her more profound and better equipped younger sister, Toru Dutt (1856-1877), whose work and worth are of lasting nature. Toru has written only one volume of original poetry culled *in Ancient Ballads and Legends of Hindustan* (1882), but this work alone is enough to give us a peep into the classical Indian tradition full of religious fervour and philosophical speculations. This work also demonstrates her deep love for the Motherland, its folklores and legends, its ancient tales of high moral and spiritual character. Her "Savitri" is simply superb both as a legend and as a piece of artistic creation. Coupled with this, Toru has also produced *A Sheaf* (a work of translations from the French poets), *Bianca, or The Young Spanish Maiden* (a fragmentary novel in English, 1878), and *Le Jounal de Mademoiselle d'Arvers* (a complete novel in French, 1879), in addition to a series of letters written to her British friend, Miss Mary Martin, and to the French authoress, Mme. Clarisse Bader.

Unlike Aru and Toru, Romesh Chunder Dutt lived a life full and whole, and produced, besides his historical treatises in prose, his remarkable verse-renderings of the two great Indian epics, the *Ramayana* and the *Mahabharata*, which are truly a triumph of condensation and, in Prof. Iyengar's words, "the best introductions in English to our great national epics."[3] Romesh is invariably convincing in his creative job. Nobo Kissen Ghose popularly known as Ram Sharma, was a sincere soul of great convictions. But he sometimes misdirected his energies by writing commemoration and topical verses which can't be claimed to be poetry pure and genuine. The authentic poet is actually revealed in such sustained pieces as *Willow Drops* (1873-74), *The Last Day* (1886), and *Shiva Ratri*, *Bhagaboti Gita*, and *Miscellaneous Poems* (1903). As a dream fantasy, *The Last Day* is a remarkable achievement. *Shiva Ratri* is conceived as an Indian Vanity Fair; it has a rich pictorial quality. *Bhagaboti Gita* is perhaps his best poem, its theme being Bhagaboti, the Eternal She, the 'home-of-all, womb-of-all Ram.' Sharma has used blank verse in imitation of Milton, but his real artistry is seen in the wielding of the ballad measure as in "Daksha Yagna." In this ballad the story of Daksha's defeat at the hands of Shiva is effectively recounted. Although extravagant claims have been made for Nobo Kissen, the truth remains that he is a poet of the middle order.

Rabindranath Tagore, primarily a Bengali writer, has come to occupy a significant position in Indo-Anglian poetry. Apart from the English versions he made of his poems and plays, he wrote in English *The Child*, which is an impressionistic description of the pilgrimage of men and women of all kinds to the hypothetical Shrine of Fulfilment. His prose works too — notably *Sadhana*,

Nationalism, *Personality*, *The Religion of Man*, etc. — were originally written in English, for they were meant for an international public. His *Gitanjali* (1913), a prose poem, compelled world-wide attention, and he was now recognised as a poet not of Bengal's only, but of India's and the world's. This great laureate of renascent India comes before us in diverse facets — the poet, the story-teller, the novelist, the philosopher, the educationist, and the prophet of enlightened humanism.

Manmohan and Sri Aurobindo received their education in England. Oscar Wilde was deeply impressed by Manmohan's poems, and wrote in the *Fall Mall Gazette* in this manner : 'Mr. Ghose ought some day to make a name in our literature.' In collaboration with Arthur Cripps, Laurence Binyon and Stephen Phillips, Manmohan published in 1890 a volume of verses entitled *Primavers*. *Ghose's Love Songs and Elegies* was released in 1898, and his *Songs of Love and Death* in 1926 (two years after his death). The latter is a work of enduring quality. His poetic sequences entitled *Immortal Eve* and *Orphic Mysteries* unquestionably irradiate the true pathos and sublimity of pure poetry. Manmohan has been rightly called by George Sampson 'the most remarkable of Indian poets who wrote in English.' And the same authority further remarks that a reader of Manmohan's poems "would readily take them as the work of an English poet trained in the classical tradition."[4] As a true poet, Manmohan has sufficient time and patience to stand and stare, to feel the heart-throb of birds and beasts, trees and flowers.

Manmohan's younger brother, Sri Aurobindo, passed the Civil Services examination, turned it down, taught for a while at the Baroda College, gravitated towards politics, and was, eventually, drawn to the discipline of *Yoga*. He was a master of many languages — Greek, Latin, French, English, German, Italian; Sanskrit and Bengali —, and in due course became a veritable Pilgrim of Eternity, a *Mahapurusa*, a *Mahayogi*. The Aurobindo Ashram founded at Pondicherry has now become a centre of pilgrimage for those interested in meditation and *Yoga*. Sri Aurobindo is fairly known today as a poet and as a critic of life and letters. The two sumptuous volumes of his *Collected Poems and Plays* give us the best of what he wrote before 1942. As a translator and narrative poet, as a metrical and verbal craftsman, as a lyricist and dramatist, as a daring experimenter and explorer in the field of literature, and as a 'futurist' poet with a meaningful utterance, Sri Aurobindo has a record of poetic achievement without a parallel in our day. *Urvasie* and *Love and Death* are his beautifully articulated narrative poems, while *Baji Prabhou* is a first-rate poem of action; *Persues, the Deliverer* is a blank verse drama which is striking in its setting and prophetic in its appeal; "Thought the Paraclete" and "The Rose of God" are among the finest mystical poems in the English language. Sri Aurobindo has also successfully employed classical quantitative meters to his own purpose and accomplished new harmonies in the use of the much maligned hexameter in his long poems like *Ahana* and *Ilion*. His *Savitri* has created a new land of epic poetry. He wrote prose works of sparkling simplicity and winning naturalness — *The Life Divine*, *Essays on the Gita*, *The Synthesis of Yoga*, *The Social Cycle*, *The Ideal of Human Unity*, and *The Future Poetry*. His shorter prose treatises are : *The Mother, Heraclitus,* and *The Renaissance in India*. Sublimity is the hallmark of Sri Aurobindo's work, and he has been aptly called the Milton of India.

Other poets active during this period were : Swami Vivekananda, Malabari, J.M. Tagore, A.M. Kunte, Brajendranath Seal, D.L. Roy, N.W. Pai, Nizamut Jung, Peroze P. Meherjee, Ardeshir M. Modi and Ezekiel Cohen. The literary activities of these poets contributed much towards the diversification of Indo-Anglian poetry.

Like Sri Aurobindo, Sarojini Naidu too started as a poet, but later drifted to politics, playing a stellar role in the Gandhian era. Her poetic style is modelled on the lines of 'Decadent' poets. She tenaciously pursued it to her last, and her poems are replete with "jewelled phrases."[5] The introduction of Indian themes provided a new vitality to her poetry. The publication of the first collection of her *poems The Golden Threshold* (1905), by M/s William Heinemann made her famous in the whole of the English-speaking world. The succeeding volumes, *The Bird of Time* (1912) and *The Broken Wing* (1917), considerably consolidated her position as a poet. Sarojini's marvellous mastery over verse forms enabled her to compose such flawless lyrics as "To a Buddha Seated on a Lotus" and "The Flute-Player of Brindavan." In 1961, her unpublished poems were collected by her daughter Miss Padmaja Naidu, and published by M/s Asia Publishing House under the heading *The Feather of the Dawn*. In all the four volumes by Sarojini Naidu we witness her unerring sense of beauty and melody. Her poems present a feast of delight to the reader. As a true lyricist, she always spoke in a 'private voice' and never bothered to express the burning problems of her day. But she is an artist of the first rank, and on the strength of her perfect rhythm and verbal felicity she has come to occupy a place near Toru Dutt, R.N. Tagore and Sri Aurobindo in the realm of Indo-Anglian poetry.

Sarojini's younger brother, Harindranath Chattopadhyaya (1898-1990), is as well known to the poetic world as his sister, though George Sampson completely ignored him in his book, *The Concise Cambridge History of English Literature.* Harindra has been a constant devotee to the Muse, and has written some brilliant pieces of poetry. He is popularly known everywhere for his varied interest and public service. Many of his poems are marked both by a devotional note similar to the one expressed in the Vaishnava lyrics and a Vedantic awareness of God's omnipresence. Despite his belief in the Marxist ideology, Harindra has remained "an idealist and a seeker of spiritual truth"[6] in his poetry. Among his published works are : *The Feast of Youth* (1918), *The Coloured Garden* (1919), *Perfume of Earth* (1922), *Collected Poems and Plays* (1927), *Five Plays* (1937), *The Dark Well* (1939), *Lyrics* (1944), *Blood of Stones* (1944), *The Son of Adam* (1946), *A Treasury of Poems* (1948), *The Divine Vagabond* (1950), *Kannappan or The Hunter of Kalahasti* (1950), *Spring in Winter* (1955), *Siddhartha: Man of Peace* (1956), *Masks and Farewells* (1961), *Virgins and Vineyards* (1967), etc. Though Harindra is not a great poet, he is a fascinating poetic personality. Some of his poems will be read for their force, clarity and message in the times to come.

II

THE CONTEMPORARY SCENE

Of all Indo-English poets of today, Nissim Ezekiel and P. Lal enjoy immense historical significance by virtue of their unflinching devotion to the Muse and their unstinted support to a number of young versifiers. While both produced a fine body of poetry on varying themes and moods, P. Lal became very active to champion the cause of contemporary Indo-English verse and launched almost a cultural crusade against the age-old taboos and doubts being associated with it. Lal's matchless enthusiasm is reflected in the founding of the Writers' Workshop at Calcutta in 1959 which has promoted a number of emerging talents by publishing their works free of charge. Ezekiel has been a source of inspiration to many young practitioners of English verse in India by setting up a salutary example of his disciplined art before them.

Nissim Ezekiel (born 1924), who is now a retired Professor of English, has been prescribed in many Indian universities. He has seven volumes of verse to his credit, which are : *A Time to Change* (1952), *Sixty Poems* (1953), *The Third* (1959), *The Unfinished Man* (1960), *The Exact Name* (1965), *Hymns in Darkness* (1976), and *Latter-Day Psalms* ('82). He is one of the most widely circulated and anthologized poets of India writing in English today. His plays brought out by the Writers Workshop indicate that he is not so successful in drama as in poetry. As a poet, he is aware of his cultural milieu and native (that is, Indian) problems. His sharp sensibility enables him to grapple with the situations around him, without nostalgically recalling his stay in England or dreaming of a foreign land (in this quite a contrast to Shiv K. Kumar, another Indo-English poet of established stature). He gives careful thought to his ideas, medium of expression and form of words and phrases, and does not attempt to depict what is gaudy and inane and mere adolescent. In him the reflective and philosophical strains are predominant.

P. Lal (born 1929), an accomplished craftsman in Indo-English verse, is well-read in modem English and American poetry and Sanskrit classics. Like Dom Moraes, his sensibility remains largely romantic, though he is strongly opposed to romantic excesses. Whatever poetry he could produce, he produced it only in the sixties, — *The Parrot's Death* (1960), *Love's the first and Other Poems* (1963), *'Change', They Said* (1966), *Draupadi and Jayadratha* (1967), and *Calcutta : A Long Poem*. Thereafter, he turned to verse translations or 'transcreations' (as he calls them), and in this context his vigorous and laudable job of rendering the *Mahabharata* in ten years must be mentioned. As a poet, Lal shuns propaganda and sticks precisely to the concise phrase and concrete imagery, as may be seen in his poem, "The Simplest Love."

Next to these stalwarts of Indo-English verse comes Dom Moraes (born 1938) with his extraordinary power of perception and expression. Educated at Oxford and having worked initially under the influence of Eliot, Auden, and Spender, he has emerged as the most successful of the 'new' poets with a number of his volumes — *A Beginning* (1957), *Poems* (1960), *John Nobody* (1965), and *Selected Poems* : 1955-65. His autobiography, *My Son's Father*, contains flashes of self-revelation. He won the Hawthorndon Prize for poetry. Moraes whose sensibility is essentially romantic is a subjective and confessional poet. But he tries to turn the personal into the universal, as in "Letter to My Mother":

> Your eyes are like mine
> When I last looked in them
> I saw my whole country
> A defeated dream
> Hiding itself in prayers
> A population of corpses...............

Some of his well-known poems are : "This Island" (in 4 parts), "The Prophet", "Kanheri Caves", "Being Married", "A Man Dreaming", etc. What appeals to the reader most is Moraes' perfect mastery over the medium, his dazzling artistry, and his sweeping rhythm ('the flow of lines,' as he terms it).

Another poet of repute is A.K. Ramanujan (1929-1993), whose four volumes published by the Oxford University Press has earned recognition of his merits and talent, — the four volumes being *The Striders* (1966), *Relations* (1971), *Second Sight* (1986), and *The Black Hen* (1995). He is also known to the literary world as a translator of the famous *vachanas* from Kannada and some of the love lyrics from the *Kurunthohai*, a classical Tamil anthology. A Professor of Linguistics and Dravidian Studies at the University of Chicago, Ramanujan handles his medium with a sure touch of an unerring craftsman devoted to glowing images and surcharged diction. The family serves as a "central metaphor"[7] to him. His favourite themes are : Indian men, women and their manners, family and relatives, love and life and death, and cultural conflicts. As a poet of love, he is warm and intimate, and his images are conveyed through memorable phrases and sensuous images, as in the following :

Flames have only lungs. Water is all eyes.
The earth has bone for muscle. And the air
Is a flock of invisible Pigeons.
But anxiety can find no metaphor to end it.

Through chiselled phrases and striking metaphors the poet has achieved the maximum success here. Ramanujan has the ability to build a whole rhythmic poem out of a trifling incident, and "The Striders" is a glaring example of it. We only hope that there is more in store to come from him in the near future to show that his poetic springs have not yet gone dry.

Deb Kumar Das is another established poet who worked for a while under the impact of T.S. Eliot, but who has now emerged as an artist deserving our consideration. His well-known poetical collections are : *The Night Before Us* (1960), *Through a Glass Darkly* (1965), *The Winterbird Wakes, The Eyes of Autumn*, *The Labyrinths* and *The Fire Canto.* Das is competent enough to offer a cosmopolitan flavour to his 'Knotted verse' and this has earned laurels for him in the West. He has also displayed his capability, like A.K. Ramanujan, to translate in verse the *Isa Upanishad.*

Pritish Nandy also enjoys considerable fame as a fiery practitioner of English verse, with an intention to give it a fresh mould and direction as an innovator. His is an irrepressible voice with verve and vigour that has emerged during the sixties and the seventies. He appears before us as a poet, a playwright, a translator, an executive (in an advertising firm at Calcutta), and an anthologist. Gauri Deshpande rightly remarks that Nandy is "innovative and profuse."[8] Amongst his published works are : *Of Gods and Olives* (1967), *On Either Side of Arrogance* (1968), *I Hand You in Turn My Nebbuk Wreath* (1968), *From the Outer Bank of the Brahmaputra* (1970), *Madness is the Second Stroke* (1971), *The Poetry of Pritish Nandy* (1973), *Dhritarashtra Downtown : Zero* (1974), *Riding the Midnight River* (1975), *Lonesome Street* (1975), *In Secret Anarchy* (1976), *A Stranger Called I* (1976), *Tonight This Savage Rite* (1977; again this title appeared in 1979 in collaboration with Kamala Das), *An Anthology of Modern Indian Love Poetry* (1979), etc. His poetry rings changes on a variety of themes and moods. There are a fairly large number of poems on Love and Romance in his volumes. Poems like "In Transit, Mind Seeks" and "Parts of

Fragmented Autobiography" are unconventional in content and treatment. He has written a number of prose poems like Thakur Rabindranath Tagore, and poems like "What shall we do with these memories," "Calcutta if you must exile me," "Beyond that rock is the silent sea," and "She wandered among the ruins" are highly experimental and original in vein and style. Occasionally, Nandy can write verses charged with passion, pulse and power, as in the following from "Wild horses rage in your tresses" :

> Wild horses rage in your tresses on this savage
>   night of desire when primal fire breaks
>   through your loins
> descend the dark mountain of sorrow tonight
>   let a black rain of stars bathe in your
>   limbs in blood
> wild virgin of death teach me the fury of the night
>   teach me to bleed and not feel pain teach me
>   to suffer the anguish of words
> and when the rivers of passion flow into your breast
>   let me discover the tender gold of your flesh
>   let me wander in a field of discreet memories
> let a black rain of stars bathe your limbs in blood
>   tonight.

This passage is to be marked for its sweepy rhythm and sensuous, even impetuous, imagery. It is on such passage that the poet Nandy's fame will rest for ever.

The seventies in particular has given us a number of talented poets whose works have added honour and prestige to Indo-English poetry, — the poets like Shiv K. Kumar, R. Parthasarathy, and K.N. Daruwalla. Of these, Prof. Kumar, a distinguished academic poet, has published to date six volumes of verse — *Articulate Silences* (1970), *Cobwebs in the Sun* (1974), *Subterfuges* (1976), *Woodpeckers* (1980), etc. Though he writes on a variety of subjects, he is more known as a poet of love and sex and of sex poised against the tabooed, traditional religion/morality than for any other theme. The irony is his *forte*, which sometimes becomes devastating and consuming; he does not spare even himself, as is clear in "Broken Columns," an autobiographical piece indeed. His work smacks of the academic atmosphere of the University and abounds in learned tricks and scholarly allusions. But Daruwalla, like Arun Kolatkar, is made up of a different fibre altogether, and breathes in the air of freshness and originality by taking resort to the open countryside landscapes and natural surroundings. His poetical collections are : *Under Orion* (1970), *Apparition in April* (1971), *Crossing of River* (1976), and *Winter Poems* (1980), and *The Keeper of the Dead* (1983). He has also brought out a collection of short stories, *Sword & Sickle* (Vikas, I979), and an anthology of Indo-English verse[9] (1980) written during the last two decades. And of the three poets mentioned here, R. Parthasarathy appears to be very fastidious and disciplined in his art. His diction tends to be chaste and tense, and his style austere and exacting. *His Rough Passage* (1977) came out after a long silence. Strangely enough, this poet decided to withdraw his *The First Step : Poems* 1956-66 (1967) after making an appearance in the poetic world, and his edited work, *Poetry from Leeds* (the place where he had gone for a Language course and training), contained none of his own poems. The book is divided into three parts, and forms the poet's "autobiography"[10] in verse. It is a compact piece of artistry replete with marble-images of integrity and observation. Parthasarathy is a conscientious poet, who aims at economy of phrases and concreteness of images. He was once the Regional Manager of the Oxford University Press, New Delhi. His anthology, *Ten Twentieth-Century Indian Poets* (1977, rpt. 1979), has been on the syllabi of many Indian universities, but the truth is that it is not only ill-titled but also a little misleading in its representation of Indo-English poets.[11] And from the poet we expect some more gems of English poetry in the near future so that he may claim for himself a place beside the immortal ones.

There are, then, two poets drawn from the world of journalism : Keshav Malik and Rakshat Puri. Admittedly, both are poets of some stature and repute. Malik is definitely the better one, with four volumes of verse to his credit — *The Lake Surface* (1959), *Rippled Shadows* (1960), *More Poems*, and *Storm Warning* (1979). Earlier he used to edit the now-defunct literary weekly, *Thought*, from New Delhi, and also *Indian Literature*, a bi-monthly journal of the Sahitya Akademi. Besides being a poet, he is also a translator, a short story writer, and an art-critic. His poems reveal a fine artistic taste and a sure touch. They move in the world of love and romance rather than in the world of harsh reality. At a later stage, the world of romance disappears, and he is seen probing into the mysteries of life and death. He is a widely travelled poet, and the experiences gained from his travels abroad get reflected in his verse. To his verses Malik often lends an "organic" touch.[12] His poems in *The Lake Surface* are cast in glowing images and symbols, whereas those in *More Poems* are mostly short and lyrical. It is but a fitting tribute to his genius that the noted English critic, David Daiches, described his poetry as representing 'a notable achievement' in English. The second poet under our discussion here, R. Puri, who has by now released at least three volumes of verse — *Poems* (1969), *The Year Like a Fuse & Other Poems* (1971), and *Nineteen Poems* (1972), betrays the impact of Eliot and Pound on his works. He seems to be crying out against the dehumanized and devitalized nature of modern man in a tone of dejection and disillusionment :

> This stretch of misshapen time
> At the morgue received its sudden
> Stop in a celebration of laughter
> And screams as picnickers passed
> On a charabanc of rolling dreams.

His agonised sensibility demonstrates that Puri is a poet of our times who is concerned about the modern man and his pressing problems.

Of all the Indian poets, perhaps, Syed Amanuddin has suffered worst due to critics' negligence and indifference. That's why he does not like to be called an "Indo-Anglian."[13] As a poet, Amanuddin has displayed a wonderful talent engaged in creativity in the fields of both poetry and drama, and he must be reckoned with as the poet of first order by virtue of his voluminous work and qualitative art. Amongst his published poetical works are : *The Forbidden Fruit* (1967), *Tiffin State Hospital* (1970), *Shoes of Tradition* (1970), *The Children of Hiroshima* (1970), *Poems of Protest* (1972), *Lightning & Love* (1973), *The Age of Female Eunuchs* (1974), *Adventures of Atman* (1977), *Gems and Germs* (1978), and *Challenger Poems* (1988). The Two plays written by him are : *System Shaker* (1972) and *The King Who Sold His Wife* (1978). He has had a wide experience of editing various creative journals in the United States, where he is busy doing his teaching-*cum*-research assignments.[14]

A few poets are there carrying forward the Aurobindonian torch. Of these poets, mention may be made of Krishna Srinivas, K.V.S. Murti, K.R.S. Iyengar, and Deb Kumar Das. Even V.K. Gokak and R.R. Menon come under this category. They are alike in their mystical and metaphysical leanings, and their primary concern is with Eternity. The works of these poets and those of many others — J.P. Das, Jayanta Mahapatra, Gieve Patel, Adil Jussawalla, K.D. Katrak, Arun Kolatkar, Subhas Saha, Pranab Bandyopadhyay, O.P. Bhatnagar, Syed Ameeruddin, Sukanta Chaudhuri, S. Santhi, P.S. Sastri, Subhas Kak, etc. — have gone a long way in establishing Indo-English poetry on a sound footing and in according it long-awaited and much-needed dimension and dignity. Although the works of these poets are quite varied in nature and merit, they cumulatively tend to establish the truth of fecundity of imagination and diversity of perception while living physically or mentally in this extraordinarily picturesque land of ours.

Besides, many 'new voices' are also heard these days, promising a better climate for the growth and expansion of this brand of English verse in the days to come. Some of these 'new voices' have already been anthologized by poets like Pranab Bandyopadhyay, Syed Ameeruddin, and O.P. Bhatnagar[15] and their separate collections of verse, like the one by Saleem Peradina and the one stipulated by this writer himself,[16] are likely to create ripples in the tense, hurried academic and poetic world of today on their appearance. And if we can't be very optimistic about the prevailing state of Indo-English poetry because of certain negative forces at work in it — *viz.*, regionalism, groupism, parochialism, etc., there is nothing to feel shy or gloomy of it in the face of the validity of our work being carried forward under adverse circumstances until the day dawns when good sense will prevail and these negative forces will be destroyed completely. And without being self-defeatists in the noble cause of the Muse, we must wage a relentless and heroic struggle against these forces to emerge on a scene of sunshine and success.

One of the remarkable developments of Indian poetry in English being composed today is the upsurge of a number of perceptive and talented women poets. As a matter of fact, women writers were almost always present on the literary scene of India right from the Vedic and Upanishadic days, and the present age appears to be no exception. In the 19th century, we had Aru Dutt and Toru Dutt who composed their rhythmical and rhymed verses in English, and in the early 20th century there was Sarojini Naidu who sang her mellifluous songs of high lyricism and emotionalism, earning thereby the prized title of 'the Nightingale of India.' The post-Independence scenario presents a richer and more fertile crop of Indian women poets, who through their wonderful creations have carved an abiding niche in the temple of the Muse. Amongst such women poets, Kamala Das stands out for her sweep of lines and great urgency of poetic purpose. Her poems like "An Introduction" and "Composition" throw light on her poetic mode and perception, and in them as elsewhere too she becomes quite witty and frankly confessional, recalling the practice of such great women writers of our age as Sylvia Plath, Anne Sexton and Judith Wright. Besides her, Gauri Deshpande, Monika Varma, Lila Ray, Margaret Chatterjee, etc. have made substantial contributions to the growth and diversification of Indian-English poetry. Others who have shown a certain amount of promise and talent are : Gauri Pant, Suniti Namjoshi, Lalita Venkateswarn, Anna Sujatha Modayil, Lakshmi Kannan, Vimala Rao, Malathi Rao, Meena Alexander, and Eunice de Souza. Taken as a whole, the works of these women poets and a few more though do not display a wide range and variety of experience as to be witnessed in their male counterparts, they still have succeeded in voicing in their own tender way the hopes, fears and aspirations of the feminine world, which is so charmingly built up with the rainbow colours of their sweet dreams and soaring visions. They may not be having the same national and political consciousness as some of the male poets of our nation, but they do show greater courage and determination in tackling certain outstanding social issues related to them (Such as dowry evil and bride-burning). Moreover, they are better equipped to deal with children and their delicate psychology as well as with their own burning problems. We come across a peculiarly delicate feminine sensibility in the works of these women poets.

III

LOOKING FORWARD

A short yet succinct account of the origin, growth and expansion of Indian poetry in English from its very beginning to this day (as seen in the first two parts of this paper) convinces us that the future of this brand of poetry is not so bleak and dismal as coloured by some West-trained academics. If we accept the premise that there exists a variety of English known as 'Indian English,' then we should also accept the fact that this variety of English is sure to flourish in diverse forms — fiction, prose, poetry, and drama, and that it shall flourish in the same manner as many other regional languages and literatures. By according recognition to English, the framers of our Constitution have shown an appreciable farsightedness and insight, and no efforts of the detractors of English toward demolishing it completely and throwing it out of the country are ever likely to succeed, — nor even the political outcry and outrage against it. The main reason is that it has now acquired an international status and recognition, and its worthwhileness in global matters can't be ruled out. One should rather adopt a realistic approach in this matter, and the reality of the situation is that Indian literature in English is as much an integral part of our common heritage as the literature being written in several regional languages today. As regards Indian-English poetry it stands on a firmer ground today than ever before. In this context, we might aptly quote the distinguished English critic, William Walsh, who pointedly remarked that the 'highest achievement' of Indo-Anglian authors was in fiction, in the work of Mulk Raj Anand, R.K. Narayan, and Raja Rao, but that the future, the promise, lay in poetry, in the work of Nissim Ezekiel, A.K. Ramanujan and R. Parthasarathy.[17] It is definitely a miscalculation to say that the sun of Indian-English literature will set around 2000 A.D. (as Uma Parmeswaran pronounced in her work[18]). It would be rather more plausible to think in terms of its continual growth and enrichment with all its Indian touch and taste in the days to follow. The distinguished Indo-English poet, A.K. Ramanujan, was once asked by an interviewer in New Delhi as to what his reactions were to the mushroom growth of some 300 poets in Indian English and his characteristic reply sounded a good deal of optimism. He simply said, 'I wish good luck to all of them,' and further added that '300 is not an awesome number.' Our Nobel Laureate, Thakur Rabindranath Tagore, was also equally optimistic about Indian literature in English. Speaking of Bengal's response through literature to the call of the West (which gave us a powerful medium of expression), Tagore remarked thus : "It has a future for it is quickened with life, and it carries within itself a hope that one day it will become a great channel for communication of ideas between the adventurous West and the East of the immemorial tranquillity."[19] I think, it is high time for us Indians to rise to the occasion and fulfil the prophecy of Tagore. But our poets must now learn to concentrate on their own feelings and thoughts, images and symbols, and on Indian themes and landscapes, and they should not try to imitate the West ape-like and to get their creative energies dried up in the process. The onerous task of a literary critic starts at this juncture, and he should not hasten to patronise or encourage a poet unduly, particularly a third-rater (and there is no dearth of him in India, alas!), until he is fully convinced about his merits. But if he really discovers a genuine poet, he should not feel diffident about him. By pursuing such a course, he will unquestionably be brightening the future of Indian poetry in English and putting it on a high pedestal.

NOTES & REFERENCES

1. T.O.D. Dunn, *The Bengali Writers of English Verse* (Bombay : Longmans, Green & Co., 1918), p. 5
2. As recorded by Gosse in *The Examiner*, dated 26th August 1876.
3. K.R. Srinivasa Iyengar, "Indian Writing in English," *Contemporary Indian Literature*, 2nd ed. (New Delhi : Sahitya Akademy, 1959), p. 40.
4. George Sampson, *The Concise Cambridge History of English Literature*, EL.BS ed. (London : Cambridge University Press, 1961), p. 914.
5. V.K. Gokak, "Introduction", *The Golden Treasury of Indo-Anglian Poetry* (New Delhi : Sahitya Akademy, 1970), p. xx.
6. P.C. Kotoky, *Indo-English Poetry* (Gauthati : Gauhati University, 1969), p. 57.
7. R. Parthasarathy, ed. *Ten Twentieth-Century Indian Poets* (New Delhi : O.U.P., 1979), p. 95.
8. Gauri Deshpande, *An Anthology of Indo-English Poetry* (Delhi : Hind Pocket Books, n. d.), p. 14.

9. Its title is *Two Decades of Indian Poetry* : 1960-1980 (New Delhi : Vikas Publishing House, 1980), which seems to me a misnomer, as it does not include any poetry from writers of other languages in India and also excludes a number of well-known Indo-English poets like Pritish Nandy, P. Lal and Keshav Malik.
10. See this author's review in *The Reviews Journal*, No. 2 (Dec. 1980, published from the Flinders University of South Australia), p. 31.
11. This should have included a few more poets to avoid the impression of having been edited for the Bombaywallahs only.
12. Manohar Bandyopadhyay, "The Poetry of Keshav Malik," *The Journal of Indian Writing in English*, 2, No. 1 (Jan.1974), p. 59.
13. Syed Amanuddin, "Don't Call Me Indo-Anglian", *Indian Verse*, 2 (1977), n.p.
14. Those interested in him should see my article on him in this very volume.
15. Pranab Bandyopadhyay has edited *Indian Verse by Young Poets* (Calcutta, 1980), Syed Ameeruddin *New Voices in Indo-English Verse* (Madras, 1981) and O.P. Bhatnagar *New Dimensions in Indian Poetry in English* (Amravati, 1981).
16. The work of Saleem Peeradina is *The First Offence* (Bombay,1980), and the project of this writer is titled *Random Reflections* (Delhi, 1994).
17. William Walah, "Introduction," *Readings in Commonwealth Literature* (Oxford : At the Clarendon Press, 1973), p. xviii.
18. See her "Introduction," *Some Representative Indo-English Novelists* (New Delhi : Vikas Publishing House, 1976), p. 6.
19. Look up the closing sentence of Tagore's "Foreword," *The Bengali Writers of English Verse*, by Dunn (1918).

2

The Poetry of Aru Dutt

Aru Dutt, the elder sister of Toru Dutt, has been a victim of Destiny as well as of proud Oblivion's curse. The long and irresistible hands of Destiny snatched her away at an early age, leaving behind her parents and sister totally depressed and broken. And coupled with this is the fate of her literary work that still remains mostly unknown and unrecognised. It is really a matter of pity that she has not been accorded her due place in a consideration of the merits and attainments of Indo-English poets.[1]

Born in 1854 in the cultured Dutt family of Rambagan (Calcutta), Aru, like her younger sister, received her education and training under the supervision of her poet-*cum*-linguist father. She inherited the poetic talent from her parents, — Govin Chunder Dutt had contributed a lion's share to *The Dutt Family Album* (1870) and written two books of verse entitled *The Loyal Hours* (1876) and *Cherry Stones* (1881), and Kshetramoni, the mother, had a refined sensibility and had rendered *The Blood of Jesus* from English into Bengali. In 1862, the family embraced Christianity. Aru was a meek and fragile child, as noted down by her father. After describing the physical appearance of his only son, Abju—'Almost a man in seeming, yet a child', Govin wrote :

> My next, the beauty of our home, is meek;
> Not so deep-loving haply, but less wild
> Than her dear brother; brow and blushing cheek
> Her nature shows serene, and pure, and mild
> As evening's early star......

After the untimely death of Abju in 1865, the sisters began to read *Paradise Lost* repeatedly for consolation. In 1869, when the family reached Europe, Aru and Toru attended a French school at Nice for a short while. From France they went to London, where they started translating French poems into English verse. In 1871, the family moved to Cambridge, where the two girls attended the so-called Higher Lectures for Women, and where they made a lasting friendship with Miss Mary Martin. In 1873, the entire Dutt family returned to Calcutta after a period of four years. Now the sisters plunged, in the words of Edmund Gosse, into "a feverish dream of intellectual effort and imaginative production."[2] But the literary strain proved fatal for the young girls; and Aru succumbed to consumption on July 23, 1874, at the tender age of twenty. On her death Toru wrote to Miss Martin : "The Lord has taken Aru from us. It is a sore trial for us, but his will be done. We know He doeth all things for our good....."[3] Mr. Govin was so grievously disturbed at her death that he wanted to go back to England and settle down there for good.

It won't be irrelevant here to recall Mr. Govin's Prefatory Memoir to the second edition of *A Sheaf Gleaned in French Fields* wherein he puts his two daughters side by side and remarks about their skill, nature and behaviour :

> In the performance of all domestic duties, Aru and Toru were exemplary. No work was too mean for them. Excellent players on the piano were they both, and sweet singers with clear contralto voices, which I still fancy I hear at times. Toru had read more, probably also, thought more, and the elder sister generally appeared to follow the lead of the younger; so that I have often been asked by strangers which of the two is Miss Dutt? And yet there was no assumption of superiority on the part of Toru. It seemed perfectly natural to Aru to fall in the background in the presence of her sister. The love between them was always perfect....
>
> Not the least remarkable trait of Toru's mind was her wonderful memory. She could repeat almost every piece she translated by heart, and wherever there was a hitch, it was only necessary to repeat a line of the translation to put an end to it, and draw

> out of her lips the whole original poem in its entireness. I have already said, she read much; she read rapidly too, but she never slurred over a difficulty when she was reading. Dictionaries, lexicons, and encyclopaedias of all kinds were consulted until it was solved, and a note taken afterwards; the consequence was that explanations of hard words and phrases imprinted themselves, as it were, in her brain, and whenever we had a dispute about the signification of any expression or sentence in Sanskrit, or French, or German, in seven or eight cases out of ten, she would prove to be right............
>
> The great ambition of the sisters was to publish a novel anonymously, which Toru should write, and Aru who was far more deft at the pencil should illustrate. Toru's part of the contract has been faithfully fulfilled. I have before me her manuscript. It is in the form of a diary written in French by a young lady. The scene is laid in France, and the characters are all French men and women. I shall publish it probably hereafter. Aru did not live to complete her part of the undertaking.[4]

The novel referred to is *Le Journal*. This long quotation is full up with remorseful remarks of a bereaved father (the Memoir was written after the death of daughters), and throws sufficient light on the conduct and talent of Aru and Toru. It may be mentioned here that Aru was a good painter.

Now to come to Aru's poetical contribution. At the close of eight poems in *A Sheaf Gleaned in French Fields*, we meet the initial 'A'. This 'A' stands for Aru Dutt, whose name is as inseparably mingled with that of Toru Dutt as the name of Coleridge with that of Wordsworth in the production of the *Lyrical Ballads*. The comparison is quite pertinent, for as in the *Lyrical Ballads* Coleridge's quota of work gave its unique character and success, so also in the *Sheaf* Aru's work gave its pungent taste and striking success. In the words of a scholar, her work rather "outshines that of her younger sister,"[5] though personally I don't agree with this view. Despite the fact that her work has a remarkable lyrical quality, Aru plays a second fiddle to her sister in the poetic venture and stands on a low pedestal in points of quantity and fecund imagination.

The eight poems that Aru translated for the *Sheaf* are : (1) "The Young Captive," (2) "The Emigration of Pleasure," (3) "Romance of Nina," (4) "Morning Serenade," (5) "Chanson," (6) "My Village," (7) "The Mother's Birthday" and (8) "The Captive to the Swallows." Her work is undoubtedly meagre, but it merits attention. We might even guess that she could have written some lasting verses, had not she died so early. She was gifted like her sister, though in no way more.

Aru's contribution to the *Sheaf* opens with "The Young Captive," which is translated from Andre Chenier's "Le Jeune Captive." Toru's notes inform us that the heroine of this well-known poem was the beautiful Aimee de Coigny, le Duchess de Fleury. Very deftly Aru conveys the longing and lingering look at life of the Duchess, who, like her poet, is a victim of the French Revolution. The first stanza of the poem runs thus :

> The budding shoot ripens unharmed by the scythe,
> Without fear of the press, on vine-branches lithe,
> Through spring-tide the green clusters bloom.
> Is't strange, then, that I in my life's morning hour
> Though troubles like clouds of the dark present lower,
> Half-frighted shrink back from my doom?[6]

The note of pathos should be marked here. It reaches the climax in the last but one stanza :

> A prisoner myself broken-hearted and crushed,
> From my heart to my lips all my sympathies rushed,
> And my lyre from its slubbers awoke;
> At these sorrow, these wishes, of a captive, I heard,
> And to rhyme and to measure I married each word
> As softly and simply she spoke. (p. 5)

Aru appear to have kept perhaps more closely to the original than Toru often did[7], but the former has hardly left sufficient work behind her to warrant a very decided opinion in this matter.

The next poem by Aru, "The Emigration of Pleasure," highlights the sorrows of France at the time of war with European enemies.

Pleasure is personified here, as may be gathered from the first stanza :

> Affrighted by the ills that war
> Had drawn upon unhappy France,
> Pleasure sought in regions far,
> Encouragement and countenance.
> Through Germany and Spain to pass
> Was weary work for miles and miles,
> The Spaniard never jokes, alas!
> And the German never smiles. (p. 8)

All the five stanzas of the poem are steeped in misery and helplessness.

The poem "Romance of Nina" is of shorter length, but it was highly welcomed when it appeared. It is so beautifully rendered into English that it deserves full quotation :

> When back the well-loved shall return
> To her who pines though once so dear,
> The Spring from its abundant turn
> Shall scatter blossoms far and near.
> I watch, I wait : — in vain, in vain,
> The loved and lost comes not again.
>
> Ye birds far sweeter shall ye sing
> When ye shall catch his tender tone:
> Then haste the well-loved back to bring,
> I'll teach ye songs of love alone.
> I watch, I wait; — in vain, in vain,
> The loved and lost comes not again.
>
> O echo whose repose I mar
> With my regrets and mournful cries;
> He comes, — I hear his voice afar,
> Or is it thine that thus replies?
> Peace! hark he calls! in vain, in vain,
> The loved and lost comes not again. (p. 23)

The beloved's piercing cry can be heard through the poem. She is totally disappointed at the disappearance of someone 'loved and lost.' Her stung heart springs its sorrows almost in every line and in every phrase. This poem and "Morning Serenade" are Aru's masterpieces. The diction in them is couched in musicality and simplicity. We can hardly think of any better translations.

The pathetic note we come across in "Romance of Nina" is also to be witnessed in "Morning Serenade" which was the first poem to be opened and read by Sir Edmund Gosse when the *Sheaf* was thrust into his unwilling hands by Prof. Minto. The poem filled the noted English critic with a sense of 'surprise and almost rapture.' He, however, wrongly attributed the piece to Toru Dutt, — a mistake which was first discovered by Mr. E. J. Thompson. The poem abounds in beauty and craftsmanship to arrest the attention of the reader, and it would be a pleasure to read it in full here :

Still barred the doors! — The far east glows,
The morning wind blows fresh and free,
Should not the hour that wakes the rose
Awaken also thee?

No longer sleep,
Oh, listen now!
I wait and weep,
But where art thou?[8]

All look for thee, Love, Light and Song,
Light, in the sky deep red above,
Song, in the lark of pinion strong,
And in my heart, true Love.

No longer sleep,
Oh, listen now!
I wait and weep,
But where art thou?

Apart we miss our nature's goal,
Why strive to cheat our destinies?
Was not my love made for the soul?
Thy beauty for mine eyes?

No longer sleep,
Oh, listen now!
I wait and sleep,
But where art thou? (p. 30)

Aru's rendering has reached a high-watermark here. The lyrical power is displayed at its best. The repetitive burden is really heart-touching. It is no wonder that the renowned English critic remarked on it as follows : "When poetry is as good as this it does not much matter whether Reuvevre prints it upon Whatman paper, or whether it steals to light in blurred type from some press in Bhowanipore."[9] The poem, as it is, stands supreme and matchless in the whole of the *Sheaf.*

The three poems that follow — "Chanson", "My Village", and "The Mother's Birthday" are not of so high order. Of these, "Chanson" — is full of romantic longings and loveful dreams. It is taken from Victor Hugo. "My Village" brings before us an exile, also the speaker, who wants to die in the land of his birth :

An exile from my earliest prime
Benumbed and chilled with cold,
I long to warm myself again,
Beside the hearth of old.
Arise each day — my native land,
In memory's longing eye!
In thee began my course of life,
In thee I wish to die. (p. 41)

The original poet of this piece is Gensoul. The poem "The Mother's Birthday" celebrates the birthday of 'Mamma' out of deep love for her. It is picked up from an anonymous author, and is found, as Toru informs us,[10] together with "My Village," in a little book entitled *Nos Souvenirs*. The last few lines from "the Mother's Birthday" are given here to evoke a favourable response from the reader :

O! what is there so good or precious
As a gentle mother's love!
On this earth, the only treasure
Sent us from the heavens above. (p. 42)

Taken together, all the three poems have a swift movement of lines and a lucidity of expression, — the qualities for which Aru will be long remembered.

And last comes "The Captive to the Swallows," a famous song of Beranger. The theme of the poem is the captivity of a soldier who has nobody else to talk to and hence welcomes the swallows from afar, from France probably. He speculates that some of them might have been born upon the roof beneath whose shade he first beheld the light of morn. He asks them to inform him about his loved country and dear people :

> 'Speak of them all, the loved, the lost,
> My sister, is she married now?
> And have they e'er your wanderings crost
> That were my playmates long ago?
> Of all the friends that came of yore
> With me, to win a soldier's praise,
> How many have beheld once more
> The cherished scenes of earlier days? (p. 44)

This is the last but one stanza of the poem.

Taking all Aru's poems together, it may be inferred that pathetic scenes and romantic yearnings, imprisonments and frustrations, caught her sensitive mind as readily as perhaps the fire catches the fuel. Whatever she rendered became aglow with her intense feelings. In her renderings she shows a wonderful command of the English and French languages and of the varied verse forms. Her movement is always smooth and her rhythm always sure. It is true that her work is very slight, but she has made her name immortal as a poet and as a translator in the annals of English poetry written by Indians.

Compared with Toru's work, Aru's is less original, less powerful and less varied, but at the same time it is equally lyrical and charged with emotion. In reviewing Aru's character one is reminded of the powerful pen-picture of Charlotte Bronte which tells us about the marked difference in the character of her two sisters — Anne and Emily. We are told that Anne's character was milder and more subdued; she lacked the power, the fire, the originality of her sister, but was well endowed with her own quiet virtues. Aru, like Anne, was more reticent and reserved than her younger sister. It is likely that in the sudden upsurge of one's emotional enthusiasm for Toru Dutt one loses sight of her elder sister, but it won't be proper in view of the sterling quality of her work. Like Toru, she was also a true child of Romanticism. This becomes quite clear when one takes into account her themes of poetry. She was always at the beck and call of whatever was touched with the pathos of the far-away, of the by-gone scenes, of reminiscences or farewell, of laments of exile and dirges for the dead.

Finally, to the concluding sonnet of the *Sheaf* called "A mon Pere" Toru attached this note : "The writer of these pages has only to add here that the pieces signed A are by her dear and only sister Aru ... Had she lived, this book with her help might have been better, and the writer might perhaps have had less reason to be ashamed of it, and less occasion to ask for the reader's indulgence."[11] But that was not to be; and Aru leaves us guessing at what she 'might have been' had she lived longer.

NOTES

1. Even the pioneer critic Dr. K.R. Srinivasa Iyengar's book, *Indian Writing in English* (2nd ed., 1973), does little justice to Aru Dutt. This might be due to the fact that she has left behind no independent work of her own. But we feel that she deserves a better treatment than that meted out to her.
2. Edmund Gosse, "Introductory Memoir," *Ancient Ballads and Legends of Hindustan* (London : Kegan Paul & Co., 1882), p. xiii.
3. See Mr. Harihar Das's *The Life and Letters of Toru Dutt* (London : Oxford University Press, 1921), p. 65.
4. Govin Chunder Dutt, "Prefatory Memoir," *A Sheaf Gleaned in French Fields* (Bhowanipore : The Saptahik Sambad Press, 1878), pp. ix-xi.
5. Kalipada Mukherjee, "Aru Dutt and Her Work," *The Calcutta Review*, XLIII (April-June 1932), 197.
6. *A Sheaf*, p. 3. All textual quotations that follow in this article are taken from the 1878 edition.
7. Harinder Das, *The Life and Letters of Toru Dutt*, p. 303.
8. The French original of the first stanza of this poem is given here for those interested in comparison :

    L'aube nit et ta porte est close!
    Ma belle, pourquoi sommeiller?
    A l'heure ou s'eveille la rose
    Ne vas-tu pas te reveiller?

        O ma charmante,
        Ecoute ici
        L'amant qui chante
        Et pleure aussi!

9. Gosse, "Introductory; Memoir," *Ancient Ballads*, p. x.
10. Toru Dutt, "Notes," *A Shead*, p. 242.
11. *Ibid.*, pp. 286-7.

3

Toru Dutt and Her Poetry*

I

Toru Dutt was an extraordinarily gifted girl, but beauty and tragedy, sunshine and darkness, crisscrossed her life. Like gold tested by fire, Toru kept shining in her work even in the midst of adversity. This "fleeting visitant"[1] to our sphere attained that excellence in poetic art which is hard to be attained even in a full lifetime. It is not till we come to her that we find "the first solid achievement"[2] in Indo-Anglian poetry, and with her we find that Indo-Anglian poetry has taken a long leap forward.

Born in a Hindu family in Rambagan, Calcutta, on March 4, 1856, Toru Dutt was brought up by her father, Govin Chunder Dutt, a good linguist and cultured man. In those days, the Dutt family had distinguished itself in the whole of Bengal for its creative activities. Toru's mother, a woman of sweet temperament, was well-versed in Indian myths and legends.

In 1862, some members of the family, including Govin Chunder, were drawn to the Gospel of Christ. However, the conversion to Christianity caused a temporary estrangement between Toru's parents.

The first calamity that befell the family was the death of Toru's only brother, Abju, aged 14, in 1865. In 1869, the family left for Europe, where Toru along with her elder sister, Aru, learned French and English. According to Margaret Macnicol, Toru's knowledge of these languages was "astonishing."[3] At Cambridge, where she was studying, Toru made a life-long friendship with Mary Martin.

---

*Reprinted with permission of the editor of *WLWE* (Nov. 1975), pp. 278-290.

In September 1873, the family returned to Calcutta. On July 23, 1874, Toru's loving sister died of consumption. The tragedy at home made Toru lonely and gloomy. In 1875, she with her father started studying Sanskrit, and within a year acquired a comfortable knowledge of it. By 1877, Toru's health had run down because of recurrent attacks of fever, cough-spasm and blood-spitting. As a result, she breathed her last on August 30, 1877, leaving her parents totally deserted and depressed. She was buried at the C.M.S. Cemetery in Calcutta, near her dear brother and sister.

II

Toru Dutt produced a small body of poetry in her brief career.[4] But her meagre poetic output is the real gem. It has enabled Toru Dutt to carve out for herself a permanent place on the Indo-Anglian poetic mount.

However, the recognition of Toru's poetic genius did not come off readily. When the *Sheaf* was completed, no publisher in Calcutta was prepared to bring it out. But when it was published and reached England and fell into the hands of Edmund Gosse, Toru's fame immediately shot up. Gosse sympathetically reviewed it in *The Examiner*, dated August 26, 1876. Opening it at random and reading Aru's rendering of Victor Hugo's "Morning Serenade" (for there were a few pieces in it by Aru too), he was filled with delight to see poetry as good as that. But he was quick to point out certain shortcomings of Toru's writing. In August 1879, a reviewer in *The Saturday Review* wrote that there was every reason to believe that in intellectual power Toru was one of the most remarkable women that ever lived. Edmund Gosse received Toru Dutt with great enthusiasm in his introductory memoir to *Ancient Ballads*. After lamenting Toru's untimely death, he said, "When the history of literature of our country comes to be written, there is sure to be a page in it dedicated to this fragile, exotic blossom of songs."[5] Another noted critic, Dunn, thought that Toru was the first of her sex to interpret the soul of India to the West, and as such she "struck a genuinely Indian note that reveals the sincerity of a mind proud of the intellectual traditions of its native land."[6] In a scholarly article published in the *Asiatic Review*, Harihar Das spoke highly of the "classical tradition" in Toru Dutt's poetry.[7] Amaranatha Jha, in his edition of *Ancient Ballads*, thoughtfully speculated about the poetess and wrote, "One cannot help regretting that time cut short prematurely a career of such promise and such fulfilment. There were few poetic glories which, given maturity, she could not have achieved .... She might have developed into a novelist or a writer of lyrics breathing grace and sweetness."[8] Another critic, K.R. Srinivasa Iyengar, says that Toru "has left behind her a body of achievement to which it will be difficult to find a parallel in the history of English literature."[9] Paying his glowing tributes to Toru Dutt, Alokeranjan Dasgupta has observed : "She was the first of our modern artists who have transmuted the nervous tension of adolescence into the saner idiom of art."[10]

III

A Sheaf Gleaned in French Fields was the only work which Toru Dutt could see published in her lifetime. Of the 165 pieces in this volume, 8 were by Aru, but the title-page carried only Toru's name, and this perhaps caused Gosse to attribute even Aru's pieces to her sister. The volume consisted of some two hundred pages, and carried no Preface or Introduction. It was dedicated to Madame Govin Chunder Dutt and was sold out very soon. In May 1878, Toru's father brought out a second edition, which was prefaced by a memoir written by himself. This was followed in 1880 by a third edition published in England by Kegan Paul & Co. Since then the volume has never been re-issued.

Broadly speaking, the *Sheaf* is a haphazard collection of translations from the French poets. Toru has carefully avoided the Classicists and chosen the Romantic and Parnassian poets. But earlier poets have not been entirely ignored. In fact, Toru starts as early as the l6th century with du Bartas and du Bellay. Evan many others of the 19th century, who cannot be associated with either of the aforesaid schools, are not omitted. But the truth remains that the Romanticists — Hugo, Soulary, and de Gramont — are the basis of the volume. There are nearly seventy-five poets represented herein, many of whom are not known to the average English reader of French literature.

What strikes a reader in this volume is its wealth and variety. Toru ably handled the apparatus of translation, and successfully showed that the translator is also the creator. Dasgupta holds "it was Toru, the first of major Indian writers, who proved that the translation is not an isolated phenomenon but an index of personality meaningful in its relatedness with greater heritage, cultural and literary. She gave a status to translation."[11] Her translation is at once exact and free, and recaptures the spirit of the original to the maximum extent. Toru, however, did not hesitate to give a twist or twang to the original whenever necessary, and this makes her translation readable and pleasant. Sometimes words, phrases and sentences in the original are rejected and substituted by new ones, such as in her rendering of Beranger's "My Vocation."

There are some delightful and moving English lyrics in the *Sheaf.* The following excerpt from Hugo's "Lines" aptly shows Toru's sensitiveness to English tones :

> Methinks, Remorse
> Hath such a cry, and such a force —
> Wail mothers thus for children gone.

Similarly, her rendering of Hugo's "The Rose and the Tomb" reveals the vigour and the beauty of her work :

> The tomb said to the rose, —
> Of the tears the night strows,
> What makest thou, O flower of the dawning?

Here the metre is as near to the original as possible.

It is noteworthy that the metre in the *Sheaf* as a whole is "smooth and suggestive of no labour or toil in its making."[12] This may be clearly seen in Berat's "My Normandy" and Peyrat's "Roland," the latter being in a form not easy to sustain evenly for a hundred lines.

In her translations Toru also tried her hand at blank verse, though not very successfully. In a note to a piece by Louise Bouilhet she recorded that she had not hesitated to render the piece in blank verse.[13] The use of blank verse is to be found in "The Death of the Wolf" (as also in *Ancient Ballads*). Her lines are all end-stopped.

It appears that Toru was inclined to the sonnet-form. This is evident in some forty sonnets among her translations. Harihar Das speaks of Toru's partiality to sonnet,[14] but he is mistaken when he says that she gave us only two poems — "Baugmaree" and The Lotus" — in that form.[15] If Das means here original sonnets by Toru, there is at least one sonnet which seems to have escaped the biographer's notice — the one entitled "A mon Pere," about which Toru wrote to her British friend, "it is not from the French, but it is original."[16]

Critics have admired Toru's notes appended to her translations. It has been suggested that she would have rivalled Sainte-Bauve, whom she praised for his critical qualities.[17] The notes sent Gosse guessing about her deep insight and critical ability. He wrote :

> Occasionally she [Toru] showed a profundity of research that would have done no discredit to Mr. Saintsbury or "Le doux Assellineau." She was ready to pronounce an opinion on Napel le Pyrenean or to detect a plagiarism in Baudelaire.[18]

Toru, in truth, possessed a seeing eye and a retentive memory. She made comparisons of old and new, of this country and that, of East and West, with a surprising boldness.

Toru's *Sheaf* is undoubtedly an admirable achievement. Critics like Andre Theuriet and Edmund Gosse spoke highly of it. Iyengar rightly thinks that in it "Toru found her vocation as well as her voice."[19]

To the success of the *Sheaf*, Aru also contributed her share. Her powerful rendering may be seen in the following :

> Still barred the doors! the far east glows,
> The morning wind blows fresh and free.
> Should not the hour that wakes the rose
> Awaken also thee?
>
> All look for thee, Love, Light, and Song,
> Light in the sky deep red above,
> Song, in the lark of pinions strong,
> And in my heart, true Love.
>
> ... ...
>
> No longer sleep,
> Oh, listen now!

I wait and weep,
But where art thou?

Besides Hugo's "Morning Senade," which is quoted above, Aru translated half a dozen other poems by different authors. She had a command over the language and verse-forms comparable to her sister's. Her delightful lyricism and smooth rhythm, as in "The Young Captive" and "Romance of Uma," are sure to please the reader.

IV

Perhaps the need to go back to native roots prompted Toru Dutt to produce *Ancient Ballads and Legends of Hindustan*. This slim volume abounds in poems about Indian myths and legends. Apart from seven non-mythological pieces, it contains nine ballads or legends. These are : "Savitri," "Lakshman," "Jogadhya Uma," "The Royal Ascetic and the Hind," "Dhruva," "Buttoo," "Sindhu," "Prahlad," and "Sita." Of these, "The Legend of Dhruva" and "The Royal Ascetic and the Hind," both translated from the *Vishnu Purana*, had appeared during Toru's lifetime in *The Bengal Magazine* (October 1876) and in *The Calcutta Review* (January 1877) respectively. Both are written in blank verse and have a continuity with the rest in their religious note.

"The Legend of Dhruva" relates the story of the prince Dhruva, the son of a less-favoured queen, who, having failed to secure his father's love owing to the interference of his step-mother resolved to scorn the position of worldly power in favour of spiritual greatness :

I shall try
The highest good, the loftiest place to win,
Which the whole world deems priceless and desires.

He left his father's house, went to the woods to live among the hermits, and eventually realized his ambition, as a result of which he still "shines a star" to be seen by men at night.

"The Royal Ascetic and the Hind" is about the failure of King Bharat's matchless asceticism. The great hermit-king of Saligram gave up all the luxuries at home and went out to the woods to practise penances and privations. But he became altogether a changed man when he developed deep love for a forlorn fawn whose thirsty mother had leapt to death out of fear caused by a lion's roar at hand. After the lapse of many years, when Bharat was about to die, his mind was still filled with anguish at leaving his little fawn behind :

> To it devoted was his last, last thought
> Reckless of present and of future both!

The poem ends with a spirited defence of Bharat's conduct and a condemnation of the ideal of asceticism. This ballad, like the previous one, is replete with personal views of the poetess, and is "altogether modern, and out of line with the past."[20]

"Savitri" is the triumph of constancy in love and purity in thought. Savitri, the only child of Madra's wise and mighty king, chose Satyavan as her companion despite the opposition of Naradji and her parents, though Satyavan was to die within a year. When the fateful day arrived, Yama, the God of Death, came to take away the soul of Satyavan. Yama did his work and moved slowly on towards his own dim dominions. Savitri persistently followed him. Yama advised her to go back and take up the funeral rites and sacrifices. But Savitri meekly told him that she must accompany her husband in woe or weal. There began a lively philosophical discussion between the two. Savitri started speaking in terms of Vedanta :

> I know that in this transient world
> All is delusion, — nothing true :
> I know its shows are mists unfurled
> To please and vanish. To renew
> Its bubble joys, be magic bound
> In *Maya's* network frail and fair,
> Is not my aim!

Hearing the words of Savitri, Yama was much pleased and granted her three boons, including the life of Satyavan, and then disappeared in a flame.

"Lakshman" is cast in the form of a conversation between Sita, Rama's wife, and Lakshman, Rama's brother. Hearing a piercing cry raised by Marichi in the voice of Rama at the behest of Ravana, the lord of demons, Sita insisted on Lakshman to take up his weapons and go to his brother's help, but the latter was unwilling to leave her alone in the midst of a forest. But when Sita passed certain sarcastic remarks like the following :

> He perishes — well, let him die!
> His wife henceforth shall be mine own!
> Can that thought deep imbedded lie
> Within thy heart's most secret zone!

Lakshman at once got ready to go to the forest, but not before drawing a magic circle on the ground for her protection.

"Jogadhya Uma" is based on a folk-tale. It recounts the sudden appearance of the goddess Uma to a simple pedlar, and not to a ritualistic priest. The poetess is at home here. Her originality finds its fullest expression in this poem. Toru's closing comments upon the story are :

> Absurd may be the tale I tell,
> Ill-suited to the marching times,
> I loved the lips from which it fell,
> So let it stand among my rhymes.

In reality, there is a delicacy of touch and a "delicate old-fashioned, essentially Indian, flavour"[21] about the poem.

"Buttoo," a story from the *Mahabharta*, deals with the rejection of Buttoo, a low-born hunter's son, as a pupil by Dronacharjya, the greater master of magic and archery, and the determination of Buttoo to attain perfection in the art of archery. Buttoo did succeed in his mission, but Aarjuna's jealousy persuaded Dronacharjya to demand as his due the right thumb of Buttoo. Immediately, Buttoo offered it to his 'guru' :

> Glanced the sharp knife one moment high,
> The served thumb was on the sod,
> There was no tear in Buttoo's eye,
> He left the matter with his God.

Dronacharjya was so much moved that he prophesied immortality for the pupil.

"Sindhu" depicts the devotion of a son to his parents. Sindhu or Shravana Kumar, the only child of his sage-parents who were weak, blind and helpless, attended to their wants at every moment. One day, he went to the river to bring water for his parents. While filling the pitcher, he was shot unwittingly by King Dasarath, who thought that a roebuck had been drinking there. Sindhu had only one sorrow at the time of his death — the helpless conditions of his parents. Dasarath carried the pitcher and the deceased to Sindhu's parents, who, on hearing the death of their loved son, gave up their lives immediately, but not before predicting the death of Dasarath under similar circumstances :

> Die — for a son's untimely loss!
> Die — with a broken heart!
> Now help us to our bed of moss,
> And let us both depart.

In due course of time, the prediction came true, as the *Ramayana* tells us.

"Prahlad," taken from the *Mahabharata*, is the story of a great boy-devotee who did not hesitate to oppose even his tyrannical father, King Heerun Kasyapyu. God Himself appeared in the shape of a ferocious half-man and half-lion ('Narasimha') to kill the tyrant and to vindicate the ways of His devotee at a time when Prahlad was tortured most. After proclaiming Prahlad king in place of Kasyapu, God disappeared in a thunder-clap. It was a time when :

> One king lay stiff, and stark, and dead,
> Another on the peacock throne,
> Bowed reverently his youthful head.

"Prahlad" shows Toru's growing skill in the selection of details. It is written in eight-lined stanzas, the lines consisting of eight syllables each, and rhyming alternately. The technique employed here is described as "far in advance of that of the earlier poems."[22]

Last comes "Sita," which is a very short piece indeed. It brings to light Sita's unmerited sufferings at the hands of Rama. Sita, exiled by Rama on flimsy ground of a slanderous rumour about her, is seen living in the hermitage of Valmiki. The picture of the sad Sita along with her children deeply moves us all :

> Not in vain
> She weeps, — for lo! at every tear she sheds
> Tears from three pairs of young eyes fall amain,
> And bowed in sorrow are the three young heads.

The poem is rich in pathos and carries a strong autobiographical touch.

Ancient Ballads, on the whole, is essentially native in *genre* and outlook. For all her Western training and faith, Toru never ceased to be Indian. The ancient legends of Hindustan were neither exotic nor alien for her. The stories of the past stirred her and touched a responsive chord within her. The call of the land evoked her sympathetic answer. The ballads are interspersed with sententious remarks that suggest Toru's familiarity with the best expositions of the Hindu view of life. This is what she makes Savitri say :

> I know in such a world as this
> No one can gain his heart's desire,
> Or pass the years in perfect bliss :
> Like gold we must be tried by fire :

And this is what we hear from Prahlad :

> Hath He a shape, or hath He none?
> I know not this, nor care to know,
> Dwelling in light, to which the sun
> Is darkness, — He sees all below,
> Himself unseen.

Of all the poems contained in the volume, "Savitri" is the nearest to the Indian temper. The poem is the most articulate expression of Vedantic philosophy.

Apart from this, the volume presents certain subtle character-portrayals. Savitri, Sita and Jogadhya Uma are the ideal representatives of Indian womanhood, and offer an opportunity to the poetess to reveal the mysterious feminine nature. Toru's intimate feelings are expressed through them. In creating them, the poetess is the happiest. There are also many memorable male characters in Toru's poems, such as Satyavan, Lakshman, Bharat, Dhruva, Buttoo, Sindhu, and Prahlad. In portraying the inner feelings and the complex moods of her characters, Toru has adopted the device of dramatic speeches in her poems.

As one reads the ballads, one is struck with the large space covered by descriptions of Nature. The following lines from "Buttoo" will substantiate the statement :

What glorious trees! The sombre saul
On which the eye delights to rest,
The betel-nut, — a pillar tall,
With feathery branches for a crest,
The light-leaved tamarind spreading wide,
The pale faint-scented bitter neem,
The seemul gorgeous as a bride,
With flowers that have the ruby's gleam,
The Indian fig's pavilion tent
In which the whole armies might repose,
With here and there a little rent,
The sunset's beauty to disclose,
... ...
All these and thousands, thousands more,
With helmet red, or golden crown,
Or green tiara, rose before
The youth in evening's shadows brown.

This is the description of a forest-scene. Similar descriptions may be found in other poems too. Toru, no doubt, was keenly sensitive to Nature and specially to colour. "Baugmaree," "The Lotus," "Our Casuarina Tree" and many others show how responsive Toru was to colour and how sharp her powers of observation were.

The ballads highlight Toru's skill in narrative verse. They lead us to believe that she would have attained distinction in it, had she lived longer. Her method of narrating the tales is appealing enough; and in the words of Jha, "She [Toru] has a rare gift of story-telling, of arousing interest and curiosity, of creating suspense, and of drawing character. But perhaps in descriptive poetry, she is even superior."[23]

As regards Toru's technical excellence, she manages the octosyllabic line with considerable dexterity, and her rhymes are rarely far-fetched. Sense glides along without interruptions. Her blank verse is somewhat wooden, but then blank verse yields its peculiar charms only to the lucky few like Marlowe, Shakespeare and Milton. Gosse is correct in his assessment that the ballads as original English poems would ultimately "constitute Toru's chief legacy to posterity."[24]

There are also seven miscellaneous poems contained in the second part *of Ancient Ballads*. They are mostly autobiographical in vein and style. Their quality has led scholars to think that but for her short life Toru might have written "beautiful lyrics"[25] and "a powerful sonnet-sequence or poetic tragedy."[26] They were composed on different occasions, extending from 1870 to 1877. In point of merit, too, they are very uneven.

Among these poems, "Near Hastings" and "France-1870" are written in a mood of sincerity. "The Tree of Life" describes a vision in sleep. "On the Fly-Leaf of Erckmann-Chatrian's Novel Entitled 'Madame Therese' " is a poem inspired by the patriotic instincts of that great heroic woman who hurled herself into the French war against the sullen Prussians. "Baugmaree" is a memorable sonnet depicting the place where Toru passed a major portion of her life. "The Lotus," another notable sonnet, deals with the birth of that charming flower. "Our Casuarina Tree" mixes memory and desire, time and eternity, and local touches and literary reminiscences. It is written in the eleven-line stanza form, rhyming *abba*, *cddc*, *eee*. Iyengar declares, "In the organization of the poem as a whole and in the finish of the individual stanzas, in its mastery of phrase and rhythm, in its music of sound and ideas, 'Our Casuarina Tree' is a superb piece of writing...."[27]

V

Obviously, Toru Dutt was the first Indian to handle English verse with ease, freedom and command. Her achievements, both linguistic and technical, were of an excellent order, and when the *Sheaf* first appeared, it was even thought that the author was an Englishman writing under the pseudonym of 'Toru Dutt.' In fact, Toru Dutt possessed an inborn poetic talent which found its best outlet in the English language. Dunn has rightly described her as "the founder of the modern School of English poetry."[28] Besides being well-versed in Bengali, Sanskrit and English, she had to her advantage a sound knowledge of French and could write that language with "ease and perfection."[29] Her tragically brief career crowded with a literary accomplishment little short of the marvelous, has left us regretting her death. Although her premature death leaves us sad, her works of lasting worth console us. Her poetry has made her immortal, and Fisher has no hesitation in enrolling "this child of the green valley of the Ganges.... in the great fellowship of English poets."[30] In the end, we may be sure that Toru's splendid poetic achievement will ever defend her from proud 'Oblivion's curse.'

NOTES

1. Arnamatha Jha, "Introductory Memoir," *Ancient Ballads and Legends of Hindustan* (1941; rpt. Allahabad : Kitabistan, 1969), p. 8.
2. B. K. Talookdar, "The Poetry of Toru Dutt," *Journal of the University of Bombay*, 6, Part 6 (May 1936), 71.
3. Margaret Macnicol, *Poems by Indian Women* (Calcutta : Y.M.C.A. Press, and London : Oxford University Press, 1923), p. 37.
4. Of Toru's poetic works, mention may be made of *A Sheaf Gleaned in French Fields*, which appeared at Bhowanipure in March 1876 and *Ancient Ballads and Legends of Hindustan* which came out in 1882. Besides the two essays written *for The Bengal Magazine* (December 1874), her non-poetic works are *: A Scene from Contemporary History* (1875), *Bianca, or the Young Spanish Maiden* (1878), *Le Journal de Mademoiselle d' Arvers* (1879), and *Letters* addressed to Miss Mary Martin and to the French authoress, Mlle. Clarisse Bader, and collected in Harihar Das's book, *The Life and Letters of Toru Dutt* (1921).
5. Edmund Gosse, "Introductory Memoir," *Ancient Ballads and Legends of Hindustan* (London : Kegan Paul & Co., 1882), p. XXVII.
6. T.O.D. Dunn, *The Bengali Writers of English Verse* (London : Longmans & Green Co. Ltd. 1918), p. 22.
7. Harihar Das, "The Classical Tradition in Toru Dutt's Poetry," *Asiatic Review* (October 1931), pp. 695-715.
8. Jha, "Introductory Memoir," p. 36.
9. K.R. Srinivasa Iyengar, *Indian Contribution to English Literature* (Bombay : Karnatak Publishing House, 1945), p. 17.
10. Alokeranjan Dasgupta, "This Fragile Exotic Blossom of Songs," *Indian Literature*, 9, No. 2 (April-June 1966), 6-14.
11. *Ibid.*, pp. 8-9.
12. Talookdar, "The Poetry of Toru Dutt," p. 77.
13. Toru Dutt, *A Sheaf Gleaned in French Fields*, 3rd ed. (London : Kegan Paul & Co., 1880) , p. 369.
14. Harihar Das, *The Life and Letters of Toru Dutt* (London : Oxford University Press, 1921), p. 298.
15. *Ibid.*, p. 340.
16. *Ibid.*, p. 112.

17. Talookdar, "The Poetry of Toru Dutt," p. 79.
18. Gosse, "Introductory Memoir," p. XVI.
19. Iyengar, *Indian Contribution*, p. 18.
20. Das, "The Classical Tradition in Toru Dutt's Poetry," p. 700.
21. *Ibid.*, p. 708.
22. *Ibid.*, p. 714.
23. Jha, "Introductory Memoir," p. 30.
24. Gosse, "Introductory Memoir," p. xxii.
25. Jha, "Introductory Memoir," p. 24.
26. Iyengar, *Indian Contribution*, p. 20.
27. K.R. Srinivasa Iyengar, *Indian Writing in English*, 2nd ed. (Bombay : Asia Publishing House, 1973), p. 73.
28. Dunn, *The Bengali Writers*, p. 20.
29. *Ibid.*, p. 21.
30. H.A.L. Fisher, "Foreword" *The Life and Letters of Toru Dutt* by Harihar Das, p. vii.

4

R.N. Tagore as a Poet*

Rabindranath Tagore wrote primarily in Bengali, but he also translated many of his poems and plays into English, often altering, telescoping, transforming the originals. Occasionally he even wrote a poem in English in the first instance, *e.g. The Child*. In addition to this, he lectured in English to audiences outside the country, and wrote many letters in English. Should we, then, consider Tagore only as a Bengali writer, or as an English writer as well? He undoubtedly belongs to Bengali literature, but he belongs to Indo-Anglian literature too. Tagore was a poet of amazing capability, enriching Indo-Anglian poetry in a significant way. He wrote a large number of lyrics in Bengali first, and then deftly rendered them into English.

One is surprised to hear Mr. George Sampson saying that Tagore's position in English literature is "less secure," and that "the great popularity of Tagore as a prose-poet can be explained by the general appetite for moral reflections, not too deep, with an Eastern setting, not too remote."[1] But this does not represent the opinion of the literary circles, and is far from the truth. The truth remains that Tagore is matchless as a prose-poet and that his prose-poems have a simple charm about them and are a "compound of day-dream and aspiration, fancy and prayerful ecstasy, naivete and profundity."[2] Tagore is well acknowledged today as an irresistible force in the world of letters, and needs no defence.

As a poet, Tagore sought beauty, and happiness through beauty, in his life. He sought beauty in children, found it and exhibited it

*Reprinted from *Indo-Anglian Poetry* (Allahabad : Kitab Mahal, 1979) with permission of the publisher.

in *The Cresent Moon*, which is a book of the beauty of innocence. He sought beauty in boys and girls, and found in them the beauty of the gradual unfolding of human personality. Tagore knew that, as a teacher, he could come into intimate contact with boys and girls at Shanthiniketan. The poet's love of the child is so clear in many of his poems. "Defamation" in *The Cresent Moon* is an example in point.

Tagore also sought beauty in Man in relation to other men and in relation to Nature. Love and Friendship and Natural piety are portrayed in many poems of *Gitanjali*, *The Gardener*, and *The Cycle of Spring*. The following piece may be appropriately quoted here :

> When, mad in their mirth, they raised dust to soil thy robe, O Beautiful; it made my heart sick....
>
> The morning light struck upon those eyes red with the revel of night, the place of the white lily greeted their burning breath, the stars through the depth of the sacred dark stared at their carousing — at those that raised dust to soil thy robe, O Beautiful! (*Fruit-Gathering,* xxxvi).

Tagore even went farther than Nature, and saw man in relation to tradition, the immemorial culture of the Hindus — the *Vedas*, the *Upanishads*, and the *Gita* — and more generally the heritage of all Indians. Art and architecture, music and dance, sent Tagore into raptures, and he discovered the beauty of profound harmony in the springs of our great tradition.

Tagore tried to see Man in relation to the Universe, to God. He sought the beauty of Holiness, and found it too. His life was, thus, one long endeavour to reach Beauty, to scale one by one its heights, and to realise unmixed happiness here on earth. It would not be wrong to say that he "tirelessly pursued the ideal of Beauty, and Beauty was to him also Love, Truth, Goodness and Power."[3] In this matter, Tagore drew inspiration from Keats, the celebrated Romantic poet of England. In fact, the poem "Chhabi" in *Balaka* repeats the theme of Keats's "Ode on a Grecian Urn" when it mentions that a work of art is as real as the "stars" and the "sky."[4] Shelley's *Hymn to Intellectual Beauty* was another potent influence on Tagore."[5]

Tagore was not only a votary of the beautiful, but also of the true and the good. *Satyam Shivam*, and *Sundaram* were his guiding principles in poetry. The postulate, "The true is good and beautiful," provides a basic criterion for the judgement of value in art which would apply to all its aspects, aesthetic and moral. It is understood that beauty is distinct from the useful or the pleasant. Both the creator and the worshipper of beauty have to approach its more universal aspects in terms of truth. Similarly, the 'good' consists in the expression of virtue which sees beyond the travail and immediate consequences of an action like Lakshman's voluntary acceptances of exile with his brother. In Indian literature the beauty of the mighty was "forgiveness," that of woman's "modesty" and not power and looks. Tagore's line of approach is typically Indian. The most elaborate expression of his views is to be had in *Saundaryabodh* collected in his *Sahitya Bichare*. It is while describing the lotus-seated : Saraswati that he quotes the phrase, "Truth is beauty, beauty truth," an exposition of the saying of the *Upanishad*, "All that is seen is His sacred and blissful Self."

Tagore's treatment of love in his poetry follows the method of Vaishnav poets. In Vaishnav poetry the human becomes godly and the celestial descends to earth. His poems in *Lover's Gift* contain flashes of it, — "Oh listen to the secrets of the world . I know that the lily is pale for the moon's love."[6] Before Tagore came to write his poetry under the Vaishnav's *rup aradhana*, he had pursued the 'formless' ideal. The denial of the old tradition is reiterated *Sandhya Sangeet* (Evening Songs), the first poems of his poetic maturity. According to Tagore, beauty is a universal attribute of the objects of the world just as mass is of matter, and it is their mutual attraction or 'love' that binds them together. The beautiful in the heart of the lover (say Krishna) attracts the beautiful in the form of the beloved (say Radha). This relationship applies to the animate and the inanimate alike. Thus beauty and love become the cause and the effect of the same principle. Love, believed Tagore, gives us immortality and youth, it is ever deathless and changeless. In one of his Shantiniketan sermons, Tagore explained the words of Maitrey in the *Upanishad* as follows — "Where do we find the touch of immortality in things mortal? Where there is love. It is love that casts the shadow of the infinite and keeps the old perpetually young and does not acknowledge death." It is literally the same kind of explanation as Shelley's in his *Sensitive Plant* :

> For love, beauty, and delight,
> There was no death nor change....

In his poetry Tagore employed ancient myths of Urvashi and the burning of Madan and the dispersal of his ashes to symbolise the spirit of love pervading the wide world. Seldom do we find the 'loudness' of passion and the 'harshness' of the real in Tagore's poetry.

As in his concept of love, Tagore is basically Romantic in his concept of Nature too. He has also been called "the direct inheritor of Vedic naturalism."[7] Tagore tells us in the memorial paper he read at the death anniversary of his preceptor, Biharilal, that the subtle harmony that exists between human emotions and Nature was first revealed to him by the poetry of Biharilal and the romance of Paul and Virginia. Biharilal's picture of Nature with gentle fawns, crystal streams, and dewy lawns, left an indelible mark on his mind. *Wild Flower*, *Evening Songs*, *Morning Songs*, *Ahalya*, *To the Sea*, *The Golden Boat*, *The Cresent Moon*, *The Gardener* and *Fruit-Gathering* : all have beautiful images of Nature. There are wonderful descriptions of landscapes and flowers, the moon and the sun. *In The Cresent Moon*, we have the following;

> Supposing I became a *champa* flower, just for fun, and grew on a branch high up that tree, and shook in the wind with laughter and danced upon the newly budded leaves, would you know me, mother?
>
> ("The Champa Flower")

Tagore's poetry, like that of Kalidasa, reveals different facets of natural beauty in all its splendour. The sights and sounds of Bengal are caught again and again in his magic verse. The varying moods of Nature are recorded in his poetry.

Tagore is one of the supreme lyric poets of the world. Sincerity of feeling and vividness of imagery combine with the moving music of his verse. This fusion of feeling, imagery and music showed very early in his life. Many of his poems are remarkable not only for their music and intensity, but also for the boldness of their images. Tagore has sung rapturously about nature, seasons, love, and life. One of his most famous lyrics is "Farewell to Heaven," in which he compares the passionate calm of heavenly bliss with the exquisite flow of joy and pain in earthly experience. In his sixties, there was an outburst of lyric poetry which can easily compare with the best work of his early youth. The poems of this period reveal a new note of deep feeling purified by suffering. The intimate quality of these poems is replaced in the next decade by a rich and mellow humanism. There is a rare economy of thought and expression in the last poems.

Though essentially a lyric poet, Tagore succeeds in giving "a rich dramatic quality"[8] to many of his poems. With his deep humanity and passionate yearning for justice, it is not surprising that he should be attracted by social and political themes. Whatever Tagore touches is lifted to a higher plane of universal meaning. He has written some bitter satires against the prejudices and superstitions of his own people, but they also show how his essential humanism rises above his indignation and wrath. Even his patriotic poems are instinct with a feeling for all humanity. For Tagore, patriotism was a positive quality of love for his own people and land, never a negative attitude of hatred for the foreigner. One of the finest examples of this is seen in his poem, *Guru Govind*, where passionate love for one's country and people is seen to deepen into love for all mankind. In fact, Tagore never recognised that anything human could be foreign to him. In his famous lyric, "The Wanderer" (*Pratashi*), he declares that man has his home in every clime and his country in every region of the world. Our National Anthem, where Tagore invokes the Lord of the heart of all the people of the world as the arbiter of India's destiny, is a fine expression of it.

In one of her talks, Maitreye Devi observed that Tagore's poetry would remain lasting, but the poet was destined to go.[9] While every poet or every man is destined to go in due course of time, it is the durability of his work that offers immortality to him. Tagore comes off successfully in this test. He is, however, to remain forever in our hearts for the spirituality of his poetry, the nobility of his utterance. There is, today, an uncertain groping in many directions, some of which are only valuable as transitional effort, and might lead to "a brilliant corruption and decadence."[10]

There is vitalistic intuitivism, sometimes taking a more subjective and sometimes a more objective form. But Tagore's is a "finer and truer spiritual vision," and his poetry floats in the complete spiritual light and finds a sight and cadence in a psycho-spiritual heaven of subtle and delicate soul-experience transmuting the earth tones by the touch of its radiance. Spiritual reality was the central theme of Tagore's poetic creation. He saw things in their essential spiritual reality, under the figure or mode of beauty. But a worshipper of beauty, unless he rises to the Upanishadic norm, is prone to become sensuous and pagan, as Keats was. The spiritual vein in Keats was secondary, but in Tagore it is primary. The world being nothing but Spirit made visible is, according to Tagore, fundamentally a thing of beauty. Tagore, no doubt, put his poetic power in the service of the great cause for the divine uplift of humanity.[11]

Related to this is Tagore's mystic poetry. When *Gitanjali* was first published in an English translation, the West hailed it for its message of peace and love in a war-torn and embittered world. The poems in this slender volume are charged with a deep sense of peace and calm. The charm of this work is "the subtle underflow."[12] It is nothing else than his "sense of life." The spirit of "curious quiet"[13] vivifies it. To readers of Tagore in Europe and America, it came with the delighted wonder of a new discovery, but to Eastern readers it was "only a natural culmination of his earlier writing."[14] The love of nature and man had by unconscious steps merged into the love of God. Deep personal suffering had given a mellowness to his images and themes. Growing experience had revealed to him the undoubted truth that all our life is surrounded by mystery. The wonder and pathos of human life had brought a new sympathy and understanding to his works of imagination. In brief, the very personality of the poet had passed into it.[15]

Tagore has often used traditional themes and drawn extensively upon the associations and assonances of classical Indian literature. He has, however, transmuted whatever he has touched. Tagore had the greatest admiration for Kalidasa, but even when he has taken a theme from him, Tagore has given it a twist that makes his treatment essentially modern : For Tagore, *Meghduta* is a message not from a mythical Yaksha to his beloved, but an expression of the yearning of all human lovers in all ages and climes.[16] Some of the traditional themes employed by Tagore in his poetry are : Urvashi, Ahalya, and the burning of Madan.

Sometimes we also find a sharp note of irony, if not satire, against the evils of society. He knew that the conventional Indian claim to spirituality is at times nothing but a refusal or inability to think. He was totally against the continuation of lifeless conventions and dead customs. The indignity and exploitation of man aroused his natural indignation. He wanted reforms in society, politics, education, and ethics.

One salient feature of Tagore's later poetry is its utter simplicity. While his earlier poems rely heavily on the rich associations and assonances of Sanskrit, his late poems, dedicated to man and God, have shed all adornment. The simplest of human situations are used to reveal his experience of the divinity. The diction also takes on the directness and simplicity of common speech. There is an immediacy of experience in them. Words have become lucid and transparent, and the purest music pleases us almost everywhere.

Critics are agreed in pointing out that the last two years before Tagore's death were a great creative period — as if his spirit flared up for a final adieu.[17] The poems composed during this period are his last proud manifestations against sorrow and pain. Here was the treatment of his abiding love for life's "richness, ripeness, ratheness." In Maitreye's opinion, Tagore's poetic power did not fail nor thoughts flickered as he grew in age, and his last poem, written a few days before his death in between some waking moments of a fatal coma, is perhaps one of his best poems.[18]

Tagore's *Gitanjali* and other English translations popularised the prose-poem form in Indo-Anglian poetry. A prose-poem has its own pattern of repetitive devices, parallelisms and contrasts. Tagore's style has been imitated by a host of Indo-Anglian poets — Anand Acharaya, Puran Singh, P.R. Kaikini, Purohit Swamy, Mrs. Budhey, Subho Tagore, K.S. Venkataramani, and L.S.C. Ramsamuj.

There have been detractors too of Rabindarnath Tagore. The objection has been made that his poetry is very subtle and remote and goes away from the broad, vital actualities of existence. Yeats is considered by some as a poet of Celtic romance and nothing more. Tagore is accused in his own country of an unsubstantial poetic philosophising, a lack of actuality, of reality of touch and force of vital insistence.[19] But this is to mistake the work of his poetry and also the missionary zeal of his life. Whether we find a complete poetic fusion in him or not, he discovered for us a new and deep manner of viewing life, a fresh mode of seeking the infinite and eternal.

Finally, Tagore is today a poet of national and international status. His poetry is born out of an amalgam of the rich classical heritage of ancient India, the spacious ways of the Mughal Court, the simple verities of the life of the common people of Bengal, and the restless energy and intellectual vigour of modem Europe. He is decidedly "an inheritor of all times and all culture."[20] It is this combination of many diverse strands and themes that gives to his poetry its resilience, universality and infinite appeal. His "internationalism" is "one of his chief claims to future remembrance."[21] He is, and will always be, one of the world's greatest international poets.

REFERENCES

1. See *The Concise Cambridge History of English Literature*, ELBS ed. (London : Cambridge Univ. Press, 1961), p. 915.
2. K.R.S. Iyengar, *Indo-Anglian Literature* (Bombay : The International Book House Ltd., 1943), p. 17.
3. K.R.S. Iyengar, *Rabindranath Tagore* (Bombay : Popular Prakashan, 1965), p. 106.
4. Baldev Singh, *Tagore and the Romantic Ideology* (Culcutta : Orient Longmans, 1963), p. 79.
5. *Ibid.*, p. 86.
6. Rabindra Nath Tagore, *Lover's Gift and Crossing*, p. 16.
7. Baldev Singh, *op. cit.* 115.
8. Humayun Kabir, "Tagorer's Poetry," *Indian Literature*, 1-2, No. I (Oct. 1958-March 1959), p. 10.
9. Maitreye Devi, *Rabindranath — The Man Behind His Poetry* (Calcutta : Published by Sudhir Das, 1973), p. 1.
10. Sri Aurobindo, "The Poetry of Tagore," *Tagore Centenary Volume*, ed. M. Kulshresta (Hoshiarpur : Vishveshavrand Vedic Institute, 1961), p. 13.
11. N.K. Gupta, *Poets and Lyrics*, p. 67.
12. Ezra Pound, "A Review of *Gitanjali*, *Tagore Centenary Volume*, p. 114.
13. *Ibid.*, p. 11.

14. H. Kabir, *loc. cit.*, p. 12.
15. Edward Thompson "*Gitangali* and the Prize," *Tagore Centenary Vol.*, p. 109.
16. H. Kabir, *loc. cit.*, p. 16.
17. S.V. Mukerjea, *Disjecta Membra* (Bangalore : The Indian Institute of World Culture, 1959).
18. See *Rabindranath — The Man Behind His Poetry*, p. 7.
19. Sri Aurobindo, *loc. cit.,* p. 16.
20. H. Kabir, *loc. cit.*, p. 20.
21. J.C. Ghosh, *Bengali Literature*, p. 173.

5

Sri Aurobindo, The Poet*

In his long life and varied career, Sri Aurobindo wrote regularly both in prose and poetry. As a poet, he displayed immense capability in handling the English language and metre. If as a prose writer he wrote letters, journalistic essays, critical reviews, philosophical treatises, and works of interpretation, he wrote epigrams, translations, adaptations, lyrics, narrative poems, poetic plays, a series of remarkable experiments in quantitative metres, and the monumental 'futurist' epic, *Savitri.* He experimented with almost all forms of poetry and prosody, and there is nothing wrong to call him primarily an 'experimentalist' and a 'modernist.'

Sri Aurobindo has also a hold on modern Bengali literature. But it is as an Indo-Anglian poet that he will be remembered in the English-speaking world. It was to his advantage that he was sent to England by his father for studies and was reared like an English child. He wrote like an English writer, not like a foreigner lisping in alien numbers, His poetry is the produce of a flawless metrical craftsmanship. He was a master of Greek, Latin and Sanskrit Literatures. He has given us a scholarly and thought-provoking 40-page essay on Quantitative Metre at the end of *his Collected Poems and Plays* in two volumes.

Sri Aurobindo, according to K.D. Sethna,[1] has done three exceedingly rare things. First, he has to his credit a bulk of excellent blank verse, a rare achievement indeed. At least five thousand lines in the *Collected Poems and Plays* are written in superb blank verse with diversely modulated beauty and power. They put him cheek

---

*Reprinted from *Indo-Anglian Poetry* (Allahabad : Kitab Mahal, 1979) with permission of the publishers.

by jowl with Keats in both essence and amount. The huge epic, *Savitri*, is a marvel which places him at once in the company of the absolute top-rankers by a sustained abundance of blank verse of the first rate. Secondly, Sri Aurobindo has used quantitative metre with great skill. What is of extraordinary import is that this metre has eluded even English poets. Sri Aurobindo has solved once for all the problem of quantity in English — a feat which gives the language "a brave new world" of poetic effects. Quantitative metre brings into English a structural music equal to that of Greek and Latin poetry. Sri Aurobindo has successfully handled the fatally alluring hexameter in his verse. And thirdly, Sri Aurobindo has laid bare a rhythmic life beyond the ranges of inspired consciousness. His mystical and spiritual utterances hail from 'planes' of inspiration higher and intenser than any usually found in the major poets, 'planes' tapped with some freedom by only the *Vedas* and the *Upanishads.* Sri Aurobindo stands as the creator of a new Vedic and Upanishadic age of poetry.[2] *Savitri* is his wonderful gift to the world; it is *mantric* and philosophical throughout. According to Sethna, "*Savitri* is from every angle the right correlate to the practical drive towards earth-transformation by India's mightiest Master of spirituality in his Ashram at Pondicherry.[3] Though the master is now no more physically present in his Ashram, his noble work of earth-transformation still continues there.

The Greek sings of the humanity of man Sri Aurobindo of the divinity of man. Under the Hellenic influence, we have forgotten that an equally poetic world exists in the domain of spiritual life even in its severity as in that of earthly life and its sweetness.[4] Sri Aurobindo has made a passion of the spiritual life. Poetry, after all, has a mission. Poetry is not merely what is pleasing and moving, but what is inspiring and elevating. Our Vedic poets always looked beyond humanity, beyond earth, and, therefore, they could make divine poetry of humanity and what is of earth. They were ever grandiose and sublime and puissant. The heroic, the epic was their natural element. Sri Aurobindo has the same outlook and this explains the ring of the old-world manner that we find in him. The Hindu legends and myths delighted him because they are always ennobling in effect. His concern was the Divine Being, who is "at once our supreme transcendent Self, the Cosmic Being, foundation of our universality, and the Divinity within which our psychic being, the true evolving individual in our nature, is a portion, a spark, a flame, growing into the eternal Fire from which it was lit...."[5] He made poetry a vehicle of expressing his positive philosophy of evolution of the human race. *Savitri* is a fine explication of his philosophy.

Sri Aurobindo held that poetry springs from a higher region. In performing his job, the poet becomes the seer and reveals to man his eternal self and the godheads of its manifestation. In other words, the true creator of poetry is the soul and the true enjoyer too is the soul; in Eternity poetry begins, in Eternity it ends. The aesthesis which deals with such poetry is called Metaesthesis or Metapoetics. In fact, Sri Aurobindo has spoken of four planes of being between the mental and the Highest consciousness which, in the order of their ascending spiritual luminosity, are the Higher Mind, Illumined Mind, Intuitive Mind, and Overmind, each producing poetry of its own particular intensity. His epic is the finest flower of 'Overmind' poetry.

Sri Aurobindo wanted poetry to be *mantric* and mystical, and poetry, to be *mantric* and mystical, must contain the following three elements : (1) the highest intensity of rhythmic movement, a kind of rhythmical soul-movement entering into the metrical form and often overflooding it, (2) the highest intensity of style — of verbal form and thought substance (the merely adequate and effective ones) and (3) the highest intensity of the soul's vision of Truth (vision being the prerogative of a poet, he loses his personality in the intense vision of Truth and establishes direct link with the soul.

As the function of poetry, to Sri Aurobindo, is neither to teach truth, nor to pursue knowledge, nor to serve any ethical purpose, but to have a life of its own, to embody beauty (intense impression) and give delight (the soul of existence), the future course of poetry as to be directed towards the fathoming of the self of man and the large self if the universe, and the discovery of the Life Divine, the Supreme Reality, and of man's own divine possibilities. The future poetry may take any or all forms — the lyric, the drama, the epic, but each form has to run along a new line and fix its own new aim. But its aim is to put forth the very heart of the Life Divine in the concrete body of the five elements of Truth, Beauty, Delight, Life and Spirit. Sri Aurobindo is, in essence, the prophet of the new age and the spokesman of the new Truth. In short, he belongs to the future.[6]

It is interesting to note that there is a marked difference between Sri Aurobindo's early poetry and the poetry of the *Savitri* period. The early poetry has been written under the influence of the Decadent poets. The aesthetic theory pursued in it is not different from that of the Romantics, Victorians, or Decadents. But poems like *Ahana*, the last poems, "Rose of God," and *Savitri*, have been composed in an entirely new world of poetic inspiration and fulfilment.[7] Sri Aurobindo's aesthetics is mainly concerned with explaining the later developments in his poetic career.

Sri Aurobindo's poetic diction is usually charged and sustained. Take the following as an illustration :

> A blaze of his sovereign glory is the sun,
> A glory is the gold and glimmering moon.
> A glory is his dream of purple sky,
> A march of his greatness are the wheeling stars,
> His laughter of beauty breaks out in green trees,
> His moments of beauty triumph in a flower :
> The blue sea's chant, the rivulet's wondering voice
> Are murmurs falling from the Eternal's harp.

(*Savitri*, p. 624)

Sri Aurobindo wrote, as is very clear in *Savitri*, under a divine inspiration. His diction, therefore, is chaste and austere, not lax and prolix as in Shakespeare or Spenser. Having successfully practised the various 'idioms' which may be characterised as Elizabethan, Neo-classical, Romantic, and Victorian, Sri Aurobindo in his later poetic phase, realised an idiom which is neither traditional nor 'modern' in the accepted sense, but typically his own. The typical idiom he realised has been branded as *mantra* — a direct and most heightened word embodying the soul's vision of the Supreme Reality.[8] He claimed that poetry is the '*mantra of the Real*' and considered the poem as the 'Rose of God.' For one thing, Sri Aurobindo, like Robert Browning, presses into service vocabulary of diverse kinds. He does not confine to mere 'poetic' words like Swinburne and the Decadent. There are passages in his poetry in which he uses technical terms, mathematical terms, words connected with the printing trade, psycho-analysis and military science. His 'poetic' words like "Soul," 'Oversoul,' 'World Soul,' 'Matter,' 'Life Divine' 'Cosmic Consciousness,' etc. have a technical import and precision about them.

A study of Sri Aurobindo's poetry is very interesting from the point of view of its style. He experimented with different kinds of style (and also rhyme, as seen earlier) in his poetic life, and the best of them are all manifested in *Savitri.* The style of this epic is flexible and varies according to its context and theme. It can be neo-classical or romantic, symbolic or modernistic. He employed a dramatic or narrative style in order to present a character or situation, an encounter or a debate. His reflective style is of three kinds — the balanced and antithetical style employed when the matter is familiar to the reader, the paradoxical style when he writes intensely and thought is subtly metaphysical, and the learned style when he presents the contours of a theme which is difficult or unfamiliar to the reader. There is also the exposition or analytical style employed in dealing with rare perceptions and mystical levels of consciousness. There is, then, the lyric style rising to a great height of intensity and passion. Lastly, there is "the allusive style."[9]

Sri Aurobindo has mentioned four levels of style or 'seeing speech' : the adequate, the dynamically effective or rhetorical poetic manner, the metaphysical or illuminating style, and the more purely intuitive or revelatory utterance.[10] These levels can be detected in many of the kinds of style noted above.

Deshbandhu Chittaranjan Das described Sri Aurobindo as "the Poet of Patriotism" in the course of his concluding argument in defence of the poet during the trial of the Alipur Conspiracy Case. Certainly the poet had taken an active part in politics before he retired to Pondicherry for long mediations. Lord Curzon's move to partition Bengal had aroused his indignation, and he had inspired certain secret societies to crop up all over the land with tens of thousands of young men as their members.[11] He drafted a scheme, practical as well as allegorical, entitled *Bhawani Mandir*. Unsigned copies of appeal were distributed to help materialise the scheme. He, in fact, gave a call for revolution under the divine inspiration of Bhawani, the Shakti. He asserted that people fail in many things for want of the Mother Shakti. What is a nation after all? The Shakti (Strength) of its millions. We make or mar our nation out of our choice. Apart from this, Sri Aurobindo had written on Bankim Chandra Cattopadhyaya while at Baroda (both in the form of a tribute and a poem). Bankim's *Bande Mataram* had shaken the very foundation of the British empire in India. Soon after coming to Calcutta, Sri Aurobindo wrote a poem on a great soul, Baji Prabhou, who was a brave soldier, devoted to Shivaji . He made Baji Prabhou say : "...make iron of your soul/Yet if Bhavani wills, strength and sword /Can stay our Nation's future from O'erthrow." He wanted to see many more Baji Prabhous in this land of ours. He also welcomed the emergent nation on its Independence in 1947.

Eyebrows have been raised against Sri Aurobindo as a poet. It is asked whether he is a poet or *yogi* primarily, although he made it plain in one of his letters that he had been first and foremost, a poet and politician, and only later a *Yogi*.[12] There is also a potent danger to identify Sri Aurobindo's verse with "pure poetry".[13] But in reality his verse is not 'pure poetry,' it rather involves the future of man and the line on which the evolution of consciousness is likely to proceed. Then there is the adverse remark of the *Times Literary Supplement*. This famous English weekly praised Sri Aurobindo as the prose-writer; but criticized him as a poet, saying, "It cannot be said that Aurobindo shows any organic adaptation to music and melody. His thought is enchants or disturbs is not there. Aurobindo is not another Tagore or Iqbal or even Sarojini Naidu" (July 8 1944). But Mr. Sethna rebuts the charge marked by its "sweeping ineptitude." He thinks, and rightly so, that it denies inspiration completely and in all its modes to Sri Aurobindo's poetry. He writes : "In poetry, music does not stand just for one particular arrangement and movement of speech — a simple dance or a rich swirl, a slow gravity or a swift puissance. It can be anything and it is born fundamentally of kindled emotion and vision setting language astir and aglow so that words and phrases become intense and harmonious in a vital suggestive way and fall into suitable metrical patterns that ring significant changes on recurrent base. In short, it is inspiration adequately expressing itself."[14] It would be really sad for humanity to ignore Sri Aurobindo and his poetry, That some of the Western papers and critics have failed to see the divine in him speaks of the their own helplessness and earthfound vision. To read Sri Aurobindo's poetry is to believe in immense human possibilities. Here is, in fact, the hope for poetry and the hope for man. With him, we have the return of the *Rishi*. It is in this light that he is not only a great poet, but the poets' poet.[15]

REFERENCES

1. See his *The Poetic Genius of Sri Aurobindo* (Bombay : Sri Aurobindo Circle, 1947).
2. *Ibid.*, pp. 2-3.
3. *Ibid.*, p. 156.
4. N.K. Gupta, *Poets and Mystics* (1951), p. 16.
5. Sri Aurobindo, *The Life Divine*, II, 513.
6. See also Sri Swatantra Swami's article in the special Number on Sri Aurobindo in *The Banasthali Patrika*, Nos. 17-18 (July 1971-Jan. 1972).
7. V.K. Gokak, "The Evolution of Sri Aurobindo's Aesthetic Theory," *The Banasthati Patrika*, Nos. 17-18 (as above), p. 10.
8. Rameshwar Gupta, "Sri Aurobindo's Poetic Idiom", *The Banasthali Patrika* (as above), p. 133.
9. V.K. Gokak, "Introduction," *The Golden Treasury of Indo-Anglian Poetry* : 1928-1965. (New Delhi : Sahirya Akademi, 1970), p. xxxvi.
10. *Ibid.*, p. xxxvi.
11. Manoj Das, *Sri Aurobindo* (New Delhi : Sahitya, Akademi, 1972), p. 29.
12. Sisir Kumar Ghose, *Sri Aurobindo : Poet and Social Thinker* (Dharwar : Karnatak Univ., 1973), p. 3.
13. *Ibid.*, p. 6.
14. K.D. Sethna, *The Poetic Genius of Sri Aurobindo*, p. 9.
15. S.K. Ghose, *op. cit.*, p. 18.

6

Sarojini Naidu's Poetry : A Thematic Study

In the rush of her romantic emotions, Sarojini became a poetess despite the wishes of her father to be a mathematician or a scientist. There is an interesting story about the beginning of her poetic career which may be, in the words of the poetess herself, recounted thus : "One day, when I was eleven, I was sighing over a sum in algebra it wouldn't come right; but instead a whole poem came to me suddenly. I wrote it down."[1] Once the beginning was made, she did not stop writing effervescent verses until she plunged into the hectic politics of the day. Her fame as a poet rests today on the four published books of poetry, which are : *The Golden Threshold* (1905), *The Bird of Time* (1912), *The Broken Wing* (1917), and *The Feather of the Dawn* (1961).

But before giving to the literary world the first flowers of her genius, Sarojini had to get cleared her own doubts and hesitations about the worth of her work. With this end in mind, she submitted her lyrics to Sir Edmund Gosse for a close critical scrutiny. Sir Gosse was, however, surprised to find them Western in emotion and imagery, built on reminiscences of Shelley, Keats and Tennyson. He counselled her to consign them to the waste paper-basket, and give up writing about robins, skylarks and English landscapes, and concentrate on "some revelation of the heart of India, some sincere penetrating analysis of native passion, of the principles of antique religion and of such mysterious intimations as stirred the soul of the East long before the West had begun to dream that it had a soul."[2] Accepting his counsel, Sarojini became completely 'autochthonous' in all that she wrote afterwards and her themes now became exclusively native.

The obvious object of the present paper is to pinpoint themes in Sarojini's poetry and to show how far she has gone in employing them. From the thematic viewpoint, her poems fall into the following categories : (1) nature poems, (2) love poems, (3) poems of life and death, (4) poems of the Indian scene, (5) patriotic poems and (6) poems on childhood and miscellaneous ones. We shall now examine her poems in the light of this broad categorisation.

I

NATURE POEMS

Sarojini's response to Nature was largely aesthetic, and not moral or spiritual as in case of Wordsworth. Still, like Wordsworth, she sought a kind of inspiration from Nature. The poetess was susceptible to lovely natural scenes and sights and bright catching colours. This is how she once wrote to her friend Arthur Symons :

> Come and share my exquisite March morning with me : this sumptuous blaze of gold and sapphire sky; these scarlet lilies that adorn the sunshine; the voluptuous scents of neem and champak and serisha that beat upon the languid air with their implacable sweetness; the thousand little gold and blue and silver breasted birds bursting with the shrill ecstasy of life in nesting time. All is hot and fierce and passionate, ardent and unashamed in its exulting and importunate desire for life and love. And, do you know that the scarlet lilies are woven petal by petal from my heart's blood, these little quivering birds are my soul made incarnate music, these heavy perfumes are my emotions dissolved into aerial essence, this flaming blue and gold sky is the 'very me,' that part of me that incessantly and insolently, yes, and a little deliberately, triumphs over that other part — a thing of nerves and tissues that suffers and cries out, and that must die tomorrow perhaps, or twenty years hence.[3]

It is evident that the poetess grew exultant and ecstatical at the mere contact of the sun. She was always in search of Beauty and her 'nerves of delight' always quivered at the contact of Beauty. In this respect, she resembled Keats, the great Romantic poet. The Spring with its fresh flowers and foliage, the streams and brooklets, the hills and mountains, the lakes and fountains, the green fields and forests, the star-studded sky and the glimmering moon and the pleasantly shining sun : all touched a responsive chord within her. She had, however, no particular attitude toward Nature, as Wordsworth or Coleridge had. She often lent her own moods to Nature, — the moods of ecstasy, hope or despair as the occasion demanded. At one time the Spring cheered her amply :

> The earth is ashine like a humming-bird's wing
> And the sky like a kingfisher's feather,
> O come, let us go and play with the spring
> Like glad-hearted children together.
>
> ("The Call of Spring")

At the other, it did not touch her heart at all :

> O Sweet! I am not false to you —
> Only my weary heart of late
> Has fallen from its high estate
> Of laughter and has lost the clue
> To all the vernal joy it knew.
>
> ("The Coming of Spring")

Because of her personal approach, her Nature poems are rarely realistic portrayals. Nature offered to her, as to Tennyson, a background for the portraiture of human emotions.

And yet she has written some charming poems on natural scenes and sights. "Leili" is one of them. Leili is a Persian word signifying Night, which is personified in the poem. A sublime atmosphere is created through the use of remarkable images in it :

> A caste-mark on the azure brows of Heaven,
> The golden moon bums sacred, solemn, bright
> The winds are dancing in the forest-temple,
> And swooning at the holy feet of Night,
> Hush! in the silence mystic voices sing
> And make the gods their incense-offering.

Night is enshrined in the forest-temple; the moon shines like a caste-mark on the brows of Heaven; the winds dance (as maidens would do in a temple) and swoon at the holy feet of Night; and in the silence mystic voices sing and offer incense to the gods. In such an atmosphere one is sure to be sublimated and exalted. "Leili" is really a remarkable piece of poetry, and critics like Dr. Cousins have praised it in full-throated ease : "The figuring of the moon as a caste-mark on the forehead of heaven is in itself a unique achievement of the imagination in poetry in the English language. It lifts India to the literary heavens : it threatens the throne of Diana (the goddess of Moon in the Roman mythology) of the classics; it releases Luna (another name for the goddess Moon) from the work of asylum keeper... and gives her instead the office of remembrancer to Earth that the divine is imprinted on the open face of Nature."[4]

Sarojini was keenly sensitive to bright colours, and "June Sunset" may be taken as an illustration. Herein the poetess speaks of a particular sunset thus :

> Here shall my soul find its true repose
> Under a sunset sky of dreams
> Diaphanous, amber and rose.
> The air is aglow with the glint and whirl
> Of swift wild wings in their homeward flight,
> Sapphire, emerald, topaz, and pearl,
> Afloat in the evening light.

In the increasing calm and silence of the evening, the 'rush-fringed rivers and rain-fed streams' weave their way through the meadows of lily and palm and catch fire from the sky. Then follows a veritable feast of delightful colours : diaphanous, amber, and rose in the western sky, which is also the sky of dreams, and birds winging in the air and producing reflections of sapphire, emerald, topaz and pearl. The poetess is conveying here through words what the artist might have done through his brush. The splendour of the colourful sunset is caught in a masterly fashion.

Sarojini has given us many more poems abounding in natural descriptions, such as "Spring," "A Song in Spring," "The Joy of Springtime," "Vasant Panchami," "In a Time of Flowers," "In Praise of Gulmohur Blossoms," "Nasturtiums," "Golden Cassia,"

"Champak Blossoms," and "Ecstasy" (from *The Bird of Time*), "The Call of Spring," "The Coming of Spring," "The Magic of Spring," "Summer Woods," and "The Time of Roses" (from *The Broken Wing*), "Spring in Kashmir," "The Gloriosa Lily," "The Water Hyacinth," "Mimicry," and "On Juhu Sands" (*from The Feather of the Dawn*).

Sarojini's nature poetry is, on the whole, glutted with soft, delicate, hundred-hued blossoms, with honey sweetness, and with cadenced carols of birds. This is what we come across in her Spring poems which form a major portion of her natural descriptions. She observed a peculiar beauty in Nature, and could not restrain herself from versifying it. Although the soft aspects of Nature occupied her attention mostly, the cruel and terrible aspects did not remain totally untouched, and we have the wild bees (as in "The Time of Roses"), the stormy oceans, and the strong winds in her poetry.

II

LOVE POEMS

Nearly one-third of Sarojini's poetry is on the theme of love. Out of a total of 184 poems in the four volumes, 66 are on love. Some real gems in this category of poetry are : "Indian Love Song," "Humayun to Zobeida," "Ecstasy," "The Poet's Love-Song," "An Indian Love-Song," "A Love Song from the North," "A Rajput Love-Song," "Song of Radha, the Milkmaid," "The Temple," "The Flute-Player of Brindaban," "Perplext," "The Gift," "The Amulet," "Immutable," and "Songs of Radha." The love trilogy called "The Temple" stands out as a class by itself. It is an epitome of conventional and sacrificial love-poetry typical of India. The following stanza from "Devotion" ("The Sanctuary") will prove the statement :

> Take my flesh to feed your dogs if you choose,
> Water your golden-trees with my blood if you will,
> Turn my heart into ashes, my dreams into dust —
> Am I not yours, O Love, to cherish or kill?

An Indian woman's imagination is more prone to the self-surrendering and self-abnegating aspect of love than to the neo-modernist's display of naked sex and Freud's subtle anatomization.

There is much is Sarojini's love poetry that is written out of personal experience. In "Humayun to Zobeida", she writes :

> What war is this of *Thee* and *Me*? Give o'er the
> wanton strife,
> You are the heart within my heart, the life within
> my life.

And though these lines have sprung direct from experience, they are not totally devoid of conventional touch. In fact, Sarojini treated love in the same manner as in the classical and medieval poetry of India, and also as it is treated in Persian poetry (which was well within the grasp of the poetess).

Sarojini's love poetry reflects her varying moods and feelings. In it one witnesses her hope and despair, her rapture and irony. Her moody approach to love becomes obvious when one reads poem like "The Festival of Memory" :

> Shall I array my heart
> In Love's vermeil attire?
> O shall I fling my life
> Like incense in Love's fire?
> Weep unto sorrow's lute?
> Dance unto rapture's lyre?

Weeping and dancing, grieving and rejoicing : these are the various moods distilled in the pages of her poetry. The land of mood or vision we come across in "the Temple" (to which we shall revert a little after) is hardly to be seen in her early poetry. The intense romantic fervour of the early days seems to have partly evaporated with the advancement of year, yielding place to a serener mood.

Sarojini has been usually emotional, yea even sentimental, in her response to love when we consider her poetry in its entirety. The heart rather than the head predominates in it. So it would be futile to attempt to trace a philosophy of love in her poetry. Inspired by the medieval devotional poets — Andal, Mira, Vidyapati, Chandidas, etc. — and the Vaishnavites, Sarojini rendered her poetry usually colourful, romantic and sensuous. For this she has been taken to task too. Dr. Dustoor rightly thinks that Sarojini's love poetry is mostly extravagant, needlessly wordy, or merely pretty, and that still it reveals a sensitive and passionate spirit.[5]

Sarojini's love poetry covers almost all aspects of Love. The union and the separation of lovers are beautifully depicted in it. "Village Song" pictures the mental tension of the Yamuna riverside belle who goes out to fill her pitcher with the Yamuna water but is detained by her lover's song against her wishes. The night is fast approaching; she is afraid of her brother and mother and the impending natural calamities — "*Ram re Ram*!" I shall die" — but the lover she can't deny. Another poem, "A Rajput Love Song," is an exquisite example of love poetry. Both aspects of love — union and separation — are painted in it. Parvati, the beloved, and Amar Singh, the lover, have been together during the night, but with the approaching dawn they will have to part for the day only to rejoin at night. Even this twelve-hour separation is unbearable to them, as one may clearly gather from the refrain :

> Haste, O wild-bee hours, to the gardens of the sunset!
> Fly, wild-parrot day, to the orchards of the West!
> Come, O tender night, with your sweet, consoling darkness
> And bring me my Beloved to the shelter of my breast!

This love-song lands us in a world of chivalry and romance. There are the beloved's tresses, golden sleeves, silken raiments, bright girdles, scents, sandal lutes, silver lamps, jades and gleaming bells.

Mysticism cannot be ruled out in a poetry of the kind Sarojini wrote. It may be recalled that three of her poems, namely "The Soul's Prayer," "In Salutation to Eternal Peace," and "To a Buddha Seated on a Lotus," found a berth in *The Oxford Book of English Mystical Verse* (1916). Sarojini's mystical genius found an outlet in her poetry, especially in "The Temple," the love-trilogy based in Vaishnavism,[6] which stresses that Nature and God are not two distinct entities, but one and indivisible. Nature transcends itself into God and God involves himself in Nature. Woman's love for man, or *vice versa*, at its intensest is a kind of self-transcendence, the realisation of the bliss of being. It is arriving at the abode of Vishnu; it is entering 'the temple'.[7]

Any consideration of Sarojini's love poetry would remain incomplete without taking into account "The Temple," which is a constellation of love songs, and which consists of three parts : "The Gate of Delight," "The Path of Tears" and "The Sanctuary," each part is a string of eight songs. The trilogy has a sub-title : "A Pilgrimage of Love," and its epigraph is suitably chosen from Rabindranath Tagore :

> My passion shall burn as the flame of Salvation,
> The flower of my love shall become the ripe fruit of
> Devotion.

The epigraph embodies the central theme of the poem. The first part, "The Gate of Delight", deals with Love's fulfilment. The woman absolutely offers herself to her Love. She tells her lover :

> Why need you sad penance or pardon or prayer
> For life's passion and folly and fears?
> My soul be your loving atonement, O Love,
> In the flame of immutable years!

(The "Late-Song")

The second part, "The Path of Tears," treats of the gradual disillusionment of the sensuous woman of the first part. Its dominant note is suffering. The faithful woman bewails her lover's pride and disdain and cruelty. At one place her rebellious spirit is aroused, and in a mood of resentment she says :

> When youth and spring and passion shall betray you
> And mock your proud rebellion with defeat,
> God knows, O Love , if I shall save or slay you
> As you lie spent and broken at my feet!

("The Menace of Love")

In utter desperation, she is prepared, in "If You Were Dead," to welcome even the death of her lover, for she expects union in death. According to Mr. Turnbull, Sarojini has achieved "a rare beauty"[8] in this poem. The third and last part, "The Sanctuary," is the plausible culmination of love's tragic drama. The woman having traversed Love's whole expanse — through the Gate of Delight and the Path of Tears — now gives herself over to martyrdom. She will build a temple for her lover to guard him from the scourge of Time and Fate. In truth, so fierce is her own love that he needs to be saved from herself :

What sanctuary can I pledge
Whose very love of you is sacrilege?
O I would save you from the revening fire
Of my own heart's desire!

("The Fear of Love")

A similar passionate devotion inspires the poem "The Illusion of Love." The last poem, "Devotion," completes the long pilgrimages of Love. In a spirit of total dedication, she wishes her love to dispense with her as he pleases. He may slay or cherish her, burn or wear her like a flower on his breast.

It seems that the poetess wrote "The Temple" at a time of great emotional disturbance. Her biographer, Mrs. Sengupta, also points out that in an agony of bitter disappointment in romance Sarojini has sacrificed her all.[9] She has now given up every sensual longing to start a new life after purging herself in the sacrificial fire of Love. But it is strange that she never made a candid confession of her emotional upheaval to anyone.

III

POEMS OF LIFE AND DEATH

Sarojini wrote several poems on the problems of life and death. "Life," "To the God of Pain," "Damayanti to Nala in the Hour of Exile," "The Poet to Death." "To a Buddha Seated on a Lotus" (All from *The Golden Threshold*), "Dirge," "Love and Death," "Death and Life," "The Soul's Prayer," "A Challenge to Fate," "In Salutation to the Eternal Peace" (all from *The Bird of Time*), "A Song from Shiraz," "The Challenge," "The Garden Vigil," "Invincible," and "Three Sorrows" (all from *The Broken Wing*) are some of the well-known poems of this *genre*. The poetess had experienced the ups and downs in life and wanted to get at the mystery of life and death, as is clear from the following :

In childhood's pride I said to Thee :
"O Thou, who mad'st me of Thy breath,
Speak, master, and reveal to me
Thine inmost laws of life and death...."

She was peculiarly attracted to different walks of life and sang gaily of them. But sometimes she was overpowered by feelings of fear, pain and death and uttered aloud of them too. Thus, in "To the God of Pain," she cried out in intense agony :

> I have no more to give, all that was mine
> Is laid, a wrested tribute, at thy shrine;
> Let me depart, for my whole soul is wrung,
> And all my cheerless orisons are sung;
> Let me depart, with faint limbs let me creep
> To some dim shade and sink me down to sleep.

Nevertheless, she faced the vicissitudes of life heroically without being cowed down by the terrors of Death. Like Robert Browning, she occasionally hurled challenges to Death and Fate.

Sarojini's approach to the problems of life and death was not the approach of a metaphysician. She did not explore these problems with the same tenacity as Sri Aurobindo or Rabindranath Tagore did. But the lack of system does not imply that she never ventured into considerations of these subtle questions. In "To a Buddha Seated on a Lotus," we have :

> And all our mortal moments are
> A session of the Infinite.

These two lines neatly summarise the Vedantic philosophy and are the outcome of a direct imaginative realisation of the Eternal. After all, Sarojini was the worthy daughter of her worthy sage father whose wisdom she had inherited.

IV

POEMS OF THE INDIAN SCENE

Several poems of Sarojini Naidu are centred round the Indian scene. All her Folk-Songs fall into this category. "Palanquin-Bearers," "Wandering Singers," "Indian Weavers," "Coromandel Fishers : "The Snake Charmer," "Corn Grinders," "Harvest Hymn," "Indian Dancers," "The Indian Gipsy," "Nightfall in the City of Hyderabad," "Street Cries" (from *The Golden Threshold*), "Village Song," "Bangle-sellers," "The Festival of Serpents," "Hyman to Indra, Lord of Rain," (from *The Bird of Time*), "Wandering Beggars" "Lakshmi, the Lotus Born," "Kali the Mother" (from *The Broken Wing*), "Raksha Bandhan," "The Festival of the Sea" and "Kanhaya" (from *The Feather of the Dawn*) : all are poems on the Indian scene and life. As stated earlier, Sir Gosse's advice has turned Sarojini a singer of native customs and fashions, flowers and fruits, birds and bees, sounds and sights. The entire pageantry of Indian life comes alive in her poetry — the carefree and songful palanquin-bearers, the wandering singers, the weavers, the Coromandel Fishers, the snake-charmers, the bangle-sellers, the corn-grinders, the merry dancers, the tameless gipsy girls and the lovely pardahnashins. Various Indian festivals — the Nag Panchami, the Reksha Bandhan, the Dipawali, the Vasant Panchami, the Kali Puja, and the Lakeshmi Puja — and songs of Radha, the Milkmaid, and Kanhaya, the Flute-player of Brindaben are embalmed in the spicy and aromatic pages of her poetry.

Of all the folk-songs penned by Sarojini, 'Palanquin-Bearers' and "Indian Weavers" deserve special mention. The first-named is based on a common sight in India — that of palanquin-bearers carrying a young, noble bride to her husband's. This poem of two stanzas only is structured on a string of touching images. Take the first stanza as an elucidation :

> Lightly, O lightly, we bear her along,
> She sways like a flower in the wind of our song;
> She skims like a bird on the foam of a stream,
> She floats like a laugh from the lips of a dream.
> Gaily, O gaily we glide and we sing,
> We bear her along like a pearl on a string.

This stanza rests on no more substantial base than the comparison of a lovely lady inside the palanquin to a flower, a bird, a dreamy laugh, and a pearl. But its appeal is immediate and direct to the heart. The palanquin-bearers' tone is in complete rapport with the heart-beats of the lady inside. No doubt, the poetess has successfully captured the emotionally surcharged atmosphere of the event described.

"Indian Weavers" presents the picture of weavers in rural areas who weave handloom cloth in variegated colours and patterns. The poem is set forth in question-answer form, the first two lines in each of the three stanzas asking the question and the last two lines giving the answer. The questions are put at three different hours — at day-break, at nightfall, and at chill moonlight time. Outwardly this poem looks to be simple, but actually it is not so. Its simplicity belies its complexity which arises out of a commingling of birds, colours, similes, images, sound patterns, different hours and moods. It is rich in symbolism too. In the words of Prof. Narasimhaiah, "Here, in twelve lines, is an elliptical, allusive, and symbolic presentation of life's journey from birth to death."[10] Very concisely the poetess has presented here her solemn thinking about life, love and death.

Sarojini seldom sang about modern industrial life. Like W.B. Yeats, she was of an old type aristocratic temperament and never felt at home with the drab of industrial Life. The slum, the street-arab and the chimney-smoke, the motor-horn and the locomotive, the labour class and the trade unionists found no room in her poetry. What appealed to her most was the old typical Indian life with its beautiful scenes and sights and with its vivacious common men and women. Her poems of the Indian scene indicate her faculty for observation. She depicted what she actually saw around her, with no mixture of her own feelings. Also, her common scenes and sights lack in particularity and no one can be sure about the place and time of their occurrence, but they always carry a human context.

V

PATRIOTIC POEMS

A fifth theme that enters into Sarojini's poetry is the theme of patriotism. There are some poems which throb with the passionate love for the Motherland and which express the poetess's hopes for India's glorious renaissance. In this connection, one may mention such poems as "To India," "The Gift of India," and "The Lotus." The first stanza of "To India" is given below for the enjoyment of the reader :

> O young through all thy immemorial years!
> Rise, Mother, rise, regenerate from thy gloom,
> And, like a bride high-mated with the spheres;
> Beget new glories from thine ageless womb!

Some of Sarojini's poems are inspired by national leaders like Gopal Krishna Gokhale, Lokmanya Bal Gangadhar Tilak, Mahatma

Gandhi, and Umar Sobani. Of these, Gokhale, Tilak and Sobani are immortalized in the opening pages of *The Feather of the Dawn*, while Mahatma Gandhi figuratively appears in the poem "The Lotus" in *The Broken Wing*. Gokhale has been remembered as a 'great saint and soldier of our national righteousness,' Tilak as a 'scholar, mathematician and saint' and as a resolute freedom fighter, Sobani as a Muslim nationalist to join Mahatma Gandhi and a 'millionaire philanthropist of Bombay, and Gandhi as a 'mystic Lotus, sacred and sublime.'

VI

POEMS ON CHILDHOOD

Lastly, Sarojini composed a few poems on childhood, such as "To My Children" (in *The Golden Threshold*), "Child Fancies" and "'The Lonely Child" (in *The Feather of the Dawn*). They simply show her delicate feminine fancy, and nothing more. There are also some miscellaneous poems inspired by a certain occasion, place or person; for example, "Ode to H.H. The Nizam of Hyderabad," "The Iman Bara," "Imperial Delhi," "Memorial Verses" (to the Nizam of Hyderbad and Gokhale), "In Salutation to My Father's Spirit" (for Aghorenath Chattopadhyaya), "Gujerat," etc. These poems are light in content and treatment and do not speak of Sarojini at her best. Evidently, Sarojini is at her best in her love poems and folk-songs.

REFERENCES

1. Arthur Symons, "Introduction," *The Golden Threshold* (London : William Heinemann, 1905), p. 12.
2. Edmund Gosse, "Introduction", *The Bird of Time* (London : William Heinemann, 1912), p. 5.
3. Symons "Introduction," pp. 17-18.
4. James H. Cousins, *The Renaissance in India* (Madras : Ganesh & Co., 1918), p. 265.
5. P.E. Dustoor, *Sarojini Naidu* (Mysore : Rao & Raghavan, 1961), p. 40.
6. Shankar Mokashi-Punekar, "A Note on Sarojini Naidu," *Critical Essays on Indian Writing in English*, ed., M.K. Naik *et al* (Dharwar : Karnatak University, 1972), p. 79.

7. Although Vaishnavism operated best in "The Temple," it is also to be felt in "Songs of Radha" (*The Feather of the Dawn*, p. 43), wherein we have :

   I am of thee, as that of me, a part.
   Look for me in the mirror of thy heart.

8. H.G. Dalway Tumbull, *Sarojini Naidu : Select Poems* (Bombay : Oxford University Press, 1930), p. 232.
9. Padmini Sengupta, *Sarojini Naidu* (New Delhi : Sahitya Akademi 1974), p. 45.
10. C.D. Narasimhaiah. *The Swan and the Eagle* (Simla : Indian Institute of Advanced Study, 1969), p. 22.

7

Toru Dutt and Sarojini Naidu : A Comparative Approach*

By common consent, Toru Dutt and Sarojini Naidu are the two distinguished daughters of modern India who have written in English. They took to an alien medium for the expression of their essentially native genius, and contributed substantially towards the expansion of the intellectual horizon by carrying to the West the hoary wisdom of the East. Coming as they did in the wake of the Indian Renaissance in the 19th century, they did their utmost to place their birth-land on the international map of letters. Their literary activities demonstrated to the world that the then prevalent Victorian belief — 'woman for the hearth' — was miscalculated. They enjoyed popularity in their lifetime as they are doing now, and are prescribed in the syllabi of Indian and foreign universities. It is high time to place them side by side and study them comparatively.

To begin with, Toru Dutt lived a short span of life on earth, while Sarojini Naidu lived a life full and whole. They produced some lasting works in their literary pursuits. Toru produced *A Sheaf Gleaned in French Fields* (1876), *Bianca, or the Young Spanish Maiden* (1978), *Le Journal de Mademoiselle d' Arvers* (1879), and *Ancient Ballads and Legends of Hindustan* (1882), besides two essays on Leconte de Lisle and Henry Vivian Derozio, translations of the two speeches delivered by Victor Hugo and M. Theirs in the French Legislative Assembly, and quite a few letters to Miss Mary Martin and Mlle Clarisse Bader, whereas Sarojini brought out *The*

---

*First published in *Commonwealth Quarterly*, 3 No. 9 (Dec. 1978), 82-94. Reprinted here with permission of the editor.

Golden Threshold (1905), *The Bird of Time* (1912), *The Broken Wing* (1917), and *The Feather of the Dawn* (1961). These publications make it clear that Sarojini came to the scene long after Toru Dutt, who in Indo-English poetry occupies a significant position historically. Before her there were only explorers in the field. Derozio mooted the idea; the Dutts dug trenches and sent out feelers here and there; and Toru gave the sound base. It is not till we come to her that we find "the first solid achievement"[1] in Indo-English poetry. When Sarojini appeared on the scene, the spadework was already done. But credit goes to her for earning recognition of this brand of poetry through her fiery lyrics, which recall Sappho to our minds.

Both Toru and Sarojini were Bengalis by birth, and both chose English as the medium of expression. Toru wrote also in French and *Le Journal* is a proof of it. Both were talented and sensitive women. Both were sponsored by Sir Edmund Gosse, the noted English critic, and to both he wrote fine Introductions. About Toru Dutt he wrote : "It is difficult to exaggerate when we try to estimate what we have lost in the premature death of Toru Dutt. Literature has no honours which need have been beyond the grasp of a girl who at the age of twenty one, and in languages separated from her own by so deep a chasm, had produced so much of lasting worth... When the history of literature of our country comes to be written, there is sure to be a page in it dedicated to this fragile, exotic blossom of song."[2] And about Sarojini he remarked : "Mrs. Naidu is, I believe, acknowledged to be the most accomplished living poet of India — at least, of those who write in English, since what lyric wonders the native languages of that country may be producing I am not competent to say. But I do not think that any one questions the supreme place she holds among those Indians who choose to write in our tongue. Indeed, I am not disinclined to believe that she is the most brilliant, the most original, as well as the most correct, of all the natives of Hindustan who have written in English."[3]

Both Toru and Sarojini belong to the Romantic school of poets, Neither of these shows any signs of modern poetry. While Toru was one of the 'early' authors, Sarojini virtually ceased to write poetry when the modern movement in English letters set in. The latter was apparently a misfit in the modern Pound-Eliotian era.

Had she read French, as Toru had done, she might have been exposed to it. Although Sarojini knew some of the modernists personally and read their works with a sense of admiration, she herself practised otherwise. For their romanticism, Toru and Sarojini have been criticised, and the Workshop poets like P. Lal and K. Raghavendra Rao have dismissed them with a snigger. But the Workshop poets must remember that the fire flies and the flowers are as much a part of human experience as the din and dust of modern metropolis, and their self-righteous attitude to poetry does not tell the entire story about it.

The two Indian poetesses under discussion often wrote in a traditional style. Toru chose for herself a simple, translucent style, whereas Sarojini picked up for her use the style of 'jewelled phrases.' In Toru we have a stanza like this one"

Once, and once only, have I given
My heart and faith — 'its past recall;
With conscience none have ever striven,
And none may strive, without a fall.

("Savitri")

And in Sarojini we have the following :

To field and forest
The gifts of the spring,
To hawk and to heron
The pride of their wing;
Her grace to the panther,
Her tints to the dove...
For me, O my Master,
The rapture of Love!

("Guerdon")

Evidently, Toru's style does not call forth a series of glowing images or similes, but states propositions, as in orthodox prose. But Sarojini has composed poems full of striking images or similes, as in the following :

Lightly, O lightly, we bear her along,
She sways like a flower in the wind of our song;
She skime like a bird on the foam of a stream;

She floats like a laugh from the lips of a dream.
Gaily, O gaily we glide and we sing,
We bear her along like a pearl on a string.

("palanquin-Bearers")

The above-given stanza rests on no other substantial base than the comparison of a lovely lady inside the palanquin to a flower swaying in the wind, a bird skimming on the foam of a stream, a dreamy laugh, and a shining pearl. The style of Mrs. Naidu smacks of the 'Decadent' practice and she remains almost matchless in word-craftsmanship and prosodical perfection. This was perhaps due to her close contact with the members of the Rhymers' Club (Yeats, Rhys, Symons and others).

Both the writers were lyricists instinctively. But Toru was not simply that. She was also an accomplished novelist (she did two novels, one complete and the other fragmentary), an impressive translator, and a fine letter-writer. As contrasted to her multi-pronged genius, Sarojini's was merely poetic. The latter was 'a singer of songs' and 'a song-bird.' That is why she is called the Nightingale of India (Bharat Kokila). Qualitatively speaking, Toru's verse seems to be more natural than that of Sarojini, who is often conventional and too sing-song. Mrs. Naidu's themes are usually girlish and repetitive, and it is astonishing that a discerning critic like Sir Gosse should have remarked that by the time she came to write *The Bird of Time*, the note of 'girlish ecstasy' had passed and a graver music had taken its place.[4] After her third book, Sarojini herself realised the real nature of her verse, and decided to part company with the Muse in a huff. On the other hand, Toru, a prodigious child of nature, never deserted the Muse in her lifetime. Her fragile physical constitution; her fever and consumption, and her pathetic circumstances did not come in the way of her literary endeavours. The tragedy of Toru Dutt lies in speculating what she 'might have been,' had not the race of her life been so quickly run, and that of Sarojini Naidu in bidding farewell to her muse at a time when she was thirty-eight and in plunging headlong into political activities directed towards the liberation of her motherland from the clutches of a mighty foreign ruler.

It may be mentioned here that Sarojini's political career is as eventful and absorbing as her poetic career, but Toru's career is purely artistic. Sarojini rose to be President of the Indian National Congress in its Kanpur sessions in 1925, and strove untiringly to infuse a sense of nationality in the minds of the countrymen so that India could be a sovereign, democratic republic. She toured the country extensively and appealed for peace and harmony in the event of a communal riot. She was a fiery orator and a brilliant conversationalist and hence her appeal never went unheeded. Her sparkling wit and humour added extra charm to her personality. She did not spare even her close associates, and used to call Mahatma Gandhi 'Micky Mouse' and 'the little man.' Once when Pt. Jawaharlal Nehru was surrounded by a bevy of gaping young girls at a tea-party, Sarojini suddenly cried out, "Jawahar, take off your cap and disillusion the girls!" On another occasion in a Congress meeting, Dr. Rajendra Prasad and Sardar Patel were sitting with their shawls covering their heads. A foreigner came and asked as to who those persons were. She immediately replied, "They are the widows of Mahatma Gandhi!"[5] The unmistakable sense of wit and humour made her a welcome speaker in colleges and universities. If Mahatma Gandhi lifted politics to moral sphere, Sarojini lifted it to artistic sphere. Pt. Nehru rightly remarked that Sarojini "started her life as a poet, but when she was drawn into politics her whole life became a poem and a song."[6] As against this bright political career of hers, Toru draws a blank.

The range of Sarojini's poetry is limited, but she moved flawlessly within her limited range, reminding us or Jane Austen's 'two inches of Ivory.' According to an Indian scholar, there is "no deep emotional conflict or spiritual upheaval"[7] in her poetry. She did not propound or uphold any particular theory, creed or philosophy. She was moved by the scenes and sounds around her which she turned into lovely lyrics. Her imagination was best suited for short swallow flights, and that is why she never attempted long verses. But Toru was capable of long, sustained flights of imagination and composed long poems like "Savitri," "Lakshman" and "Jogadhya Uma." Unlike Sarojini, she remains mostly objective in her poetry. Only in her Miscellaneous Poems she becomes somewhat personal. In "Our Casuarina Tree," she writes :

But not because of its magnificence
Dear is the Casuarina to my soul :
Beneath it we have played; though years may roll,
O Sweet companions, loved with love intense
For your sakes shall the tree be ever dear!
blent with your images, it shall arise
In memory, till the hot tears blind mine eyes!

Even here, desire is mixed with memory, the present with the past, and the line 'For your sakes shall the tree be ever dear' is very significant in raising the poetess above purely personal considerations. But Sarojini remains personal in her poetry through and through. Take the following as an illustration :

Hide me in a shrine of roses,
Drown me in a wine of roses
Drawn from every fragrant grove!
Bind me on a pyre of roses,
Burn me in a fire of roses,
Crown me with the rose of Love!

("The Time of Roses")

'I' and 'me' and 'mine' are to be pointedly marked in the above poetic passage. As for Toru's range of poetry, it is not so limited as Sarojini's is. She could as easily move among the best pieces of French poetry as among the inexhaustible treasures of Sanskrit literature and the moralising tales and myths of Hindustan. She sometimes talked of social manners and stigmas, as in "Savitri" :

And think upon the dreadful curse
Of widowhood; the vigils, fasts,
And penances; no life is worse
Than hopeless life, — the while it lasts.

and of political opportunism, as when speaking about Sonda Marco in "Prahlad" :

A man
Among the flatterers in the court
Was found, well-suited to the plan
The tyrant had devised. Report
Gave him wisdom owned by few,
And certainly to trim his sail,

And veer his bark, none better knew
Before a changing adverse gale.

and of Vedantic philosophy at some length, as in "Savitri" :

I know that in this transient world
All is delusion, — nothing true;
I know its shows are mists unfurled
To please and vanish. To renew
Its bubble joys, be magic bound
In *Maya's* network frail and fair,
Is not my aim! The gladsome sound
Of husband, brother, friend, is air
To such as know that all must die,
And that at last the time must come,
When eye shall speak no more to eye
And Love cry; — Lo, this is my sum.

Of course, Sarojini could also write lines like these :

And all our mortal moments are
A session of the Infinite.

("To a Buddha Seated on a Lotus")

But she was incapable of giving a thoughtful exposition of Indian philosophy.

Sarojini wrote no epic, no dramatic or narrative poetry, no blank verse. Being a songster solely, she had no aptitude or talent for them. She had, of course, once dreamt to be a Goethe or a Keats for India,[8] but she could not be that despite her perfect metre and haunting melody. Instead she became a far more living entity,— a sensitive poet of her own people and country. As regards Toru Dutt, she also attempted no epic, but did write descriptive and narrative verse. In the words of a noted Indian scholar, it may "be reasonably said that had she lived longer she could have attained distinction in narrative verse and in descriptive verse. She has a rare gift of storytelling, of arousing interest and curiosity, of creating suspense, and of drawing character. But perhaps in descriptive poetry she is even superior."[9] Though Toru had a propensity for sonnet-form, she tried her hand at blank verse too. It is used in "The Death of the Wolf" *(A Sheaf)* and in some of the legends of *Ancient Ballads*. Her blank verse is somewhat wooden, but it yields its peculiar charms only to the lucky few like Marlowe, Shakespeare and Milton.

The two writers also differed in their observations of Nature.[10] Toru's description of trees is not the same as we find in Sarojini, who seemed always to feel, maybe because of Gosse's advice, that all she described *must* be Indian. To Toru, the trees just happened to be her own — her mango-groves, bamboos and casuarinas. To Sarojini, the trees must be described with an Oriental background. This is how Toru describes a beautiful natural scene in her "Sonnet — Baugmaree" :

> But nothing can be lovelier than the ranges
> Of bamboos to the eastward when the moon
> Looks through their gaps, and the white lotus changes
> Into a cup of silver. One might swoon
> Drunken with beauty of them or gaze and gaze
> On a primeval Eden, in amaze.

And this is how Sarojini write in her "Champak Blossoms" :

> Amber petals, ivory petals,
> Petals of carven jade,
> Charming with your ambrosial sweetness
> Forest and field and glade,
> Foredoomed in your hour of transient glory
> To shrivel and shrink and fade!

It is clear that Sarojini filled up the gap of her natural description with plenty of words and phrases, whereas Toru became profuse and luscious in revealing the beauties of Nature.

It has been stated that Nature to Sarojini was what it was to Tennyson — a background for the portraiture of human emotions, but it appears that she never quite excelled in understanding or portraying human nature. Her characters are usually clothed in dreamlike vagueness, in religious symbolism, and in flowery phrases and glowing similes. In her poetry a human being does not stand out as a loving person baldly confronting his problems in the world around and sharing the joys and sorrows of his follow-beings. Toru has, however, presented certain subtle character-portrayals through the device of dramatic speeches.[11] In *Ancient Ballads* alone (nothing to speak of her novels), we have such ideal representatives of

Indian womanhood as Savitri, Sita and Jogadhya Uma. These characters are delineated with nobility and feminine mystery. There are also many memorable male characters in this work, such as Satyavan, Bharat, Dhruva, Buttoo, Sindhu, and Prahlad.

Finally, both the writers have certain plus and minus points with them. It would be hazardous to glorify one at the cost of the other.[12] In matters of artistry weaving the tender fabrics of dream and fantasy, of finished form and touching rhythm, of placing together a series of coherent images and similes, Sarojini is decidedly the better one, but in portraying living human characters with subtle motives and mysterious nature, in having the range and depth of poetry, and even in displaying the originality of approach and the variety of subject-matter, Toru relegates Sarojini to the background. Moreover, literature or poetry was a whole-time vocation for Toru, but it was mostly a matter of diversion for Sarojini. Toru never parted company with the Muse, whereas Sarojini deliberately deserted her at a crucial moment in her life. And this makes a vital difference between the two.

REFERENCES

1. B.K. Talookdar, "The Poetry of Toru Dutt", *Journal of the University of Bombay*, Part 6 (May 1936), 71.
2. Edmund Gosse, "Introductory Memoir," *Ancient ballads* (London : Routlege, Kegan Paul & Trench, 1927), p. xxvii.
3. Edmund Gosse, "Introduction," *The Bird of Time* (London : William Heinemann, 1912) , pp. 1-2.
4. *Ibid.*, pp. 6-7.
5. Taken from Sahib Singh Ahuja, "The Humour of Mrs. Sarojini Naidu," *The Modern Review* (February 1962), p. 152.
6. Jawaharlal Nehru, "Sarojini Naidu : A Tribute in India's Parliament," *The Hindustan Review*, 82 (April 1949), 205.
7. K.K. Mehrotra, "The Poetry of Sarojini Naidu," Essays and Studies, (Allahabad : I.okbharti Publications, 1970), p. 88. As regards 'spiritual upheaval' Prof. Mehrotra's statement is quite correct, but it is difficult to agree with his statement that there is 'no deep emotional conflict' in her poetry. Right from the beginning of her career, she was rather emotionally disturbed. Her earlier songs published privately by her father in 1896 bear it out. Later, she wrote "The Temple : A Pilgrimage of Love" under a severe emotional strain. Her biographer, Mrs. P. Sengupta, also holds this view. She says, "There seems to have been some great disappointment in romance, for

which she has sacrificed her all. She now abandons every romantic sensual longing and starts a new life so to speak." — *Sarojini Naidu* (New Delhi : Sahitya Akademi, 1974), p. 45.

8. E. Gosse, "Introduction," p. 7.
9. Amaranatha Jha, "Introductory Memoir," *Ancient Ballads* (1941; Allahabad : Kitabistan, 1969), p. 30.
10. P. Sengupta , *Sarojini Naidu*, p. 95.
11. See this writer's article, "Toru Dutt and Her Poetry," I *World Literature Written in English*, 14, No. 2 (November 1975), 287.
12. As Prof. H.H. Anniah Gowda did by stating that Sarojini was "perhaps a better poet" than Toru Dutt. See his article, "Toru Dutt and Sarojini Naidu as Poets," *The Literary Half-Yearly*, 9, No. 1 (1968), 22.

8

Imagery in Nissim Ezekiel's Later Poetry*

The images are beautiful birds
and colourful fish : they fly,
they swim in my Jewish consciousness

(*Latter-Day Psalms*, p. 47)

I

A. Alvarez once remarked that "the experimental techniques of Eliot and the rest never really took on in England because they were an essentially American concern."[1] While agreeing with Alvarez that the literary movement called 'Imagism' is clearly 'experimental' in nature and unmistakably 'American' in origin, it is to be submitted that the shores of England did not remain untouched by this great movement and that through England it also spilled over to India and other parts of the world. Originally, Ezra Pound gathered the scattered experimenters in a group and published *Des Imagistes* in America in 1914 (through the financial investment of Albert and Charles Boni), which included such names as Richard Aldington, 'H.D.,' F.S. Flint, Skipwith Cannell, Amy Lowell, William Carlos Williams, James Joyce, Ford Maddox Hueffer, Allen Upward, John Cournos, and Pound himself. It was quickly followed by three annual Imagist anthologies, *Some Imagist Poets* (published by Houghton Mifflin Company in 1915, 1916 and 1917 respectively), but the Imagist *pronunciamentos* were carried in the very first anthology. The Imagists announced some six principles for themselves to

*This paper was written before the publication of Ezekiel's *Collected Poems* (New Delhi : O.U.P., 1989).

practise — (1) to use the language of common speech, but to employ always the exact word, not the nearly exact, nor the merely decorative word; (2) to create new rhythms — as the expressions of new moods and not to copy old rhythms, which merely echo old moods, insisting on the use of 'free verse' for the sake of liberty and individuality; (3) to allow absolute freedom in the choice of subject; (4) to present an image in order to avoid vague generalities; (5) to produce poetry that is hard and clear, never blurred nor indefinite and (6) to believe that concentration is the very essence of poetry.[2]

Now, what does an 'image' mean? In the simplest terms, it means "a picture made out of words."[3] It is usually expressed through a phrase, an epithet, a metaphor, and a simile. C. Day Lewis has observed thus about it : "An epithet, a metaphor, a simile may create an image; or an image may be presented to us in a phrase or a passage on the face of it purely descriptive, but conveying to our imagination something more than the accurate reflection of an external reality."[4] Of all these constituents of imagery, Aristotle gives priority to metaphor.[5] Broadly speaking, imagery tends to be graphic, visual or expressive in effects, and is used for conveying some similarity, analogy or congruity. It is very useful toward 'concretization of emotions' and 'obliquity of expression'. Vividness, compactness and concentration constitute its hallmarks. It is very effective in avoiding direct statements in poetry, as Hugh Kenner has pointed out in one of his essays — "Any image is by its nature more vivid than any statement."[6]

II

Here in this paper I want to dwell on the imagery of Nissim Ezekiel, a major Indian English poet of today, as employed by him in his later poetry. By 'later poetry' I mean his two OUP publications — *Hymns in Darkness* (1976) and *Latter-Day Psalms* (1982). I do not want to suggest here that Ezekiel is as much addicted to the drug of imagery as the Imagists proper were. But it is also true that imagery is not entirely absent from his poetry. He rather uses imagery sparingly and judiciously. As a result, his images remain strictly functional rather than decorative. Some images in Ezekiel's poetry are repeatedly used, and they acquire symbolic overtones. But such images are not too many in number, and they will be examined in a separate section (VI) in this paper.

III

Consisting of twenty-seven poems and dedicated to Keku and Khorshed Gandhy, *Hymns in Darkness* moves along with deeper thoughts and surer techniques. In his Foreword, the poet has explained that these poems were written between 1966 and 1975 and that they are largely cast in free verse[7] (except for two poems — "Subject of Change" and "Mind"). This poetical volume is notable for employing imagery at appropriate times. Its opening piece, "Subject of Change," makes a beautiful use of simile, metaphor and figurative expression in barely twenty lines. For metaphor and figurative application of language, one may mark the very first stanza :

> The evening walk proved not to be
> Along the shore of memory.
> I edged towards a different light :
> The fevers of a future night.

(*H.D.*, p. 9)

Here 'the shore of memory' is a striking metaphor and 'The fevers of a future night' is both provocative and figurative. The last stanza of the poem brings in a very apt comparison :

> The waves
> Rise and fall like nightmare graves
> That cannot hold their dead. The sky
> Is smaller than this open eye.

(*H.D.*, p. 9)

Obviously, Ezekiel appears to be searching for the objects and their exact description. To a common reader, the last line may appear to be hyperbolical or startling, but it is definitely a very apt description of the geography of Bombay, which is so inescapably surrounded by the sea-water.

In certain other poems, too, Ezekiel employs metaphors and similes exceedingly well, such as in "Poem of the Separation" and sixth section of "Hymns in Darkness" (for metaphors) and in "Guru," "Distance," "London," "Tone Poem," the fourth and ninth sections of "Poster Poem," and the third, sixth and thirteenth sections of "Hymns in Darkness" (all for similes). One or two illustrations of metaphor and simile will suffice here to indicate Ezekiel's poetic and evocative powers. In his "Poem of the Separation," the poet says :

> Any man may be a whirlwind,
> any woman lightning ....

(*H.D.*, p. 29)

and in his "Hymns in Darkness," he combines metaphor with simile in order to extend the domain of 'old friends' and their mutual 'relationships' :

> His follies are familiar,
> accepted
> like old friends.
> Incapable of quarrelling with them,
> he maintains the old
> stale
> unredeemable relationships.

(*H.D.*, p. 56)

One may guess at the aptness and precision of Ezekiel's comparisons by looking at the following passage from the poem "Guru" :

> We too one day
> may grow like him,
> dropping our follies
> like old clothes or creeds.

(*H.D.*, p. 25)

or at the following from "Tone Poem" :

> Your breasts are small,
> tender
> like your feelings.

(*H.D.*, p. 38)

In the last-quoted passage, the poet does not go anywhere beyond the subject of his treatment for an arresting simile. This shows the alertness of the poet's mind. Clearly, Ezekiel has compared the 'tenderness' of a woman's — the beloved's — breasts with the 'tenderness' of her feelings. But while the 'breasts' are tangible and visible, 'feelings' are not. By this analogy the poet has tried to explore 'the universe of quality' and to chart 'the non-measurable world,' as J. Middleton Murry would have it :

> All metaphor and simile can be described as the analogy by which the human mind explores the universe of quality and charts the non-measurable world. Of these indefinite qualities some are capable of direct sensuous apprehension, while others can be grasped only by a faculty which, though obviously akin to sensuous apprehension, yet differs from it. Sensuous perception is of the qualities of the visible, audible, tangible world; of the spiritual qualities of the more recondite world of human personality and its creations there is intuition. Both faculties are necessary to the great poet....[8]

Perhaps one cannot find a better example combining these two 'faculties' — of the visible and the invisible, of the world of direct 'sensuous perception' and 'the non-measurable world' — than in the quoted extract from "Tone Poem," and it is in this that one discovers the real greatness of Ezekiel as a poet.

IV

Dedicated to Daisy, Kavita, Kalpana and Elkana, the latest poetical collection of Ezekiel — *Latter-Day Psalms* — offers us a delicious feast of functional imagery at appropriate places. Talking of the genesis of this collection, Ezekiel has observed thus :

> ...though first of all the idea is an accident. In response to an invitation, I travel to that poetry festival in Rotterdam...taking no books with me, so as to give myself a chance to *see* and *hear*. I arrive at my hotel, and am immensely struck by the total silence of the place. We're so accustomed to noise in India. I sleep for a few hours, get up, and it's tea again ... The only thing to read in the hotel room is the Giddon Bible... I read something from the Old Testament. I turn to Job... Still plenty of time for dinner, and I read the first Psalm.

> I think I realised suddenly that I had never accepted the Psalms, and this crystalised into an answer to the first one. Within ten minutes I'd written the first Latter-Day Psalm and formed the idea of writing ten. I completed nine Latter-Day Psalms in Rotterdam (June'78). The tenth is a commentary on the other nine, written in modern English.

About the kind of idiom used by the poet herein, he further informs us : "The idiom is important. It had to be a very special kind of English, not old-fashioned and dead, but also not ultra-modern and sparkling either. The characters had to speak functional, idiomatic, non-dated English."[10] As for imagery in *Latter-Day Psalms*, it is usually concrete and sensuous, pointed and pertinent. The title piece contains some fine flashes of fancy through simile and metaphor, mostly simile. Here is a passage containing a striking simile in this longer poem :

> The ungodly are in the same con-
> dition, no more like the chaff
> which the wind driveth away
> than the godly.[11]

and another drawn from the world of nature :

> I am like a pelican of the wild-
> erness, like an owl of the de-
> sert, like a sparrow alone
> upon the house top —
>
> (*LDP*, p. 45)

and still another derived from the world of human experience :

> I wax old as a garment,
> as a vesture I am changed.
>
> (*LDP*, p. 46)

The simile is also to be found in the lines— "Children are as arrows in the hands of a mighty man" (LDP, p. 46). In one place in this poem, at least, the poet has used metaphor in a striking way :

> The images are beautiful birds
> and colourful fish... etc.
>
> (*LDP*, p. 47)

Here the poet has hinted at the process of image-making, aiming at the concretization of details. In this poem, the poet has used some beautiful figurative expressions; for example :

> Rare is the man whose fruit is
> in his season. Yet, his leaf
> must wither, and that which
> appears to prosper, is often
> dying at the root.

(*LDP*, p. 39)

In this passage, man is likened to a fruit-bearing tree, which is bound to decay in due course. Such expressions as "the wine of astonishment" (p. 42) and "the bread of sorrow" (p. 46) are very aptly handled.

There are some more poems in this volume which clearly display Ezekiel's imagistic skill and evocative power. Of such poems, mention may be made of "Warning," "Two Sonnets," "Furies" (the third of the Postcard Poems), and "Nudes 1978" (especially sections 3, 9 and 14). In the first-mentioned poem, the poet compares the 'middle age' with the non-crucifying 'cross' in the opening sonnet, while in the second one he brackets poets with sellers who cheat their customers (*i.e.*, readers) with cheap words instead of money. But he also warns them that they will not go scot free, for they have to be caught by 'critic-cops' sooner than later- "Counterfeiters/caught by critic-cops at dead of night" (p. 16). The second poem noted above — "Furies" — likens the poet to "a maddened/dog or horse" (p. 31), and the third one — "Furies 1978" — employs a metaphoric language in "I love/your body too, though you're hardly/my cup of tea" (p. 33) and bodies forth an abstract thing like 'desire' in "desire/dared, sent forth Zen-eyed/to bring her in, saying,/'Yes,' this is me as I am'..." (p. 38). In the ninth section of "Nudes 1978," the poet comes out with all the creative resources at his command and recounts a series of 'landscape images' in a single breath, almost Whitman-like in shoring up details. The first eight lines cataloguing a number of visible objects are being given below to enable the reader to form his own idea about this poetic piece :

> Hills, valleys, swelling river-banks,
> all those landscape images,
> praise of breasts and buttocks
> seen as fruit, thighs as tree-trunks;
> flower, moon, fire, bird
> of desire, fish of sex
> remotely tell a small
> fragmented part of the story.
>
> (*LDP*, pp. 35-36)

Besides landscape images, one may unfailingly discover sensuous and natural images herein. No doubt, eroticism cannot be ruled out of a poem depicting 'nudity' and 'nakedness' — "naked seen, seeing nakedness" (p. 38).

V

It won't be irrelevant here to take stock of the imagery used by Ezekiel in the poems culled from *The Unfinished Man* (1960) and *The Exact Name* (1965) and incorporated in the texture of *Latter-Day Psalms* (which is now under review) and to proceed in the matter in chronological order. Ezekiel has incorporated in *LDP* some six poems from *The Unfinished Man* out of a total of ten and some eight poems from *The Exact Name* out of an output of twenty. *The Unfinished Man* has been described as "the most perfect book of poems written by an Indian in English" wherein Ezekiel is "at his most honest and lyrical best."[12] Commenting on the 'laconic precision' of the poems in this volume, David McCutchion has observed thus :

> The virtuosity and technical brilliance strongly suggest Auden... we find the same deft precision, the same mastery of a colloquial idiom, the personifications and generalised efforts, the stock phrases in new contexts, the juxtaposition of the commonplace and the erudite, the same compactness, startling appropriateness.[13]

Chetan Kamani, who has also admired this book of poems, remarks : "*The Unfinished Man*, then, is an inspired work, prolific in its proper fruits. Ezekiel here showed a mastery of song which he was never to match again."[14] All these scholars highlight Ezekiel's precision, compactness, appropriateness and mastery of idiom and diction in his poetic utterance, and one has to see here how far his imagery is responsible for these artistic qualities.

Of the six poems derived from *The Unfinished Man* and contained in *Latter-Day Psalms*, "Urban" is the first one dealing with the city life and mechanical movements and actions of its inhabitants. The city here becomes a symbol of distracting noises and 'kindred clamour' and 'shadows of the night' and serves as "the purgatory before blessedness."[15] A very graphic picture of it has been painted by the poet in the following lines :

> The city like a passion burns.
> He dreams of morning walks, alone,
> And floating on a wave of sand.
>
> (*LDP*, p. 58)

These lines bring in both simile (in the first line) and metaphor (in the third line) together, producing a harmonious effect on the reader's mind. In truth, the city of Bombay is a brooding figure throughout the volume and seems to haunt the poet inescapably. It comes out as the central metaphor in this work. This is quite evident when one reads a poem like "A Morning Walk" which pictures the banal and despairing influence of the city on the poet's perception. Ezekiel calls this city "cold and dim/where only human hands sell cheap" (p. 60), this "barbaric city sick with slums/ Deprived of seasons" (p. 60). He then goes on to describe the city-dweller and his pitiable conditions by means of a series of similes :

> His will is like the morning dew.
> The garden on the hill is cool,
> Its hedges cut to look like birds
> Or mythic beasts are still asleep.
> His past is like a muddy pool
> From which he cannot hope for words.
>
> (*LDP*, p. 61)

The poem ends on a note of disenchantment and disillusionment by specifically pointing out that the busy man of the city, where "fame is cheap," plays "an active fool" throughout his life (p. 61).

The poems like "Morning Prayer" and "Marriage" do employ imagery in a minor key. While the first-named poem gives us "Secretive as a mole' (p. 61), the second one offers a simile in the following lines :

> Wordless, we walked among the trees,
> And felt immortal as the breeze.
>
> (*LDP*, p. 62)

In the second poem, Ezekiel shows his enviable power of evoking an image with the help of a single word — "The darkened room/*Roars* out the joy of flesh and blood" (p. 62; italics mine). Does not the word 'roars' immediately bring 'a lion to our imagination? Yes, it does.

The poem "Enterprise" is significant for our brief study here inasmuch as it uses the metaphor of pilgrimage. According to Garman, "it is a journey from city to primitive hinterland,"[16] and the poet is ill at ease here because his 'copious notes' and use of 'too many words' (as he says in "In Retrospect") lead him in his journey only to his 'home' — "Home is where we have to gather grace" (*LDP*, p. 59). Ezekiel has undoubtedly used this metaphor elsewhere in a better way, *e.g.* in "A Time to Change" (the title-piece of the first volume), "Something to Pursue," "Communication" and "The Worm," though he seems to point out to his readers that the pilgrimage without love is more of a myth than reality — "the pilgrimage is unable to get under way until the love-theme is developed sufficiently to allow the over-rehearsed sex to result in the situation of woman, home, a child or two, and land to plough."[17] What one finds in "Enterprise" is actually a fine illustration of this, — a reversion of the role of the poet-pilgrim for its creator.

Let us now examine the eight poems in LDP taken from *The Exact Name* in the light of our discussion here. The first poem, "Philosophy," considers history and its movements and conflicts as of no consequence in the total perspective of time with the help of a fine image :

> I think
> Of each historic passion as a blink
> That happened to the sad eye of Time.
>
> (*LDP*, p. 48)

Each period of history is regarded as 'a blink' only in the Heraclitean flux of time. In this poem, an appealing figure is to be had in the line : "Here, the mills of God are never slow" (*LDP*, p. 48). The second poem in this poetical volume, "Night of the Scorpion," treating a sad yet familiar family situation — that of the stinging of the poet's mother by a poisonous scorpion — depicts the superstitious peasants as 'swarms of flies' :

> The peasants came like swarms of flies
> and buzzed the Name of God a hundred times
> to paralyse the Evil One.
>
> (*LDP*, p. 49)

The verb 'buzzed' extends the metaphor of 'flies' in the second line. The third poem, "In India," applies a charming and proper figurative expression in the lines —

> I ride my elephant of thought,
> A Cezaanne slung around my neck.
>
> (*LDP*, p. 50)

While the fourth poem, "Poet, Lover, Birdwatcher", is more known for "its association of ideas"[18] than for its imagistic quality, the fifth one, "Poetry Reading", makes a very good use of an audible image — "An image fell/like a silver coin upon the floor" (*LDP*, p. 53). No other poem but "The Visitor" deserves a passing mention here for the simple reason that it brings out the artistic credo of the poet in concrete terms and imagistic details :

> Outside the miracles of mind,
> The figure in the carpet blazing,
> Ebb-flow of sex and the seasons,
> The ordinariness of most events.
>
> (*LDP*, p. 55).

The second and third lines in the above-given poetic passage present picturesque, audible and fluid images to the reader. The economy of language and the poet speaking in figures (and not making direct statements) add to the charm of the poem. Ezekiel remarkably demonstrates here his preference for figures and his choice of ordinary events as the subject-matter of his poetry. From the viewpoint of our topic, this book is not so rich artistically and imagistically as *The Unfinished Man*. At times it lapses into abstract philosophical speculations and unnecessary theorisings about the process of poetry.

VI

It has already been indicated that not too many of Ezekiel's images assume the nature of symbols in his poetry, and that such images are few and far between. Of such recurring images, we may mention the images of journey or pilgrimage, the woman, the city, nature, and the basement room. Since we have already examined the image (through metaphor) of pilgrimage while discussing the poem "Enterprise," we shall confine ourselves here to a consideration of the remaining four recurrent images only.

In Ezekiel's poetry, early as well as later, the image of woman is generally associated with animality and sexuality, with corruption and defilement. The pagan woman as frequently painted by the poet becomes an embodiment of sensuousness and sensuality and beastiality. The image of woman as a sexual beast or seductress appears repeatedly in his verse. Some of the significant poems in this context are : "The Couple," "Poem of the Separation," "Tone Poem," the section called "The Couple" in "Passion Poems," and sections 7 and 9 in "Hymns in Darkness" (all from *HD*), "Nudes 1978," "Poverty Poem," and "Poet, Lover, Birdwatcher" (all from *LDF*). Here is an example of the pagan woman :

Her false love became infused
with truest love
only in making love.

("The Couple," *HD*, p. 15)

In this very poem, the poet speaks freely about her indolence and arrogance, about her deception, passion and possession. She comes out as a seductress in "Poverty Poem" :

She didn't know beggars in India
smile only at white foreigners.

(*LDP*, p. 13)

The picture of the woman in "Nudes 1978" betrays her sensuality and nakedness and nudity :

'Yes, this is me as I am',
naked seen, seeing nakedness,
named, flamed in detail,
womanly and vulnerable.

(*LDP*, p. 38)

It is not that the poet depicts her mate counterparts as saints, nor that he does not paint virtuous women at all (as in "Marriage" or in the earlier poems like "A Woman Observed" and "Platonic"), but that the pagan woman overshadows the ideal woman. Occasionally, Ezekiel concentrates on the physical organs of the female, such as breasts, buttocks, thighs and hair. Take the following as an illustration :

And breasts, thighs, buttocks
swinging
now towards
now away from him.

(*LDP*, p. 57)

or the following :

I want you back
with the rough happiness you lightly wear,
supported by your shoulders,
breasts and thighs.

(*LDP*, p. 30)

Such physical details of the woman only add to the eroticism and beastly urban atmosphere of the poems concerned.

Another recurring image is that of the putrid city, which together with the image of the pagan woman completes the picture of debased and defiled human life. Both the interrelated images, thus, become symbols of corruption and banality. On the one hand, the image of the city confirms the poet's strong sense of commitment, robust sense of 'belonging,' to it : "I have a strong sense of belonging, not only to India, but to this city,"[19] on the other, it shows that he is not blind to its filth and squalor, its debasement and distractions. Most of the poems in *The Unfinished Man* have the city as the dominant metaphor, such as "Urban," "A Morning Walk," and "Case Study." Ezekiel sees the city of Bombay burning "like a passion" ("Urban," *LDP*, p. 58); he also looks upon it as "cold and dimm" "barbaric" and "marshy" ("A Morning Walk"), as also the place where labour and fame are so cheap. The following extract from "Minority Poem" will tell a lot about the poet's general attitude towards the city :

> Polish up your alien
> techniques of observation,
> while the city burns.
>
> (*LDP*, p. 21)

This extract recalls T.S. Eliot's *The Waste Land* to our minds, particularly the lines :

> To Carthage then I came
> Burning burning burning burning[20]
>
> ("The Fire Sermon," 11.307-308)

Keeping the above fact in view, critics have rightly remarked that the "urban theme forms an important strain in Mr. Ezekiel's verse,"[21] and that he "is a poet of the city, Bombay..."[22]

Nature is another recurrent image in Ezekiel's poetry, standing all for purity and tranquility in contradiction of the image of the city. For Ezekiel, nature is a manifestation of the glory and greatness of the Almighty, and it is through her that a man can understand the essential truth and 'see into the life of things' (to borrow a Wordsworthian phrase). The tension to be witnessed in a number of Ezekiel's poems often results from a juxtaposition of the defiled city and the pure nature. This may be best seen in the poem "Urban" :

> The hills are always far away.
> He knows the broken roads, and moves
> In circles tracked within his head.
>
> (*LDP*, p. 58)

Ezekiel goes to the world of nature time and again and draws the fresh and vital images of hills, river, wind, skies, sun, moon, and rain in his poetry. In his poem "Morning Prayer," he prays to the Lord thus :

> God grant me certainty
> In kinships with the sky,

Air, earth, fire, sea —
And the fresh inward eye.

(*LDP*, p. 61)

According to K.D. Verma, the nature images are the archetypal life-symbols : "They project a pastoral vision of a fully refulgent and harmonious life, a pattern in which man enters into sacred communion with his cosmos, including objects of nature, as a metaphorical condition of his integrated humanity and of his desire to foster a community of being."[23]

The image of the basement room is also frequently employed by Ezekiel in his poetry. When Ezekiel was away to England for his higher courses in Philosophy during 1948-1952, he had lived in a basement room in London with his three professed companions — poverty, poetry and philosophy :

Twenty-two : time to go abroad.
First, the decision, then a friend
To pay the fare. Philosophy,
Poverty and poetry, three
Companions shared my basement room.

("Background, Casually," *HD*, p. 1)

The poem "London" throws sufficient light on the conditions of the basement room, wherein the poet states :

That basement room
remains a true place

in my chronology.
Cold and bare, it held

a rare turbulence
in check, for growth

(*HD*, p. 33)

He tells us that two of his friends shared it with him at different times. Further, he reveals that —

Sometimes I think I'm still
in that basement room,

a permanent and proud
metaphor of struggle

for and against the same
creative, self-destructive self.

(*HD*, pp. 33-34)

The 'basement room' thus becomes a metapahor of the poet's relentless struggle for artistic creation and introspection even at the cost of personal health ('self-destructive' as he characterizes it). In another poem entitled "The Room," Ezekiel has clarified that the 'room' was a placc "without a fever or exaggeration" and that it was his "ready cash of doctrine and deliberation" (*HD*, p. 42). Besides the philosophical pursuits that the poet undertook here, he also makes it plain that —

I have to name anew
the things I see. (*HD*, p. 42)

despite "too many contradictions and books" (*HD*, p. 42) at hand. The "basement room' has thus become a symbol of a place of refuge, a shelter from the distracting external world, a place where the poet can reflect and create and 'name things' in a fresh perspective. For him, it is the 'home' where he has 'to gather grace,' where he has to embark on a voyage of self-exploration and self-contemplation, where he has to perform his new and noble deeds. About this place the poet has no misgivings or confusions, though, otherwise, he has been a "trader in paradoxes," an "ally of the dialectic" (as he himself confesses to be in one of his "Postcard Poems" in "Dilemma"— *LDP*, p. 30).

VII

To sum up : Ezekiel's imagery is usually undecorative and functional, and in his later poetry (as well as in his earlier poetry) he uses it wherever necessary. As J. Middleton Murry remarks, "...the greatest mastery of imagery does not lie in the use, however, beautiful and revealing, of isolated images but in the harmonious total impression produced by a succession of subtly related images,"[24] Ezekiel is definitely successful in producing 'the harmonious total impression,' the intended artistic effect, on the mind of the reader by means of his 'subtly related images.' His images of the city and the pagan woman, and of nature and the basement room, are, as noticed in the foregoing pages, closely connected with one another.

Ezra Pound once remarked that "it is better to present one image in a lifetime than to produce voluminous works,[25] and by now we know that Ezekiel has created more than one image of lasting worth to make him immortal in the annals of contemporary Indian-English poetry.

NOTES AND REFERENCES

1. A Alvarez, "Introduction," *The New Poetry*, rev. ed. (Harmondsworth, Middlesex, England : Penguin Books, 1966), p. 21.
2. Louis Untermeyer, *American Poetry Since* 1900 (New York : Henry Holt & Co., 1942), p. 305.
3. C. Day Lewis, *The Poetic Image* (Cambridge : At the University Press, 1955), p. 4.
4. *Idem*.
5. Commenting on the significance of the use of metaphor by a poet, Aristotle observed as follows :

   But the greatest thing by far is to be a master of metaphor. It is the one thing that cannot be learnt from others; and it is also a sign of genius, since a good metaphor implies an intuitive perception of the similarity in dissimilars. — Cited from Ingram Bywater, *Aristotle : On the Art of Poetry* (Oxford : At the Clarendon Press 1967), p. 78.
6. Hugh Kenner, "The Image : What the Words Actually *Name*" *Twentieth Century Poetry*, eds. G. Martin & P.N. Furbank (Walton Hall, Milton Keynes : The Open University Press, 1975), p. 28 :
7. Nissim Ezekiel, "Foreword", *Hymns in Darkness*, 3rd impr. (Delhi : Oxford University Press, 1981), p. 6. All textual quotations from this book are given in the essay itself and are invariably referred to as *HD*. .
8. J. Middleton Murry, "Metaphor," *Twentieth Century Poetry*, p. 12.
9. Cited from the original typescript of Imtiaz & Anil Dhar Kor's "Interview : Nissim Ezekiel", pp. 1-2 (which was supplied to me by the poet himself).
10. *Ibid*., p. 2.
11. Nissim Ezekiel, *Latter-Day Psalms*, 2nd impr. (Delhi : Oxford University Press, 1984). p. 39. All textual quotations are absorbed in the essay itself and are invariably mentioned as *LDP*.
12. Adil Jussawalla, "The New Poetry," *The Journal of Commonwealth Literature*, No. 5 (July 1968), p. 69.
13. David McCutchion, *Indian Writing in English* (Calcutta : Writers Workshop, 1969), pp. 101-2.
14. Chetan Kamani, *Nissim Ezekiel* (New Delhi : Arnold-Heinemann, 1974), p. 73.

15. Michael Garman, "Nissim Ezekiel — Pilgrimage and Myth," *Critical Essays on Indian Writing in English*, ed. M.K. Naik *et al*, 2nd ed. (Dharwar : Kanatak University, 1972), p. 133.
16. *Idem.*
17. *Ibid.*, p. 126.
18. C. Kamani, *op. cit*, p. 91.
19. See the typescript of John B. Boston, "An Interview with Nissim Ezekiel," which later appeared in *WLWE* (April 1977), especially its second sentence, p. 1. The poet was kind enough to have supplied the original typescript of this interview to me.
20. T.S. Eliot, *The Waste Land, Collected Poems*, 5th impr. (London : Faber & Faber Ltd., 1970), p. 74.
21. Rajeev Taranath & Meena Belliappa, *The Poetry of Nissim Ezekiel* (Calcutta : Writers Workshop, 1966), p. 6.
22. Linda Hess, "Post-Independence Indian Poetry in English," *Quest*, 49 (Spring 1966), p. 30.
23. K.D. Verma, "Myth and Imagery in *The Unfinished Man* : A Critical Reading," *JSAL*, XI, Nos. 3 & 4 (Spring & Summer 1976), p. 231.
24. J.M. Murry, *loc, cit.,* p. 13.
25. Cited from C.D. Lewis, *op. cit.*, p. 25.

9

Theme and Form in Ramanujan's Poetry*

In his Introduction to *Readings in Commonwealth Literature* (1973), William Walsh wrote that the 'highest achievement' of Indo-Anglian authors was in fiction, in the work of Mulk Raj Anand, R.K. Narayan, and Raja Rao but that the future, the promise, lay in the poetry, in the work of Nissim Ezekiel, A.K. Ramanujan, and R. Parthasarathy.[1] Evidently, Walsh graded Ramanujan with Ezekiel and Parthasarathy for writing tense and taut poetry. Of all practising poets of today, Ramanujan occupies a prominent place by virtue of his intellectual stamina, his ability to depict the inner struggle, and his ineluctable language. Though his poetic output is meagre — only two volumes : *The Striders* (1966) and *Relations* (1971), it is of enduring quality. Now, we shall examine Ramanujan's poetry in relation to its theme and form.

I

One of the distinguishing features of Ramanujan's poetry is its *autochthonousness*. Indian myth and history, her people and customs, her rich cultural and spiritual heritage : these form the dominant themes of his poetry. Even a cursory glance at it convinces the reader that Ramanujan has not severed his associations with India despite his long residence in the United States of America. He rather frequently resorts to native themes and traditions. His three

*This article first appeared in the *Rajasthan Journal of English Studies* (Dec. 1980). The original shape of the article remains unchanged.

Hindoo poems — "The Hindoo : he doesn't Hurt a Fly or a Spider either," "The Hindoo : he reads his GITA and is calm at all events," and "The Hindoo : the Only Risk" — are essentially Indian in background and treatment. They take us to the core of the Hindu philosophy, to the *Gita*. The poem "A River" focuses our attention on the role of the river Vaikai which flows through Madurai, particularly on its destructive role. Another poem, "A Hindu to His Body," shows that the body is as important to a Hindu as the soul; the phrases and expressions confirm it — 'Dear pursuing presence/ dear body' and 'do not leave me/behind'. "Poona Train Window" brings out the observations of a train traveller looking out of the window. "Some Indian Uses of History on a Rainy Day," which keeps on shifting scene from Madras to Egypt and to Berlin almost in a cinematic fashion, forcefully satirises the visiting Professor of Sanskrit. Some other poems like "Small town, South India," "Old Indian Belief' and "Prayers to Lord Murugan" have also a direct bearing on Indian ways of living, Indian beliefs and prayers. The last-named poem is dedicated to Lord Murugan, the ancient Dravidian god of fertility; joy, youth, beauty, war, and love, having six faces and twelve hands. The Indianness of Ramanujan's poetry is to be marked also in a poem like "Conventions of Despair," wherein the poet says :

> But, sorry, I cannot unlearn
> conventions of despair.
> They have their pride.
> I must seek and will find
> my particular hell only in my hindu mind.[2]

Even his poems on family relationships reveal a good deal of Indian life and atmosphere.

The *family*, for Ramanujan, is "one of the central metapahors with which he thinks,"[3] says the noted Indo-Anglian poet Parthasarathy. Ramanujan depicts his family life almost untiringly, as is clear from the poems collected in the second volume, *Relations*, particularly "Of Mothers, among other things," "Love Poem for a Wife 1," "Love Poem for a Wife 2," and "Small-scale Reflections on a Great House." The family relations always haunt the poet, and there are many good poems which owe their origin to the recollected personal emotions. These poems deal with the memory of his relations and the ambiguous freedom that life away from them confers. The sense of loss is most poignantly connected with the reminiscence of the mother. Viewed in this light, "Of Mothers, among other things" is a soft, soothing poem, which encompasses the mother's youth, her unerring care for the 'crying cradles,' her devotion to her work unmindful of the rains and the fluttering loose saris, and her painstaking domestic responsibility. The stanza which works is the last one :

> My cold parchment tongue licks bark
> in the mouth when I see her four
> still sensible fingers slowly flex
> to pick a grain of rice from the kitchen floor.[4]

The metaphors in the first two lines emphasise the futility of the poet's language to express the rough, bitter taste of the memory, and the last two lines provide an irresistible 'objective correlative' of the emotion. It is not that the poet deliberately intended to illustrate the inadequacy of poetic language, but that the simple picture of the last two lines makes the previous imagery of the poem seem laboured and incoherent. "Love Poem for a Wife 1" highlights the poet's sense of estrangement from his wife, and the reason for this is indicated in the very first stanza :

> Really what keeps us apart
> at the end of years is unshared
> childhood. You cannot, for instance,
> meet my father. He is some years
> dead. Neither can I meet yours :
> he has already lost his temper
> and mellowed.[5]

The 'shared childhood' should have added spices to the sentimental attachment, and the want of this writhes the poet's heart. In some of his translations, too, Ramanujan airs out a similar concern, such as in "What He Said" :

> What kin was your mother
> to mine? What was my father
> to yours anyway? And how
> did you and I meet ever?[6]

But in "Love Poem of a Wife 2" there is no such writhing of the heart, and the tone has softened considerably in portraying the lean, lovely face of the wife :

> my wife's face still fast
> asleep, blessed as by
> butterfly, snake, shiprope,
> and grandmother's other
> children,
> by my only love's only
> insatiable envy.[7]

The poem "Small-scale Reflections on a Great House" tells us about the wonderful assimilative and digestive powers of the house, which absorbs not only good things but also bad things. On the one hand, it is very warm to guests, sons-in-law, wives coming from poor houses, daughters married to short-lived idiots, sons returning in grandchildren, nephews killed in war on the borders; on the other, it tethers others' cows, matures 'unread library books' in two weeks, does not return neighbours' dishes brought up/with the greasy sweets. The pretentious shame of the girls of the house is beautifully brought out in the first few lines :

> Sometimes I think that nothing
> that ever comes into this house
> goes out. Things come in everyday
> to lose themselves among other things
> lost long ago among
> other things lost long ago;
> lame wandering cows from nowhere
> have been known to be tethered,
> given a name, encouraged
> to get pregnant in the broad daylight
> of the street under the elders'
> supervision, the girls hiding
> behind windows with holes in them.[8]

The expression 'with holes in them' speaks more than what actually meets the eye.

Apart from the above-mentioned themes, Ramanujan explores certain others too in his poetry, such as childhood, the experience of love, and the exposure to contemporary urban life. In truth, some of the poems pertaining to his family life concentrate on the recollections of childhood. "Love Poem for a Wife 1" is one such poem. "Looking for a Cousin on a Swing" recalls the innocent days of a premature girl of four or five and a little bigger boy of six or seven. The swing having created a sensation in them inspired them to climb a small fig tree full of leaves. Children and their happy state of existence come to the fore in "Love Poem for a Wife 2." In another poem, "Entries for a Catalogue of Fears," he writes :

> I'll love my children
>   without end,
> and do them infinite harm
> staying on the roof
> a peeping-tom ghost.....[9]

The poem "History" mentions children thrice and tells us about the change wrought on the petite little aunt by death and children's failures.

Ramanujan's best love poem is perhaps "Still Another View of Grace," which successfully captures the heat of passion in the heart of the poet. "Looking for a Cousin on a Swing" is also a pleasant love poem. The following lines in it are specially arresting :

> Now she looks for the swing
> in cities with fifteen suburbs
> and tries to be innocent
> about it.[10]

The tone becomes ironical here, and the girl now having grown into a woman on the look out is taken to task for perpetrating her initial corrupt impulse and practice. The two pieces on his wife are really delightful to read. The two dominant strains of love — union and separation, attachment and alienation — are marvellously depicted in them. Hatred is the occasional feature of love, and this is what we find in "Routine Day Sonnet" : 'she hates me, I hate her/I'm a filthy rat and satyr' (p. 28). True love is not to be found in the traffic of flesh, but in the concord of the souls. If a man cherishes the former sort of love, he is sure to be fear-ridden, say at the age of seventy, for his dwindling physical strength and for his utter futility in the face of 'the fascination/of passing/old women,' and he will be left with no option but to handle his thing helplessly —

this is precisely what we find in the sixth stanza of "Entries for a Catalogue of Fears." The predicament of the helpless lover reminds us of that of Prufrock in Eliot's poem, "The Love Song of J. Alfred Prufrock," with the difference of age no doubt.

The exposure to contemporary urban life is to be witnessed in the poem "Still Another View of Grace," which recounts the painful hesitancy on the part of the poet and the upright boldness on the part of the Christian lady in their approaches to love. The poems "Still Another for Mother" and "Conventions of Despair" handle this subject in one way or the other. In the first, we have :

> And that woman
> beside the wreckage van
> on Hyde Park street: she will not let me rest
> as I slowly cease to be the town's brown
> stranger and guest.[11]

And, in the second :

> Yes, I know all that, I should be modern.
> Marry again. See strippers at the Tease.
> Touch Africa. Go to the movies.
> Impale a six-inch spider
> under a lens. Join the Test-
> ban, or become the Outsider.[12]

Of the two passages quoted above, the first demonstrates that one can hardly attain the peace of mind in the midst of a metropolis like London, and the second that one has to be mobile and modern to fit in the present-day world and to avoid the bitter sense of agony and frustration.

II

Ramanujan once wrote: "English and my disciplines (linguistics, anthropology) give me my 'outer' forms — linguistic, metrical, logical and other such ways of shaping experience; and my first thirty years in India, my frequent visits and field trips, my personal and professional preoccupations with Kannada, Tamil, the classics and folklore give me my substance, my 'inner' forms, images and symbols. They are continuous with each other, and I no longer can tell what comes from where."[13] The 'outer' and 'inner' forms, which have been equated with "the linguistic and cultural determinants of a poet's imagination,"[14] combinedly allude to the nature of Ramanujan's poetic art.

As a Professor of Linguistics, Ramanujan shows no weakness of language or expression. In the opinion of Parthasarathy, "In no other poet before Ramanujan is there his scrupulous concern with language. He has been able to forge...an oblique, elliptical style all his own... It is an attempt, I believe, to turn language into an artifact."[15] In his poetic use of language, Ramanujan has been able to 'extend the resources of the English language' and to add a peculiar pungency to it by Indianising it. Occasionally, it tends to be colloquial and topographical. At places it becomes epigrammatic, as in the short piece "Warning" :

> Poverty is not easy to bear.
> The body is not easy to wear.
> So beware, I say to my children
> unborn, lest they choose to be born.[16]

Like Thomas Hardy's "To An Unborn Pauper Child", this poem issues a warning to unborn children out of sheer compassion. The apparent simplicity of his language, however, conceals the depth of his thought. The poem "Some Indian Uses of History on a Rainy Day" is an illustration in point; the poet speaks sarcastically about the Professor of Sanskrit, who comes home —

> in English, gesture, and Sanskrit,
> assimilating
>   the swastika
> on the neighbour's arm
> in that roaring bus from a grey
> nowhere to a green.[17]

The simple, lucid language of this passage provides a little cover for the subtle dig at the Professor, who has all along been memorising 'a foreign paradigm of lanterns, landmarks' and imitating in a parrot fashion the foreign tongue and gesture.

As for the handling of rhythm and rhyme, Ramanujan displays an interesting variety and skill in his poetry. Most of his poems are accent-based and rhythmical. Usually, the lines in a passage are not arranged in any uniform pattern, and one witnesses alterations in the rhyrhmic pitch. There is no scope for monotony in his verse. Unlike Ezekiel, Ramanujan does not employ regular rhyme (which definitely needs some rigour and discipline); he rather employs *vers libre* (which allows immense liberty to a poet).

It is not that Ramanujan's poetry is totally free from limitations. Many poems in the second volume suffer to some extent from a kind of "intellectual thinness."[18] There are some good poems too, for instance, "History." But in a poem like "The Last of the Princes" the question of intellectual adequacy is neatly skirted, and the poem simply states an experience or provides a portrait. The reader is left to draw his own conclusions. The relative failure to offer an intellectually satisfying comment upon his experience is attributed by the poet to his inability to achieve a coherent pattern in his being and experience as an Indian; he is at the moment over-mastered by his personal dilemma.

Furthermore, some of Ramanujan's poems are not logically concluded. He seems to draw conclusions which do not amount to much. A glaring example in this connection is the first poem of the first volume — "The Striders." In it the thought on 'water bugs' is disrupted in order to force a comparison with 'prophets' :

> See them perch
> on dry capillary legs
> weightless
> on the ripple skin
> of a stream.
> No, not only prophets
> walk on water.[19]

A short lyrical piece like this one hardly allows such ramblings. S. Nagarajan has drawn our attention to the 'chanciness' in Ramanujan's conclusions. One simply doubts the logical coherence of someone's 'search for certain thin-stemmed, bubble-eyed water bugs' and 'this bug sits on a landslide of lights.'

Ramanujan has employed images and symbols in his poetry abundantly. Thus, in "Breaded Fish," we have 'a hood/of memory like a coil on a heath opened in my eyes,' in "Still Another View of Grace," 'I shudder to the bone at hungers that roam the street beyond the constable's beat;' in "Poona Train Window," the tea that 'darkens like a sack traveller's urine' and a man between two rocks recalling the image of 'the symmetry/of human buttocks;' in "Some Indian Uses of History on a Rainy Day," 'a gothic lotus on the iron gate,' etc. One of the fine pieces of imagery is "Smalltown, South India," especially in the second stanza :

> I sink to the seabed in a barrel.
> Water-layers salt and pickle the sun.
> Toes mildew green, trees are porous coral,
> ambus of city shark and wifely dolphin.[20]

It has been argued that a poet who writes in images and symbols takes chances, and that some of the chances that Ramanujan takes do not quite come off because there are different levels of achievement in the same poem. For instance, in "The Hindoo : he reads his *Gita* and is calm at all events," the poet after stating that he does not marvel when he sees good and evil, writes : 'I just walk over them as over the iridiscene/of horsepiss after rain.' The vehicle and the tenor do not seem to have any special appropriateness or inevitability here. This becomes quite evident when we contrast it with the image in 'Yet when I met on a little boy's face/the prehistoric yellow eyes of a goat/I choke for a second as if hands were at my throat.'

III

In conclusion, the sound application of theme and form in Ramanujan's poetry invariably results in a forceful, meaningful utterance. His poems reveal with telling detail the specific physiognomy of an object or a situation. The poet does not hang on certain chosen literary devices at the cost of his meaning or communication, the sole end of all good poetry. There is a dynamism in his art, and one has but to agree with K.R. Srinivasa Iyengar that Ramanujan has established himself as "one of the most talented of the 'new' poets."[21]

NOTES AND REFERENCES

1. William Walsh, "Introduction," *Readings in Commonwealth Literature* (Oxford : Clarendon Press, 1973), p. xviii.
2. A.K. Ramanujan, *Selected Poems* (New Delhi : Oxford University Press, 1976), p. 12.

3. R. Parthasarathy, *Ten Twentieth-Century Indian Poets* (New Delhi : Oxford University Press, 1976), p. 95.
4. *Selected Poems*, p. 22.
5. *Ibid.*, p. 25.
6. A.K. Ramanujan, *Fifteen Poems from a Classical Tamil Anthology* (Calcutta : Writers Workshop. 1965), n.p. (Kur 40).
7. *Selected Poems*, p. 35.
8. *Ibid.*, p. 40.
9. *Ibid.*, p. 39.
10. *Ibid.*, p. 8.
11. *Ibid.*, p. 6.
12. *Ibid.* p. 12.
13. Cited from *Ten Twentieth-Century Indian Poets*, pp. 95-96.
14. Chirantana Kulshrestha, "The Self in Ramanujan's Poetry," *The Indian Journal of English Studies*, XVIII (1978-79), 110.
15. R. Parthasarathy, "How It Strikes a Contemporary : The Poetry of A.K. Ramanujan," *The Literary Criterion*, XII, Nos. 2 & 3 (1976), 195-196.
16. *Selected Poems*, p. 18.
17. *Ibid.*, p. 32.
18. S. Nagarajan, "A.K. Ramanujan," *Contemporary Indian Poetry in English*, ed. Saleem Peeradina (1972; New Delhi : Macmillan, 1977), p. 20.
19. A.K. Ramanujan, *The Striders* (London : Oxford University Press, 1966), p. 1.
20. ——, *Relations* (London : Oxford University Press, 1971), p. 44.
21. K.R. Srinivasa Iyengar, *Indian Writing in English* (1962; Bombay : Asia Publishing House, 1973), p. 671.

10

The 'Tongue in English Chains' : The Poetry of R. Parthasarathy

I

R. Parthasarathy is one of the few gifted Indian poets writing in English today. His constant, sincere devotion to the Muse has added new depth and dimension to Indo-English poetry. Before he came to publish a book of poetry, he had already made appearances in several prestigious magazines and anthologies.[1] In 1967, he had attempted to set his first step into the world of versification, but later he retraced it.[2] Then followed a decade-long silence of preparation for the poet that was broken only in 1977 when his *Rough Passage* came out from the Oxford University Press under the Three Crowns scheme. This poetical volume, which is described as "Parthasarathy's poetic autobiography,"[3] is the outcome of his painstaking "revision and elimination" where "all the poems form part of a single poem, as it were."[4] In his Preface to it, the poet remarks : "It should be considered and read as one poem. In it twenty years' writing has finally' settled."[5]

Dedicated to Shobhan and Gautam, *Rough Passage* indicates more of a journey than of an arriving at a destination, more of continuity than of completion of efforts. The poet is conscious of this fact, and observes : "I have at last composed, but perhaps not completed it."[6] And the journey that he has taken is more full of obstacles and hardships than the one of smoothness and easy-going. The title of the book is, therefore, aptly chosen, in other words, it is a telltale title.

This slender collection of poems speaks volumes of

Parthasarathy's ceaseless experimentation with the English language as well as of his predicament as a poet. He is somewhat torn within by the incompatibility of the twin pulls of the English tongue and the patriotic urges. On the one hand, he can't undo the labour of some two decades in learning a foreign language; on the other, he can't ignore the call of the land, the need of the hour. The Tamil past asserts its own claim on him, and assures him a safe anchorage. Ultimately, he comes to a kind of compromise between the two diverse pulls. But this compromise leaves its marks on his poetic art and mind. He has to undergo the trials and tribulations of a traumatic experience to be felt by many bilingual creative writers, though not so acutely expressed by them. This adds a peculiar pungency to his poetry and turns out to be the touchstone of his personality and perception.

II

The general reception to Parthasarathy's poetry has been warm and welcome. It met with an instantaneous approval of the press and the public alike. In this respect, Parthasarathy is luckier than several Indo-English poets with a greater number of books to their credit. Speaking of him, K.R.S. Iyengar has remarked : "Of the poets who cultivate an extreme austerity in style, R. Parthasarathy is probably the most successful... Parthasarathy's best poems reveal an uncommon talent and a sensibility that deliberately puts shackles on itself."[7] William Walsh, a perceptic critic of Commonwealth Literature, makes the following observations about him : "He has found, after writing for ten years in English, that this very exercise helps to alienate himself from his own civilization... One has the feeling that Parthasarathy's discomfort is purely intellectual. His own language, his own poetry, seems a living contradiction of his own case."[8] Gauri Deshpande, a well-known practising poetess, comments on him thus : "It is obvious even from a cursory reading of Parthasarathy that he pursues his craft seriously... His sense of language is competent enough for him not to be obtrusively bizarre. It is also sensitive and lively enough to allow him to come up time and again with delightfully surprising and unerring images... There is hardly any sense of joy in the fact of his poetry."[9] Adil Jussawalla, another practising poet of recognised stature, comes out with the following statement about him : "The strength of his poetry lies almost entirely in its visual juxtapositions and the startling images. His lines do not sing. He cultivates the deliberately prosaic style, an undertone of rhythm itself. So, at their best, his poems become memorable individual images themselves. But occasionally the prose ignites no metaphor, is almost purely descriptive."[10] V.A. Shahane gives his verdict like this : "He is perhaps alone among contemporary Indo-English poets to intensely explore this essential poetical predicament, the perplexing literary and cultural situation of bilingualim and biculturalism... One may hope that this dilemma will continue to remain unresolved, at least for its aesthetic potential."[11] And in the opinion of Godavari Sharma, Parthasarathy is "a skilful poet who pursues his craft seriously and who has a mode of expression — which is distinct from that of any other Indian poet today. He is an Indian trying to be an Indian, quits with the indigestible alien culture, grieving at the degeneration of his native culture."[12]

III

Rough Passage follows a neat, clean three-tier structure. It consists of three sections in all — (i) Exile, (ii) Trial, and (iii) Homecoming. The threefold structure of the book corresponds with the threefold pattern of experience. This fact strikes home when we remember that the poet's past and present mingle in it beautifully. In the course of his development, the poet seems to shift his euphoric attitude towards the English tongue to one of bitter disenchantment. His quest for identity, his search for the self, leads him step by step to this peculiar enchantment. In a way, the poet's development along his art is the development of his 'situation.' The 'situation,' in fact, becomes poetry for him. He depicts his 'situation' with immaculate skill and fidelity.

The three-tier structure of *Rough Passage* has not gone unnoticed by critics. M. Sivaramakrishnan maintains that the native whoring after English gods is the thesis, the discovery of root through those very gods is the antithesis, and the resulting synthesis is the Tamil house lass 'replaced by the exact chronometer of Europe.'[13] So far as thesis and antithesis are concerned, there is nothing objectionable, but Sivaramakrishnan errs in seeing a synthesis where there is actually none. Unto the last, the poet's predicament remains unresolved. Where is, then, the synthesis? Another critic, V.A. Shahane, seems to be nearer the truth when he states that the threefold structure of the book has a corresponding pattern of experience. He interprets this structure in terms of "the educated, Westernized Indian's threefold mode of development."[14] Even from the thematic viewpoint, the threefold structure holds good. The three sections of the book are, so to say, the articulations of the poet's cultural, amorous, and linguistic predicaments. The predicament or tension is the red thread that runs through all the sections. It provides the book with a pattern and a logical cohesion.

IV

The first section of the volume, "Exile," opens with "As a man approaches thirty he may," wherein the poet having attained the age of thirty starts taking stock of himself. Not that at this age something significant happens, but that the experience of life and the world around thickens and a clearer picture of one-self emerges — 'At thirty the mud will have settled' (p. 15). Even at this age, one continues to 'make the same mistakes.' The 'images' of the past get slowly dissolved as the poet begins scrutinising himself. He has arrived at the tether-end of his belief and conviction. He feels an exile in his own country because of his easy command of the English language, which is usually linked with the colonial past and with an alien culture. His `whoring after English gods,' as Parthasarathy puts it, entails an acute sense of estrangement from his own land and culture. In a suppressed tone, he says :

> There is something to be said for exile :
> you learn roots are deep.
> That language is a tree, loses colour
> under another sky. (p. 17)

But the recognition of 'deep roots' in Tamil does not improve his situation. His loyalty remains divided between the two great repositories of Eastern and Western cultures, between Tamil and English. His English writings come between himself and the city of his birth. There is nothing to rest his eyes on soothingly :

The streets are noisy, and trees,
on Malabar Hill blind with dust.
Spring had gone unnoticed... (p. 19)

The return of the exile (*i.e.*, the poet) to his native city is painful and uneventful. The foreign tour taken to promote the linguistic learning in Leeds merely disappoints him. His dreams are now shattered, his hopes are now belied. So, he returns 'a euphoric archipelago' (p. 21), and his native city greets him with nothing but fog and smoke, regulated traffic and buzzing crowd, the scorching sun and the struggling birds, the incolate babbles and the distracting noises, the tired sea and the littered lanes. In such a surrounding, he feels exhausted, and asks :

What have I come
here far from a thousand miles? (p. 24)

As in England, here too he comes across the frowning faces and the scowling glares of the people, and feels ill at ease inescapably — 'A grey sky oppresses the eyes' (p. 26).

Fed up with the unhappy life at home and expecting some sort of relaxation in the bosom of the beloved, the poet starts off for Jadavpur, where she supposedly lives. Here he hurtles himself into a tense and passionate experience with her. The second section, "Trial," commences at this point. It is a series of 15 love songs suffused with passion and sensuousness. The images grow golden and glowing herein, and the details concrete and picturesque. They are very charming songs indeed, stirring the reader to the depths. The poet-lover accepts love because it offers him an 'unspeakable relief at the most needed moments. He looks over the family album and finds her bewitching photo of childhood and shares it engrossingly. The sense of shared childhood leads him to the sense of oneness with her. It was the lack of this 'shared childhood' that caused an unbridgeable chasm between the poet Ramanujan and his wife (see his poem "Love Poem for a wife 1" in *Relations*, O.U.P., 1971). The concrete, sensuous, even sensual, images abound in these songs. Here are only two illustrations for the enjoyment of the reader :

But in the dark, hands and lips
have marked the spot

> We touched. Still as crockery,
> now, rinsed and dried
> after half-a-day's legitimate use. (p. 33)

and :

> The touch
> of your breasts is ripe
> in my arms. They obliterate my eyes
> with their right parabolas of gold. (p. 39)

The first poetic passage evokes the image of the 'crockery' breaking, and suggests the cracking sound in a hot bed of lovers who are involved in sex-act, while the second one focuses our attention on the ripe, full breasts of the beloved now in the hands of the lover who stands dazzled by her golden, tight parabolas. The diction tends to be economical and minimal in them, without the profusion of words and phrases as in a Romantic poet. But the poet feeds it abundantly with his glowing images. These images are employed time and again in order to effect austerity and discipline in Parthasarathy's poetic art. They render the dark alleys and chambers of obscurity illumining and the truncated expressions meaningful. But in the end, even love seems to face a rough weather, and in the last poem of this section we have : "The straw has come between us" (p. 45).

The third section. "Homecoming," completes the gradual growth of the poet's personality. After his none-too-happy trial with love, he emerges on a congenial home scene to encounter once again the burning issue of language. Explicitly, the focus now shifts from love to language. The 'homecoming' does not allow him 'peace of mind, all passion spent.' He finds his bilingual context irritatingly irreconcilable. He loves Tamil and its great cultural heritage, but he is more at home in English for creative purposes. This insoluble dilemma is aptly conveyed in the following :

> My tongue in English chains,
> I return, after generation, to you.
> I am at the end

> of my dravidic tether,
> hunger for you unassuaged.
> I falter, stumble. (p. 49)

This dilemma has almost entirely overpowered the poet. In a mood of utter helplessness, he says :

> There is little you can do about it,
> except throw up your hands. (p. 50)

His sense of helplessness increases with reflections over the death of his grandfather and father, the reality of becoming his own father, his image now seen in his son, his mother's youthful turmeric days, the degeneration of the holy river Vaikai, his tedious office-routine — something for which he has exchanged the freedom of the free, large world outside, his rueful past and wastefulness, and the strain involved in the 'last refinement of speech.' All these reflections come to him with a bang, not with a whimper. He is bewildered at his unusual situation :

> Later, I watched my forty years
> Swim effortlessly ashore in a glass of beer.
> However, there is no end
> to the deceptions I practise on myself : (p. 62)

The practice of shams and deceptions can give him no lasting peace or real pleasure. It can, of course, bring him a kind of complacency or compromise with his self :

> Hereafter, I should be content,
> I think, to go through life
> with the small change of uncertainties (p. 63)

His 'contentment' born of a compromising attitude is actually contrived to pull him through the 'uncertainties' of life. That's where *Rough Passage* ends.

V

It would be in place to speak a little about Parthasarathy's artistic excellences and weaknesses. One of the salient features of his art is the use of startlingly sensuous and concrete images. These images are often evocative, erotic and suggestive. They evoke the picture of a person, place, or thing seen and visualised, tend to elaborate a point, expand an idea in a little space, and make clear the meaning of the otherwise inexplicable. They are often arranged in such a manner as to capture the reader's attention at once. The following image graphically portrays the loneliness of a man on his beloved's going away :

> you will be alone like the stone benches
> in the park.... (p. 16)

and this image is taken from the world of reptiles :

> and streets unwind like cobras
> from a basket.... (p. 22)

and this one is concrete and visual in a moving manner :

> And words, surely, are no more than ripples
> in the deep well of the throat. (p. 41)

and this is yet another striking image :

> The balloon
> of poetry has grown red in the face
> with repeated blowing. (p. 63)

In truth, the whole book abounds in apt and memorable images — 'I have put aside the past/in a corner, an umbrella/now poor in the ribs' 'through the eye of this needle/of forgetfulness,' 'I rise, as sleep melts/on the Himalaya of bed-clothes;' 'the many-clawed sea;' 'A bus spits me out at my doorstep;' etc. Parthasarathy has a fertile imagination to conjure up a string of images at a stretch and fit them in their proper contexts. He has the necessary poetic capability to employ suggestive and evocative images, such as in :

> Through holes in a wall, as it were,
> lamps burned in the fog.
> In a basement flat, conversation
>
> filled the night, while Ravi Shankar,
> cigarette stubs, empty bottles of stout
> and crisps provided the necessary pauses.
>
> He had spent his youth whoring
> after English gods. (p. 17)

The cultural predicament is very well articulated suggestively in this passage. Ravi Shankar, the famous Indian musician, represents the East, whereas cigarette stubs and empty bottles of stout and crisps provide the Western atmosphere. The poet tries, for personal reasons too, to unite the two, but he does not wholly succeed. His efforts only create 'holes in a wall' but cannot pull down the cultural wall altogether.

Another interesting feature of Parthasarathy's poetry is its eroticism and sensuousness. The very opening poem abounds in sensuous and sensual details. In a tone of remonstration and repentance the poet begins to say :

> The woman you may have loved
> you never married. These many years
>
> you warmed yourself at her hands.
> The luminous pebbles of her body
> stayed your feet, else you had overflowed
>
> the banks, never reached shore.
> The sides of the river swell
> with the least pressure of her toes.
>
> All night your hand rested
> on her left breast. (p. 15)

He speaks of the beloved's 'breasts/sharp with desire' that hurt his fingers. The following extracts from his poetry are being given here for the delight of the reader :

> The body sputters : your flesh
> was the glass that cupped its hands
> over me. Hours glowed to incandescence. (p. 34)

and :

> My hands fill up, slowly,
> with your breasts.
> Curve to the pressure of spheroids.
>
> Your hair tumbles in the dark,
> instantly gathers
> the room in a knot.
>
> Our bodies scrape home
> for passions, older
> than the stones of Konarak. (p. 38)

and again :

A knock on the door :
you entered.
Undressed quietly before the mirror

of my hands. Eyes
drowned in the skull
as flesh hardened to stone.

... ...The touch
of your breasts is ripe
in my arms. They obliterate my eyes
with their tight parabolas of gold.

... ...

The sweet water
of your flesh I draw
with my arms as from a well,
its taste as ever
as on the night of Capricorn. (p. 39)

In these extracts, the reader finds absorbing descriptions of woman and her body, her hair and breasts, her undressing and her sweet flesh. A wave of passion wells up within him as he goes through them. They are suffused with love, life, and lust, and send electric sensations. They are surely the glowing examples of erotic and sensuous poetry. They also serve as a rebuttal of the charge of drabness and prosaicness being levelled against the poetry of Parthasarathy. They demonstrate that he is not only a serious poet of cultural and linguistic tensions, but also a delightfully readable poet of love and sex.

We need not quote any further extracts to show Parthasarathy's propensity for tense and lively diction. In the view of Gauri Deshpande, "His sense of language is competent enough for him not to be obtrusively bizarre. It is also sensitive and lively enough to allow him to come up time and again with delightfully surprising and unerring images."[15] Parthasarathy is choosy in matters of words, phrases, and expressions. His expressions are direct and dashing, more cerebral than spontaneous. He hardly ever indulges in unnecessary details. His command of the English language is so complete that many Indo-English poets envy him. He has had the necessary apprenticeship to make his words, phrases, and metaphors living and captivating. He could do so because he had mostly drawn upon his experiences. One of the notable traits of his diction is that it is tampered equally with emotion and reason.

Parthasarathy is a skilled practitioner of an extremely austere style. He has, therefore, resorted to the literary device of monosyllabism. Take the following as an illustration :

I see him now sitting at his desk.
The door is open. It is evening.
On the lawns the children play. (p. 60)

Most of the words used here are monosyllables. Parthasarathy is a conscious craftsman, and his austerity is the outcome of his intention to be concise and precise. Iyengar brands it as "austerity indeed with a vengeance."[16] This style is quite in keeping with the complexity and tension of modem life, and also with the great personal dilemma of the poet, and tends to be unadorned, direct, and matter-of-fact. Adil Jussawalla has characterized it as "deliberately prosaic."[17] Obviously, it undergoes the rigours of conscious selection or rejection of poetic wares.

Added to this is the fact that Parthasarathy employs three-lined stanzas (or tercets) throughout. The want of variety in metric form renders his poetry somewhat monotonous and dull, though this may be due to the continuity of the same mood and tone in it. The adopted stanza form, however, contributes significantly to the affected attitude of detachment by the poet.

Some of the weaknesses of Parthasarathy pointed out by scholars are that he is a disconcerting poet and a reluctant one at that, that he is a poet of no serious commitment like Nissim Ezekiel or A.K. Ramanujan, that he lacks a sense of joy in the fact of his poetry, that he is unduly ironic about his motherland and mother tongue, that he is too deliberate to be interesting, and that he unduly delves deep in rueful and nostalgic situations, leaving aside the sunny side of life. It has also been pointed out that his personal poems are "slight and strictly *sotto voce*;" that most of his love poems are "regretful, wry, even cynical,"[18] and that the poet is a pessimist through and through, without a vision for the future.

VI

To sum up, the poetic output of Parthasarathy is meagre, but it is of lasting value. He is graded with Ezekiel and Ramanujan to form a triumvirate in Indo-English poetry.[19] These three, according to William Walsh, hold the future, the promise, of the Indo-English muse. Parthasarathy is verily a fastidious and disciplined craftsman, and even his detractors, who are not too many, admit that he is a serious poet by all means. Though his poetic thrift is deliberate,[20] his art is ever engrossing and his tone ever gentle. His sensibility, like Dom Moraes's, is essentially romantic, but he tries to keep it under control. Like Gieve Patel's, his use of language is spare and unambitious, without much of cadence, rhyme, or melody. The unresolved dilemmas of language and colonial alienation are the real charms of Parthasarathy's poetry, and they provide him with the necessary situations to keep it going.

NOTES

1. His *Rough Passage* (Delhi : Oxford University Press, 1977) lists these magazines and anthologies in "Acknowledgments."
2. In his *Indian Writing in English* (Bombay : Asia P. House, 1973), K.R.S. Iyengar refers to it as *The First Step : Poems* 1956-66 by R. Parthasarathy. Strangely enough, *Poetry from Leeds* edited by R. Parthasarathy and J. Healy contains no poem of this poet.
3. Godavari Sharma, "The Poetry of R. Parthasarathy," *The Indian Journal of English Studies*, XIX (1979) p., 45.
4. R. Parthasarathy, "Preface," *Rough Passage*, p. 9.
5. *Idem.*
6. *Idem.*
7. K.R.S. Iyengar, *Indian Writing in English*, p. 673.
8. William Walsh, "Introduction," *Readings in Commonwealth Literature* (Oxford : Clarendon Press, 1973), p. xx.
9. Gauri Deshpande, "R. Parthasarathy," *Contemporary Indian Poetry in English*, ed. Saleem Peeradina (Delhi : Macmillan, 1972), p. 51.
10. Adil Jussawalla, "The New Poetry," *Readings in Commonwealth Literature*, ed. William Walsh, p. 83.
11. V.A. Shahane, "The Return of the Exile : The Poetry of R. Parthasarathy," *Osmania Journal of English Studies*, XIII, No. I (1977), 149.
12. G. Sharma, *loc, cit.*, p. 52.

13. M. Sivaramakrishnan, "That Last Refinement of Speech — The Poetry of R. Parthasarathy," *The Literary Criterion*, XII (1976), 153.
14. V.A. Shahane, *loc. cit.*, p. 150.
15. G. Deshpande, *loc. cit.*, p. 51.
16. K.R.S. Iyengar, *op. cit.*, p. 673.
17. A. Jussawalla, *loc. cit.*, p. 83.
18. G. Deshpande, *loc. cit.*, p. 52.
19. W. Walsh, "Introduction," *op. cit.*, p. xviii.
20. A. Jussawalla, *loc. cit.*, p. 83.

11

Kamala Das as a Poetic Artist*

Kamala Das, who took the literary world by storm in the mid-sixties, has created a permanent place for herself in contemporary Indo-English poetry. Though she has produced only three volumes of verse to date, which is a clear indication of her poetic energies getting dried up to some extent, she has been one of the most popular poets of India who have gained ground even in the West. And such Indian poets are not too many; in fact, they can be easily counted, — A.K. Ramanujan, Dom Moraes, Nissim Ezekiel, Pritish Nandy, K.N. Daruwalla, Shiv K. Kumar, and herself. It is not, therefore, surprising that the noted English poet, Geoffrey Hill, was prompted to remark that the one poet who stood out in P. Lal's *Modern Indian Poetry in English : An Anthology and a Credo* (1969) was Kamala Das. In points of enjoyment and applause, she stands next to none in the whole length and breadth of Indian poetry in English today.

Kamala Das as a poet treads on familiar grounds, and she never tries to transgress her self-imposed restrictions. She is, after all, a woman with a narrow range of experience in life, but she makes the best of the crippling situations around. In this context, she reminds us of another woman writer, Jane Austen, who is so well-known for her 'two inches of ivory.' Like Austen, Kamala Das also moves within her limited range with grace and skill. The advantage of this range is that it offers to the reader only what the writer has personally felt and realised, and nothing borrowed from another source.

As a poet of sharp feminine sensibility, Kamala Das gives vent

*Reprinted from my book, *Kamala Das and Her Poetry* (Delhi : Doaba House, 1983), pp. 115-130, with permission of the publisher.

to the hopes, fears and desires of womankind. She has been the champion of woman's cause in all her writings, and there is no point in challenging this statement which amounts to an altruism. In a seminar held in Lucknow in December 1980, I was questioned on the proposition that there is a 'feminine sensibility at work' in her poetry. I am still convinced that this sensibility is amply in evidence in her work, and no frivolous argument against such a self-evident truth can dislodge me from my stand. Now, what can one say about such lines as the following?

Love is not important, that makes the blood
Carouse, nor the man who brands you with his
Lust, but is shed as slough at the end of each
Embrace. Only that matters which forms as
Toadstool under lightning and rain; the soft
Stir in womb, the foetus growing, for,
Only the treasures matter that were washed
Ashore, not the long blue tides that washed them
In. ("Jaisurya")

This comes from a sensitive woman having experienced maternity and throes of delivery. Kamala Das's poems like "A Relationship," "Summer in Calcutta," "An Introduction," "Marine Drive," and several others bring to the fore her boldness and freedom in speaking aloud the secret longings and aspirations of womankind. The following extract from "Summer in Calcutta" is inspired by a woman's hectic search for the desired love under the scorching sun :

My worries
Doze. Wee bubbles ring
My glass, like a bride's
Nervous smile, and meet
My lips. Dear, forgive
This moment's lull in
Wanting you, the blur
In memory.

Not only in her poetry, but also in her essays Kamala Das comes out as an unofficial spokesman of the Indian counterpart of the women's 'lib' movement in the West, and her essays like "Why

Not More Than One Husband?" "What Women Expect Out of Marriage And What They Get," and "The She-Mouse Returns Home" bear it out.

But Kamala Das can't be as emancipated as Germaine Greer, or as wild as Tennyson's Princess (in the poem of that name), or as socially active as Sarojini Naidu, to do away with the injustices meted out to womankind, and she readily accepts the limitations of a family life. In this connection, she is comparable to the well-known Australian poet, Judith Wright, who too sees the experience of love ennobled in marriage and family rather than degraded in any way. In Kamala Das we find much that is conventional and feminine, and she speaks aloud of the needs and fears of a common woman and pleads for authentic love and sense of security for her out of her own knowledge. And yet, the woman in her cannot be completely shadowed, and so she cannot help expressing an ambivalence proceeding from her own duality, from the combination in herself of a need for domestic security and the inborn desire to be liberated. As we know, she was married at an early age and she did not find her married life altogether happy or satisfactory (as the tone of her poems suggests and as reaffirmed by her autobiography, *My Story*), and so her life story, notwithstanding its sensationalism which seems to be partly contrived, makes a poignant reading. Marriage and love forming the dominant theme of Mrs. Das's poetry need not be mutually exclusive, but for her it has invariably proved to be so. When she speaks of love outside marriage, she does not necessarily propagate the institution of adultery or infidelity, but seems to be merely searching for a relationship which gives both genuine love and impenetrable security. That's why she sometimes gives a mythical framework to her search for true love, and identifies it with the Radha Krishna syndrome or with that of Mira Bai relinquishing the ties of marriage in pursuit of Lord Krishna, the true divine lover :

> Vrindavan lives on in every woman's mind,
> and the flute, luring her
> From home and her husband
> Who later asks her of the long scratch on the brown
> Aureola of her breast, and she shyly replies,
> hiding flushed cheeks,

It was so dark outside, I tripped and fell over
the brambles in the wood....

The poem "Ghanshyam" is a relevant example in this context. Like Sarojini Naidu in her poem on Ghanshyam, Kamala Das ventilates her mystical longings and mythical leanings in this beautiful piece.

Kamala Das is primarily a poet of love. Evidently, she is not so much preoccupied with a metaphysical quest or with a formulation of poetic theory as with an intense search for love. In a letter to Devindra Kohli date 10th December, 1968, she admits that 'I began to write poetry with the ignoble aim of wooing a man. There is therefore a lot of love in my poems,' and that the poems contained in *Summer in Calcutta* were composed with the sole objective of making 'a man love me' and of 'breaking down his resistance.'[1] As a poet of love, Kamala Das looks most naive, honest, and frank, almost in the fashion of Sappho, though she does not possess the 'intellectual pride' and the 'open-hearted ease' of Judith Wright. But it must also be mentioned here that Kamala wrote her poetry against a conservative and tabooed society, and not against a free and uninhibited society of Australia, and this accounts for the difference between the two celebrated poetesses. As compared to some other women poets of the confessional mode (which is definitely Kamala's due by all means), such as Anne Sexton and Sylvia Plath, Kamala Das may fall short of intellectual vigour and witty tit-bits, but she does not lag behind in lyrical outburst of unpremeditated thoughts and feelings and in emotional intensity. In truth, she is more aware of the pathos in the life of a common woman playing a very passive role in our tradition-bound society than some of these women poets highlighting a different cultural and moral ethos. And how bold and courageous is this lady of our land may be clearly judged from the fact that she articulates the theme of sexual love in such a frank manner that we are left wonderstruck at it. There is an air of unconventionality about it.

Related to the theme of love is the celebration of the 'body' in Kamala Das's poetry. This celebration is not in the style of Gieve Patel who makes a clinical analysis of the body in a general way. Kamala's approach is perfectly personal, adding a touch of delicacy and charm to it. Her poems indicate that she both likes and dislikes her body. Physically she is dark-complexioned with 'ordinary features,' and her loathing for body is partly due to this and partly due to her protracted illnesses. In liking the body, she is led by the pleasures it affords to her and to her companion. In this matter, she resembles another distinguished Indo-English poet, Nissim Ezekiel, who is also a 'poet of the body.' In case of Kamala Das, the tensions actually issue forth from the pressures of her complex family background; neither she was properly cared for by her parents, nor by her office-going husband after her marriage. This is how she conveys her feelings at her parental and husband's homes :

> I was a burden and a responsibility; neither my parents nor my grandfather could put up with for long. Therefore with the blessings of all, our marriage was fixed.[2]

and :

> My husband was immersed in his office-work, and after work there was the dinner, followed by sex. Where was there any time left for him to want to see the sea or dark buffaloes of the slopes?[3]

Evidently, the failure of love and the birth of poetry seem to be related to each other in Mrs. Das. Her poems like "The Suicide," "The Prisoner," and "Advice to Fellow Swimmers" are the glaring examples of it. This is what she says in "The Prisoner" :

> As the convict studies
> His prison's geography
> I study the trappings
> Of your body, dear love,
> For I must someday find
> An escape from its snare.

In singing of the body, she finds no true love from her legitimate source and she tells us that her intimacy with her husband was 'purely physical.' Under such circumstances, love degenerates into lust, loud and savage, with which she is fed up in her life, and she makes a fervent appeal to her readers —

> When I die
> Do not throw
> The meat and bones away

> But pile them up
> And let them tell
> By their smell
> What life was worth
> On this earth
> What love was worth
> In the end.

The naked body became more acceptable to her during her illness than in her normal health, and she has spoken of this in one of the excerpts of her best-selling autobiography :

> Whenever he tried to strip me of my clothes, my shyness clung to me like a secondskin and made my movements graceless. Each pore of my skin became at that moment a seeing eye, an eye that viewed my body with distaste. But during my illness, I shed my shyness and for the first time in my life learned to surrender totally in bed with my pride intact and blazing.[4]

Perhaps in the moments of her convalescence, she needed her man's tenderness and reassuring love, which she accepted most heartily.

Kamala Das is a poet not so much of the countryside as of the city. In this regard, she is like most of Indo-English poets, for, in the words of Gauri Deshpande, there is "nothing...pastoral or rural in the pre-occupations of these poets,"[5] and this is a failure of Indian poetry in English in general. As a result, Nature that formed so great a stimulus in the writings of the English Romantic poets is almost completely banished from its domain. K.N. Daruwalla with his powerful rural paintings is one obvious exception, and his poems like "In the Tarai," "The Ghaghra in Spate," "Haranag," "Boat-ride Along the Ganges," and many others testify to this truth. In the second-named poem, we have :

> And through the village
> the Ghaghra steers her course :
> thatch and dung-cakes turn to river-scum,
> buffalo floats over to the rooftop
> where the men are stranded.

Three days of hunger, and her udders
turn red-rimmed and swollen
        with milk-extortion :

Now, if one looks for such poems in Kamala Das, one will be disappointed. But she is not totally ignorant about lively Nature; after all she knows the sea and the sea-waters very well, and they also figure in her verse. She also deplores her moving away from the sights and sounds of the idyllic countryside surrounding her parental house to the 'dusty cities' with their din and disturbance. Like Nissim Ezekiel, she depicts the squalor and the heat, the crowd and the slum-life, with a precision marked with reality that is really enviable, and at the same time she remains true to her experience and realisation without being over-idealistic or cynical like the Romantics. Her first volume, in particular, strikes a remarkable harmony between her private, burning passion and the dazzling, scorching sunlight. And this she achieves without taking recourse to the biting social irony of Nissim Ezekiel or savage subjective irony of Shiv K. Kumar, and she is certainly not alienated from her social milieu as Dom Moraes, for instance, is.

As a poet of the city, Kamala Das constantly employs the metaphor of the city for life, such as in the poem "A New City." There is an anguished awareness on the part of the poetess to have lost something in adopting the city as her home, but she is also aware of the joys and amenities to be found in a city. Thus, she discovers that 'all the Delhi streets' are 'fragrant and murky' rendering her 'very young, very lovely and delightfully carefree.' Elsewhere, she contrasts the inviolable peace of the Delhi landscape with the disturbed mind of the poet. She bids a touching farewell to the city of her long residence, Bombay, which she loves so deeply :

I take leave of you, fair city, white tears
Hide somewhere in my adult eyes
And sadness is silent as a stone
In the river's unmoving
Core....
It's goodbye, goodbye, goodbye,
To slender shapes behind windowpanes,

Shut against indiscriminate desire
And rain .....

This departure is as painful as the parting of a loved one, as the city forms an integral part of the emotional make-up of the poet.

The later poetry of Kamala Das shows her intense concern with death and decay in human life, and the element of discontentment is pervasive in it. The poem "Lines to a Husband" contains two parallel strands in it : the obsession with physical decay and destruction, and the obsession with love which remains unrequited in her life. And the poem "The Suicide" moves a step ahead in visualising not only the death of the body but also of the soul. Here she writes :

Bereft of soul
My body shall be bare.
Bereft of body
My soul shall be bare.
Which would you rather have
O kind sea?

and further :

O sea, I am fed up
I want to be simple
I want to be loved
And
If love is not to be had
I want to be dead, just dead
While I enter deeper.....

Out of deep anguish, she cries out in another poem :

From the debris of housewrecks
Pick up my broken face,
Your bride's face,
Changed a little with the years.
I shall not remember
The betrayed honeymoon;
We are both such cynics,
You and I.

The poem "The Sorcerers and Exorcists of Kattumadam" informs us that the poet suffered a nervous breakdown at the age of nineteen as a 'neglected wife' and a stay in Malabar with her loved grandmother could cure her. For a different reason, Sylvia Plath also had suffered a similar nervous breakdown almost at the same age, — that was due to an intense, nearly unbearable, love for her adored father. But whereas Kamala could be cured, Sylvia could not.

One of the central characters in Kamala Das's work is her grandmother who is inseparably linked with her memory of the parental home now more than three hundred years old. Here she felt at home, and got her diseases cured. She describes it as 'a paradise on earth for me'. In "My Grandmother's House" (*Summer in Calcutta*), she celebrates this house as the seat of her great comfort and abounding in love and life :

> There is a house now far away where once
> I received love... That woman died,
> The house withdrew into silence, snakes moved
> Among books I was then too young
> To read, and my blood turned cold like the moon
> How often I think of going
> There....

The poem "Blood" is an apotheosis of the house — 'this old house beside the sea'— as well as of the grandmother. Mrs. Das's fascination with the images of the old house besides the beating sea can be clearly traced back to her childhood associations with it. We know, A.K. Ramanujan also delineates his impressions about his parental house in his well-known poem "Small-scale Reflections on a Great House," but here Ramanujan's attitude is unmistakably ironic, whereas Kamala Das's attitude remains reverential and affectionate throughout.

In Kamala Das's poetry one comes across the intensity of passion which renders words irrelevant for articulation. Obviously, silence and not words is the true language of love, and Kamala Das shows her distaste for the abstract and her preference for the elemental by laying stress on the role of silence as a dramatic device in a poem charged with pulse and power. She cannot say, like Yeats, that 'words alone are certain good', or as Nissim Ezekiel says that 'the best poets wait for words.' Though Kamala is conscious of the fact that words 'grow on me like leaves', she knows well that they can ever play their semantic mischiefs and thus be a 'nuisance' :

> ...beware of them, they
> Can be so many things, a
> Chasm where running feet must pause to
> Look, a sea with paralysing waves,
> A blast of burning air or
> A knife most willing to cut your best
> Friend's throat ...

The poem "Substitute" suggests that words are a source of discord and disharmony after love-making. In another piece, "Convicts," words are submerged in the dark of passions and the music of silence, and Kamala Das writes :

> When he
> And I were one, we were neither
> Male nor female. There were no more
> Words left, all words lay imprisoned
> In the ageing arms of night. In
> Darkness we grew as in silence
> We sang.....

The lack of words does not, in any way, create the impression of inadequacy, it rather produces the desired effect of haste and urgency, especially so in Mrs. Das's poetry. She once observed, 'I like poetry to be disciplined and tidy.' But she feels, the words are merely a medium of expression, and as such they should not be allowed to be treated as an absolute truth *per se*. As words are the products of conscious selection or rejection of the writer, they are usually opposed to the essential need of expressing the dark side of passion or the onrush of intense feelings. In her poetry Kamala Das shows the inadequacy of language to cope with the heavy weight of experiential records. Even a poet like T.S. Eliot, who has been a conscious artist throughout, is also preoccupied with this problem when he remarks that 'words' reach 'Word' and are, thereafter, heard no more, and he too treats them as a means of approaching the Eternity.

Gauri Deshpande, a reputed poet herself, brackets Kamala Das with Nissim Ezekiel for "the deft touch in the medium."[6] No doubt, her control over the medium of expression is almost sure and sound, but sometimes it slips off lamentably, giving the impression of a weak and self-indulgent writing. Occasionally she also indulges in repetitions of words, lines and even sections of a poem. This device has been used by D.H. Lawrence, Dylan Thomas, and the Bible, but Kamala Das does not satisfy us on this score. This is what we find in "The Testing of Sirens" :

> Ah, why does love come to me like pain
> Again and again and again?

This tendency of the poet is also amply evident in her poem "Substitute", wherein she says :

> It will be all right when I learn
> To paint my mouth like a clown's.
> It will be alright if I put up my hair,
> Stand near my husband to make a proud pair.
>
> It will be all right if I join clubs
> And flirt a little over telephone.
> It will be all right, it will be all right
> I am the type that endures.
>
> It will be all right, it will be all right
> It will be all right between the world and me.
> It will be all right if I don't remember
> The last of the days together....

Here the repetition is made so unnerving that the reader gets almost bored and uninterested. Writing for *Quest* in April-June, 1966 (p. 38), Linda Hess also remarked thus :

> There are major weaknesses in Mrs. Das's book. These can be characterized as a general carelessness in composition, a looseness typified by the alarming number of ellipses, three lazy dots thrown in at the end or middle of a line and seeming to say, 'This matter could be elaborated much further, but I lack either the wit or the energy to do it.' There are frequent repetitions of words and phrases, another quick solution to the problem of filling up a line but one that has disastrous effects on intensity and

> precision. There are patches of triteness and lapses of balance. Too often the end of a line brings an unnatural break in the diction which seems to have no excuse except the whim of the author.

Sometimes Kamala sounds theatrical in her verse, as in the poem "A Request," wherein she is busy visualising, like Thomas Hardy in his "Afterwards," what people should do with her after her death. She actually lacks the sense of proportion in her poetry, — that is, she does not know where to stop in the hurried mood of urgent expression. But a good poet (of her stature) must know it. The last thing to be said against her is that mere salubrious details of love and sex will not convince the reader about the fecundity of her imagination or about the continuity of her creativity. For one thing, she has produced no poetical volume independently since 1973.

When all her weaknesses have been pointed out, it remains to be observed here that Kamala Das in her best poems moves us deeply through her "passionate urge and drive of the rhythm" and through her "haunting images of sterility"[7] The poem "The Looking-Glass" is to be specially marked for its honesty and openness in the expression of a woman's inner thoughts of love and sex. Here she says :

> Getting a man to love you is easy
> Only be honest about your wants as
> Woman. Stand nude before the glass with him
> So that he sees himself the stronger one
> And believes it so, and you so much more
> Softer, younger, lovelier....Admit your
> Admiration.

This is a very fine example of her 'passionate urge' for making love to the man of one's desire. For the drive of her rhythm, one may quote a poem like "The Invitation," where she writes :

> I have a man's fist in my head today
> Clenching, unclenching...
> I have got all the Sunday evening pains.
>
> The sea is garrulous today. Come in,
> Come in. What do you lose by dying, and
> Besides, your losses are my gains.

Oh Sea, let me. Shrink or grow, slosh up,
Slide down, go your way,
I will go mine.

The lines are almost even here, but the employment of monosyllabic or short words produces a tilting cadence in this piece, especially in the second and third stanzas. The poem "An Introduction," which is a brief autobiography of the poet, has the rhythms of a conversational speech :

Be Amy, or be Kamala. Or better
Still, be Madhavikutty. It is time to
Choose a name, a role. Don't play pretending
games....

"The Wild Bougainvillea "is another poem remarkable for its beauty and charm of continuously alternating long and short lines :

I walked, I saw and
I heard, the city tamed
Itself for me, and then my hunger for a
Particular touch waned
And one day I sent him some roses and slept
Through the night, a silent
Dreamless sleep and woke up in the morning, free.

While there is not much of symbolism in Mrs. Das's poetry (as one surely finds in Sri Aurobindo's work), some arresting images are to be witnessed in it. These images make her verse really delightful, graphic, and pictorial. In this connection, we may cite "The Stone Age" as an illustration :

Fond husband, ancient settler in the mind,
Old fat spider, weaving webs of bewilderment,
Be kind. You turn me into a bird of stone, a granite
Dove ....
With loud talk you bruise my pre-morning sleep,
You stick a finger into my dreaming eye. And
Yet, on daydreams, strong men cast their shadows,
they sink
Like white suns in the swell of my Dravidian blood,
Secretly flow the drains beneath sacred cities.

When you leave, I drive my blue battered car
Along the bluer sea.

The details offered here immediately evoke the picture of a sexually disconsolate wife getting enamoured of some other stronger men who come her way. Das's concrete and sensuous imagery recalls Keats to our minds. The following poetic passage will confirm the veracity of this statement :

He talks, turning a sun-stained
Cheek to me, his mouth, a dark
Cavern, where stalactites of
Uneven teeth gleam, his right
Hand on my knee, while our minds
Are willed to race towards love;
But, they only wander, tripping
Idly over puddles of
Desire.....

The 'desire' definitely gets kindled here.

It is pertinent to talk here of Kamala Das's diction, which usually tends to be lyrical and musical. Simplicity is the hallmark of her language, and she does not indulge in unnecessary verbal jugglery or pedantry, as some Indo-English poets are prone to do. One does not smack of the impact of Hulme-Pound-Eliot coterie that so insistently pleaded for 'variety' and 'complexity' in a literary work. T.S. Eliot once pronounced emphatically thus :

> Our civilization comprehends great variety and complexity and this variety and complexity, playing upon a refined sensibility, must produce various and complex results. The poet must become more and more comprehensive, more allusive, more indirect, in order to force, to dislocate, if necessary, language into his meaning.[8]

Kamala Das does not bother about such things, and her only concern seems to be the urgency of expression unclosed by any allusions or intricacies. Her poems exactly boil over; for instance, "The Freaks," "Convicts," "The Old Playhouse," and "The Looking-Glass." This is the truly charged diction of an intense love-making :

That was the only kind of love,
This hacking at each other's parts
Like convicts hacking, breaking clods
At noon. We were earth under hot
Sun : There was burning in our
Veins and the cool mountain nights did
Nothing to lessen heat. When he
And I were one, we were neither
Male nor female.

The language grows fiery and flaming here, and the reader inescapably feels the burning of his/her body while poring over these lines. The kind of frankness we witness in Mrs. Das is hardly to be had in many women poets of India and abroad. Thus, in "Substitute," she tells us rather cynically about her experience of love in a language suffused with warmth and worldliness :

After that love became a swivel-door,
When one went out, another came in.

Poets like Judith Wright and Anne Sexton would have loved and told candidly about it, but here is a poet who opens out her very heart, its burns and aches, in a highly lyrical and amorous language.

Kamala Das, with her three poetical collections, is quite secure in the realm of Indo-English verse. She may not have written much like Pritish Nandy or Nissim Ezekiel, like Monika Varma and Lila Ray among the Indian women writers, and she may also not be as witty or intellectual as some other Confessional poets of the world, or as some 'academic' Indian poets like Shiv K. Kumar and A.K. Ramanujan, but she excels them all in popularity and feminine sensitivity. She has her own range, her own cosy bower to relax in, and she moves therein with perfect ease and felicity. Explicitly, nuns and spinsters might seek reasons to attack her, but she is a poet who has the power to hold her readers spell-bound right from the start. Devindra Kholi is right in pointing out that there is "something in the tone and temper of Kamala Das's work which made one sit up from the very first poem."[9] Linda Hess, a ruthless critic of Mrs. Das, also concedes that "a genuine poetic talent is at work here."[10] And, finally, we fully agree with the noted Indo-English poet, R. Parthasarathy, when he remarks that "Kamala Das impresses by being very much herself in her poems," and that her "tone is distinctively feminine."[11]

NOTES AND REFERENCES

1. See D. Kohli's book, *Kamala Das*, pp. 29 & 58 respectively.
2. Kamala Das; *My Story*, p. 85.
3. Kamala Das, "I Have Lived Beautifully," *Debonair*, III, No. 5 (May 15, 1975), p. 41.
4. *My Story*, p. 118.
5. G. Deshpande, "Foreword," *An Anthology of Indo-English Poetry* (Delhi : Hind Pocket Books, n. d.), p. 12.
6. G. Deshpande, *op. cit.* p. 14.
7. Eunice de Souza, "Kamala Das, Gauri Deshpande, Mamta Kalia," *Contemporary Indian Poetry in English*, ed. Saleem Peeradina, p. 86.
8. T.S. Eliot, "Th

12

Beyond 'Sighs and Thighs' : The Poetry of Monika Verma

Monika Varma, who may be claimed as a 'major' Indo-English poetess of today by virtue of her sedate and sober nature, her unique artistic sensibility and her love of glowing words and phrases, deserves a serious consideration in the face of lack of adequate critical attention to her poetical works. Poetesses like Kamala Das and Gauri Deshpande may outshine her in the delineation of love and sex, Lila Ray in the depiction of life's miseries and death, and Margaret Chatterjee in the choice of philosophical themes, but she remains unchallenged in covering a wide spectrum of experiences and in treating her subjects through arresting visual and sensuous imagery and living language. In her love songs, Monika does not transgress the limits of decency and decorum, as Kamala Das usually and Gauri Deshpande occasionally do, nor does she weep too much in nostalgia which is a Western hangover, and thus rises above "sighs and thighs"[1] (to apply her own phrase to her). Monika's position as a 'major' poet can hardly be questioned, taking into account both her quantity and quality. While the quality is to be judged in the pages to follow on the basis of her excellent art and disciplined mind, the quantity is reflected in her vast poetic corpus which comprises no fewer than seven volumes — *Dragonflies Draw Flame* (1962), *Gita Govinda and Other Poems* (1966), *Green Leaves and Gold* (1970), *Quartered Questions and Queries* (1971), *Past Imperative* (1972), *Across the Vast Spaces* (1975), and *Alakananda* (1976). These volumes immediately place her head and shoulder above many other Indian women poets and very close to some outstanding male poets.

The first collection of Monika's verse consisting of 10 poems carries a brief Preface by Nissim Ezekiel and a still briefer Writer's Note, with dedication to C.R. Mandy, Nissim Ezekiel and P. Lal. Opening with "In the Domino Dusk" (which is about a reading of Rimbaud) and closing with "No Meaning Any More" (which emphasises the 'meaninglessness' of Time for the poetess at an advanced age, the volume is slight and slender in appearance. What strikes us here is the truth that it is almost entirely free of romantic longings, plaintive notes, grievings and sexualism. Most of the poems present a feast of vivid and visualised images, delightful natural scenes and sights — the dusk, the dawn, the evening, the night, the hills and the mountains, the rains and the rivers, the sun and the moon, the green leaves and the lovely flowers. The happy mood of the poetess emerges in poems like "Mountains let rest the head," "Glad Light Green" (best of all in this volume). "The Bahsoli," "This gift of a morning," whereas her sobriety surfaces in such poems as "In the Domino Dusk," "From very thinking," "The Question," "In This Loud World" and "No Meaning Any More." Curiously enough, we do not find the poetess lamenting the loss of her love or youth or the shattering of her dream of the millennium as the Romantic poets often do. The only subdued complaint of hers is against Time in the last poem wherein she declares :

> I who once ran through fires of field and field
> Walk in planetary rhythm,
> For time has no meaning any more
>
> ("No Meaning Any More", p. 16)

But in the poem "In This Loud World," she boldly speaks out her thought :

> why should I grieve —
> There is laughter in a silver thread of breeze.
>
> (p. 15)

Here 'why should I grieve' is of special significance to us because it points to a characteristic mode of her thinking, to her typical mental attitude, which is quite free of 'sobs and sighs.' As contrasted to these utterances, there are some others of utter gay abandon in certain pieces — in "Glad Light Green" and "This gift of a morning," for instance. The fancy seems to have run riot in them, but without indulging in an aesthete's decadent impulses or in a romantic's dreamy desires. Explicitly, too much weeping or naked sex display is not her concern, and as a normal and healthy human being she rather hails the beauty of the morning and the stars. This is quite evident in "Glad Light Green" and "This gift of a morning." Monika does not feel shy of talking of love and passion, as in the following :

> My reluctant sight, victim of the falcon rose,
> plumets earthwards;
> And the sun whispers : Will it be the falcon or
> the dove?
> Vexed, I answer : Give me love.
>
> ("The Question," p. 14)

but it is not allowed to be nerve-breaking or neurotic. Taken as a whole, this volume, which to Nissim Ezekiel is "less successful in building whole poems with the inner movement,"[2] fares well in the light of this discussion and smacks of a sober and trained sensibility at work here.

Gita Govinda and Other Poems is not different from the first volume in matters of content and form and love of words and nature. It has barely 14 pieces in total. The four "Bagatelle" poems recapture the fast-changing phases of Nature and the varying moods of the poet in striking words and phrases. In truth, there are a number of poems in it to demonstrate Monika's unusual interest in the selection of right words and phrases and epithets for purposes of poetic creation, — the poems like "Recherche," "No title, no name," "Words," "Bagatelle I," "Bagatelle III : Spectrum," and "Monsoon" —, and in "Words" she announces :

> I taste the flavour of words,
> the bouquet permeates from the palate to the lips.
>
> (p. 8)

And in a volume concerned deeply with certain subtle artistic questions and structural delicacies, as this one is, there is hardly scope enough for the articulation of sobs and tears and salacious sexual details. On the contrary, there are some remarkable vignettes of life vented with all seriousness and sincerity, *e.g.*, "The essence of living," "An Answer" and "It is ten o'clock night." The last-named one gives us the following :

> Am I crying tonight?
> No, It is only smoke from cooking,
> the stream-coke I use when friends drop in,
> or the neighbour's husband.
>
> (p.14)

That she is 'not crying' is a sign of her mental composure, which goads her on to a consideration of the 'essence of living' :

> The essence of living is beauty.
> Grapes and wine may have a more subtle flavour
> but the flavour of love is living.
>
> ("The essence of living," p. 15)

The only piece of great emotional fermentation is "Gita Govinda," a translated fragment from the Sanskrit original of Jayadeva, which is definitely tension-ridden and action-packed but least symptomatic of Monika's creative talents (later on, the whole of Jayadeva's classic got translated and published by her as an independent work).

Green Leaves and Gold, a poetical collection of 26 pieces and dedicated to P. Lal, abounds in charming natural descriptions which remind us of the well-known English poet, William Wordsworth, in their precision and fullness. So much so that Monika's moods apparently spring from natural sources like 'the autumn' and 'the mountain' (see the poems "Autumn Mood" and "Mountain Mood" respectively in this context). Evidently, Monika's great interest in 'green leaves and gold' is amply clear in this volume. For her the green grass becomes a symbol of her 'life' and her 'breath' (*Green*, p. 10), and gold that of her 'love' (*Gold*, pp. 34-35). In the poem entitled "Gold", she does extend her invitation to her love but without exulting in saccharine sexual details (which are in plenty in Kamala Das and Gauri Deshpande). She also does not throw a gloss of imagination over the concrete realities of life, and thus shuns, as against the Romantics, to call 'swallows' her 'sisters, brothers, lovers and love' ("Detrition", p. 28). Her metaphysical awakening is evident in the following lines from "Autumn Mood" :

Ko jagarita? Who is awake?
It is fearful Autumn moon to night.

(p. 12)

and again in :

I saw, Am I that important?
No, but my seeing is

("The Flower," p. 14)

As a grown up, wisc woman, she quickly counsels the young ones :

Hold your lamentations,
in secret their Ariadne waits.
The lowering clouds with slaveting mouth
may give tongue,
under the mountain love is a cave....
the spool unwinds on and on.

("The Young Ones," p. 11)

What is being suggested here is the fact that Monika is more alive to the vital issues of life, including spiritual life, and to her immediate situations than to the 'old, unhappy, far off things/And battles long ago.'

The fourth volume, *Quartered Questions and Queries*, comprising 27 pieces *in toto*, signals no distinct departure from the trodden usual path for the poetess and considers mainly the question of the place and value of 'words' in an artistic composition. For one thing, Monika is hardly ever 'girlish' in the treatment of her material, as Sarojini Naidu, the Nightingale of India, often tended to be. The two symbols of 'sensation' and 'passion' employed in the poem "So Many Opinions..." are not allowed to have their way, and emphatically she declares :

Fire and water? — no,
the Cabalistic sign is not enough. (p. 18)

There are two excellent love poems in this work —"Gold-Mulched Hours" and "My Loves." The first one is very brief, vivid, and arresting in imagery and deserves full quotation :

Gold-mulched hours
those days of rain,

I remember you, my love
beside me,
held in your arms, loves,
but now the sombre clouds
hide
my gold-mulched hours....

(p. 40)

It has the qualities of a good poem — well-stated theme, simple yet tense diction, suggestive technique, economy of words and phrases, and neat, clean structure. The beloved here recalls the hours and days spent in the balmy company of her lover, but suddenly a serious and sombre mood grips her hard. This mood does not allow her to escape into a world of "romantic oblivion,"[3] as Syed Ameeruddin puts it; instead, it takes her to a world of hard-pressing reality. The other poem under consideration, "My Loves," amply bears it out, wherein Monika not only universalises her love, but also keeps it away from the imaginary romantic world of elfs and nymphs and knights :

My loves are strewn upon the ground :
birds and leaves, seeds and song,
my love the heron's flight
a shadow upon the ground,
swift running of dog,
the blue jay's accepting nod.

(p. 41)

Here the poetess depicts 'love' as something related to 'life' and 'living' and 'light,' — a point illustrated by that long piece called "Quartered Questions and Queries," which offers us the following :

There is no darkness,
only light :
gold, gold, as my love for you,
my love.

(p. 37.)

Some of the poems in this collection are highly philosophical and metaphysical, such as "Silence," "The Dispossessed," and "Quartered

Questions and Queries." The poem "In This Darkness" is also of the same nature, where Monika says :

> I always asked for, prayed
> and demanded wisdom...
> and wisdom is light
> but I want darkness,
> do not give me light.

(p. 39)

'Darkness' in our *Upanishads* signifies both 'knowing, and 'unknowing,' and this poem seems to play on its ambivalence, as T.S. Eliot also did in his monumental *Four Quartets*.

The next collection of Monika's verses, *Past Imperative*, is a body of 35 poems written between 1953 and 1964. The poet's wide-ranging experience of life and nature comes to the fore here, crowding up its pages with unforgettable memories of persons and places, of past youth and lost loves. Monika says in "It is forgotten" :

> But I have grown wise, and will now delve,
> Into memories of long ago.

(p. 18)

Another poem, "The Heritage of Years" (a little longish), forcefully reaffirms it all. But the poem "You and I" is cast in a different shape and brings in the motherly love of the poetess for her son :

> Once all of you was mine,
> As mine was yours, for you and I were one.
> Within me you lived, as I within your mind.
> While your hands, softer than petal dust,
> Caressed, and my blood thrilled a thin shrill scream.

(p. 10)

The only poem in this volume abounding in love and life is "Sun, Do Not Grieve" wherein we have such moving lines as :

> Hush, Sun, do not grieve, you are loved.
> I shall not speak, I have your kiss upon my finger
> tips.

And, O Sun, you are gold, gold,
within the precincts of my heart.

(p. 34)

Here the 'Sun' is a symbol for the lover whose lusty kisses are imprinted on the cheeks and 'heart' of the beloved; it is a metaphor for the expression of her love and passion, and also a means to avoid direct utterance.

Across the Vast Spaces, which is largely a collection of her previous poems, barring a few fresh ones, is dedicated to Rita and contains some 27 odd pieces. Of the nine (according to my calculation) fresh pieces, most are about the sun, the gold, this land or foreign land, rocks, and skies, the spaces and the market-days, and the birds and the beasts. But the poem "Hammering heat of our summer sun" is quite different from them in at least treatment, and tends to be somewhat melancholic and romantic, but even here she does not have that 'summer' or 'heat' or 'boiling point' which we come across in Kamala Das, especially in her poem "Summer in Calcutta". This is Monika Varma :

Like the earth
I, too, am exhausted by hammer heat.
I am parched.
I call.
Give me love,
give me rain.

(p. 30)

And this is Kamala Das :

What is this drink but
The April sun, squeezed
Like an orange in
My glass? I sip the
Fire, I drink and drink
Again, I am drunk,
Yes, but on the gold
Of suns.[4]

The image of the April sun in the latter brings to the poet a sense of sensuous repletion and warm intoxication similar to the one we find in John Keats's "Ode on Indolence," but this is lacking in the former where we have a sense of exhaustion and dryness. Both the passages have rich suggestiveness and marked economy of expression about them. But Monika is no match to Kamala Das in matters of love and sex, and her *forte* is her serious, cerebral control over the medium of expression.

The last collection of Monika Varma's verses entitled *Alakananda* consists of 25 pieces in all and toes the line of her earlier works with regard to theme, mood and tonc. Thc two really remarkable pieces in it are : "The Time of Green Leaves is Gold" and "Alakananda," which are preponderant with natural imagery and sweeping rhythm. One notable feature of the love poems in it is their rich quality of indirection and obliquity. But "The Time of Green Leaves is Gold" is a definite exception to this general statement. While "Alakananda" is about the beauty and rush of the Ganges over the rugged high rocks in the North down to the sprawling plains and the mighty sea, "The Time of Green Leaves is Gold" is all about the poet's sacred love for her lover, being superb and unsurpassable in its delicacy of feeling coupled with marvellous natural imagery. Monika's keen sense of colours and sounds, of birds and beasts, of rains and rivers, of 'gold' and 'green leaves,' comes out vividly in this poem. The 'sun' and the 'tree' serve as symbols of love and passion (as usual with the poetess) in whose expression she is frank and honest (though not in the same degree as Kamala Das or Gauri Deshpande). There are some deeply moving passages in it, such as the following :

> Why then do you tremble, my love,
> you ask what have my eyes said :
> it was a vulnerable moment, my love,
> and now it lies shivering,
> Or is it aquiver?
> Come, my love, let your eyes
> unafraid of battle
> smile.

(p. 27)

and again the following :

> Shelter in my arms and I shall enclose you
> in a veil of green-feather love
> winging to the skies.

(p. 29)

No one, obviously, can call in question the sincerity of the poetess in these passages, though her fancy seems to be exulting in 'purple patches' here recollecting the practice of Keats and Shelley in utter romantic vein and style, or that of Kalidasa, the greatest Sanskrit poet-*cum*-playwright, in making natural objects carry human emotions (as in his matchless *Meghadoot*). Speaking of this poem, Syed Ameeruddin observes : "On the whole, it is a very rich poetry, each line is enchanting, resounding, lilting with music, pregnant with meaning and abounds in rich erotic and visual imagery."[5] The poem is shaped as a dramatic monologue, where the solo speaker is the poetess herself. It is decidedly a much better poem than many others composed by her previously or in this volume, as she has admirably succeeded here in maintaining a balance between content and form, between the changing seasons and the varying moods of love. She is surely at her best here in stirring the inner chords of a sensitive reader without any aid of erotic acts displayed on the stage.

Monika has been, as noticed above, a sober and sincere artist all through who does not believe in exploiting the general public tendency to read cheap literature or that kind of literature which indulges in sensual and sexual accounts. It is not that she treats Love as an outcast in Indian society, nor that she would be committing perjury by writing about it. She knows it well that it is as valid a theme as any other, and she resorts to it at proper moments. But it is not the be-all and the end-all for her. In this she stands apart from some other women writers of her day, — from Kamala Das, Gauri Deshpande and Sunita Jain, to name only a few. She scores over them by her rational approach to her subjects and by her maintenance of a notable equilibrium between sound and sense. She rather shuns treading on stinking and slippery grounds of sex.

Finally, we are not to accept the verdict of Murli Dass Melwani when he remarks that Monika Varma "failed to live up to the promise of her first collection, *Dragonflies Draw Flame,*"[6] as Melwani has pronounced it hastily and mercilessly without taking into account her succeeding volumes. As seen above, her works rather reveal "a growing sensitiveness to English speech and rhythm,"[7] and her impressive, fanciful transcreation of Jayadeva's classic, *Gita Govinda*, needn't detract us from a correct and judicious appraisal of her poetic worth. Notwithstanding "a saltish simplicity"[8] that we encounter in her love poems, she emerges unscarred and untainted out of the crippling atmosphere of romantic inertia and sex-exhibitionism created by some well-known women writers of Indo-English verse today, and thereby gives a clear indication of her healthy mental attitude towards the knotty problems of love and life. In striking this original and individualistic attitude as reflected in her poetry, she remains unique among her fellow practitioners. She also clarifies her position partly when she declares —

> There is a rage in creating,
> and I say "Stop...cease your lamentation, doves,
> there is more to it than this."[9]

REFERENCES

1. Monika Varma, "Gauri Deshpande," *Facing Four* (Calcutta : Writers Workshop, 1973), p. 24.
2. Nissim Ezekiel, "Preface," *Dragonflies Draw Flame* (1962; Calcutta : Writers Workshop, 1966), p. 4.
3. Syed Ammeruddin, "Monika Varma," *Commonwealth Quarterly*, 3, No. 9 (Dec 1 1978),13.
4. Kamala Das, "Summer in Calcutta," *Tonight, This Savage Rite* (New Delhi : Arnold-Heinemann, 1979), p. 31.
5. Ameernddin, *loc. cit*., p. 13.
6. Murli Das Melwani, "Indo-Anglian Women Poets," *Themes in Indo-Anglian Literature* (Bareilly : Prakash Book Depot, 1977), p. 70.
7. K.R. Srinivasa Iyengar, *Indian Writing in English* (Bombay : Asia Publishing House, 1973), p. 680.
8. See this author's book, *Indo-Anglian Poetry* (Allahabad : Kitab Mahal, 1979), p. 263, in this connection.
9. Monika Varma, "Words," *Gita Govinda and Other Poems* (Calcutta : Writers Workshop. 1966), p. 8.

13

Between Two Worlds : The Poetry of Margaret Chatterjee*

Margaret Chatterjee, a British by birth and an Indian by citizenship, combines in her artistic personality the two worlds of experience, the two planes of reality — poetry and philosophy. She offers equal opportunities to the fanciful flight of her creative talent and to the controlling rod of her disciplined thought. Her poetry, therefore, hovers between two polarities of imagination and contemplation, of colourful depiction of persons, places and things and single-minded devotion to the channels of reasoning. That she is well aware of her paradoxical situation becomes quite evident when we take up and examine a poem like "The Spring and the Spectacle," which partly runs thus :

> You in your wisdom never pose the impossible question
> That has been my life,
> The task of isolating the dance
> From the dancer,
> The kernal from the fruit,
> The flame from the fire;
> Bear with me then while I confess
> The crowning paradox —
>
> (*The Spring and the Spectacle*, p. 30)

This comes from Margaret in a very suggestive tone and amounts to nothing short of confession.

---

*Reprinted from *Indian Literature*, xxv, No. 5 (Sept.-October 1982), 72-85, with permission of the editor.

The idea that Margaret moves between the two worlds gets reinforced by yet another evidence, — an evidence that may be termed 'internal' being provided by her own poetry. She appears before us as a strange sapling of the integrated twin cultures of the West and the East. This, in no way, questions her allegiance to India, but surely states a simple and self-evident truth about her. She can, understandably, accommodate Christ and Krishna, the *Bible* and the *Gita* and the *Upanishads* in the pliable body of her verse, and thereby permitting the two hemispheres of the globe to come closer.

Educated at Oxford, Margaret has been a teacher of Philosophy by vocation and a poet by option. Her poetic career commenced with *The Spring and the Spectacle* (1967), which was followed in due course by *Towards the Sun* (1970), *The Sandalwood Tree* (1972), and *The Sound of Wings* (1978). She has shown her interest in a number of subjects, namely in music, art, poetry, philosophy, short story writing, public speaking, piano recital, and broadcasting. Presently she holds a chair in Philosophy in the University of Delhi. Uptil now, her poems have appeared in such anthologies as *Mahfil* (Michigan), *Span* (Canberra), *Hers* edited by Mary Ann Das Gupta (Calcutta), *Indo-English Poetry in Bengal*, edited by K.C. Lahiri (Calcutta), *Indian Literature* (Sahitya Akademi, New Delhi), *World Anthology* compiled by Miller (Illinois), *Nineteen Poets* edited by Malik and Bandyopadhyaya, and *An Anthology in Greek* edited by Vasilis Vitsaxis. Although some articles on, and occasional notices about, her poetry have come out so far, it has not received, surprisingly, adequate critical attention that it deserves. It is, therefore, in the fitness of things to take stock of her poetical work and worth here and now.

Margaret's first book of verse published by the Writers Workshop and dedicated to E.M.G. and N.H.G. contains only eighteen poems[1] in all. Most of the poems in it are about the changing months and seasons, varying persons and places, subjective moods and fancies, — about January, August, and September, about the rain, the winter, and the spring, about Boris Pasternak, Adam, and Delhi, and about some arresting, precious moments in the poet's life captured beautifully in her lovely lyrics. The poem "Homage to Boris Pasternak" opens the volume in a worthwhile gesture of paying a glowing tribute to the master, who declined the Nobel Prize in 1958. In "Winter in Delhi," one of her finest pieces indeed, the poet nostalgically recalls, through immediate experience, the benumbing chill of London in the winter season. While the poem "For Adam," is purely erotic in theme, "Incarnation" displays the poet's preoccupation with Christian theology and doctrines. In the latter, she appears as a devout Christian offering her prayer to the Son of Mary in the following manner :

> We who are trackless,
> Cushioned with half truths
> And never living abundantly,
> Pygmied by the innumerable enemies
> Within and without the gate,
> See now the way, the Truth and the Life.
> Broken through and transformed today
> By this scandal
> —The scent of incense and the scent of hay—
> We worship Thee in our hour of despairing.
> —O son of Mary, enter this clay.
>
> (*The Spring and the Spectacle*, p. 26)

As contrasted with this poem, we have quite a few in this volume which are perfectly Indian in content and background, — the poems like "August 15," "Winter in Delhi," and "Rajinigandha." Of these, the first-named one celebrates our Independence, a red-letter day in the history of this country replete with nostalgic reminiscences, and highlights the poet's sense of disillusionment at our mishandling of the long-desired liberty. It clearly expresses the feelings and frustrations of a bygone generation — the generation of freedom fighters who waged a relentless and heroic struggle and suffered considerably in the wake of their struggle — which stands much maligned and misunderstood in the altered circumstances today. Though the poet tells us in the very beginning of the poem that this is no occasion for 'heart-searchings or diagnosis' and still less for 'judgement,' she does not hold her ground and apparently indulges in these, as is evident from the following :

> Time came
> When obsessed with the furniture of living

—The having or the getting —
We only looked to the sky for rain,
And the flight of birds
The lilt of leaves
And the scent of grass escaped us
Because we were always awaiting
The sky's bounty.
So we tilled the land
Laying by enough for the morrow,
And if you asked us what we were building
Or where we were going,
Stricken dumb,
We could have given no answer.

(*The Spring and the Spectacle*, p. 8)

On the surface, the poem looks to be simple and straightforward in statement, but deep down it there flows an undercurrent of irony and sarcasm.

For one thing, the approach of the spring touches the inmost depths of the poet's heart, rendering her ecstatic and eloquent at the sudden burst of unusual beauty around. The charming season brings in its train 'the splendour of the spectacle,' and in her mood of sheer delight she exclaims :

For here there is no shadow-time
Between light and dark—
Aflame the sky the urgent sun
Shoots blossom from the top of every tree
And every leaf stands stiff with eager sap.

("Poem in Springtime," *The Spring and the Spectacle*, p. 16)

There is nothing spectacular if the poet's fancy runs riot at the mere approach or sight of the spring, but it is really spectacular that she absorbs into her verse Indian thought and culture, Indian customs and surroundings, in a splendid manner. There are a number of poems spread over her four volumes which lead the reader to this conviction, — the poems like "Winter in Delhi," "August 15," and "Rajnigandha" in *The Spring and the Spectacle*, "Calcutta 1970," "On Reading an Eighteenth Century Bengali Poet," "Bihar," and "Variation on a Theme from the Mundaka Upanishad" in *Towards the Sun*, "Near Howrah Station", "Taj Mahal," "For Sankho," and "Agni" in *The Sandalwood Tree*, and "Khus Khus," "Himalayas," "To Chandigarh by Road," "Vayu", "Night as Karuna," "Karma," "To a Carvaka Philosopher," "Glosses on Brhadaranyaka Upanishad, IV, 4," "Gloss on Bhagavadgita, VI, 21," "Pari Mahal," "Kashmir Valley," and "Danihama" in *The Sound of Wings*. This long listing of so many poems here indicates the extent to which Margaret has gone in naturalishing Indian air and surroundings in her verse. Insistently she employs the monsoon and rain imagery in her poems, as may be gathered from the following lines of "Urban Love" :

> And now I know the rains have come
> From the salt taste of your skin.
>
> (*Towards the Sun*, p. 10)

And in "Ballad of the Earth and the Rain", which is a really memorable piece in the first volume, she addresses the rain in an intimate tone :

> Long have I known you, old rogue rain
> —You uncertain creature —
> With your thick wet curls a blow in the wind
> And the loins of you
> Thundering with fountains
> Astride the ripe sky like a lover —
> Enough of your tantalising!
> Long have I known of your doings
> —You darling rascal......
>
> (p. 14)

In one place, Margaret observes : "There is not a great deal about rain in the verse of England. The 'small rain' of the mediaeval poet became the 'big rain' of a poem in my earlier book and the monsoon provides one of the root-metaphors in this collection."[2]

The collection she speaks of here is *Towards the Sun*, which comprises some 28 odd poems in all, and which is dedicated to Malay, Nilima and Amala. This collection definitely brings in some fine sketches of seasons, and discloses a good deal about the poet's likes and dislikes of them. This is what we find in the poem "Monsoon" :

The winter is my time
Of most consent,
Autumn its happy messenger.
But most of all your presence
Is like drenching rain :
I stand beneath the water-spouts,
My body languorous....

(p. 11)

To the poet, explicitly, the winter is most welcome, but not the rainy season, when the thick patches of cloud loom large over our heads. Her British sensibility is unmistakably in conflict here with her Indian sensibility. By the time she comes to "Woman and Monsoon Sky," she is almost ready to hail the monsoon and the rain :

I have changed
My mind.
Do come.

(p. 12)

Now the expressions become economical and words purposive; the diction tends to be shorn of all complexities and superfluities. An excellent rapport is established between thought and feeling, — a thing with which T.S. Eliot was greatly concerned in his essay on "The Metaphysical Poets" in order to arrive at a "unification of sensibility."[3] The collection has some really charming lyrics in it, which are very much personal in substance, presenting the poet before the reader in diverse roles — as a woman in love, as a wife comforting her husband, and as a mother fully prepared to suffer and sacrifice for the sake of her child. In the third lyric of the sequence called "Lyrics," she comes out, in a stoic and resigned attitude, as follows :

You, the leaven in me
Live and grow
And only such can I be bread
So paradoxical this
That through you
Being what I am
And now completely so

By you alone
Can be quite utterly
Devoured.

(p. 16)

The same attitude persists also in the poem "Analogy," where she compares herself with a kite that is held fast by a tender filament. There are, further, some poems in this collection which deal with musical instruments and exercises, such as "Tonality" and "Piano Lesson." Margaret seems to be at her ease in them, and the rhythmic lines bubble up there effortlessly, as may be seen in the following passage from "Octave" :

My fingers span these notes,
The top one you
And this one me,
So we are pitched
Quite differently
And yet we are in tune
Most perfectly,
And in between
These many notes
If struck
Make melody.

(p. 7)

This passage bears out the fact that the poet has now developed substantially in her artistic powers. In truth, the whole of the second book abounds in short, crisp, and lively poems as contrasted with the cumbrous, lengthy ones of the first book. To elaborate this point, it is suggested that the title-pieces of the two books be taken up and studied comparatively. It would have been all the more creditable to Margaret had she turned out many more pieces like "Towards the Sun" which is brief, compact, and thought provoking.

The third book, *The Sandalwood Tree*, consists of 31 poems *in toto*, several of which are on different trees, flowers and animals, and several others on varying places and persons. But, curiously enough, the title-piece dealing with Bangladesh lists a fairly good variety of trees — the tal, bamboo, mango, jackfruit, tamarind, and sandalwood — and thereby combines the traits of the two themes.

The scale of the poem weighs heavily with what the poet has seen and learnt about the scented sandalwood :

So the sage
Told the woodcutter
As the legend goes,
Before he found
The tree of trees,
The sandalwood,
Which only when most bruised
Can fragrant be.

(p. 11)

It is cast against a wholly Indian setting. Pieces like "On Pruning Roses," "Tortoise," "The Cat," "Elephant," and "Flying Fox" bring out Margaret's keen sense of observation and her altruism. And of them all, the last-named stands out as an exquisite piece of poetry :

The flying fox
Climbed pinewards
In the Indian night,
The flaked bark roseate
Held his claws,
The resin-laden wind
Flaring his nostrils,
His sharp sharp eyes
Skimming the monsoon valley
Cupped like a milky sea,
His ears assailed by
Cricket's morse code
Syncopate.
... ...
He flew,
His flight fantastic far
—To the next tree.

(p. 26)

The poem has a neat, clean structure and a fine network of alliterative lines. The last lines are specially to be marked in this connection. Those poems which describe various places and persons are : "Near

Howrah Station" "Taj Mahal," "On Reading Marianne Moore," and "For Sankho." Of these, "Taj Mahal" expresses the poet's sense of amazement at the rare craftsmanship of the sculptors as reflected on the walls of the Taj, one of the seven wonders of the world. She puts forth this sense in poetic form in her own characteristic manner :

> It is not Shah Jehan
> Who haunts these walls.
> I met the man
> Who wrought this tracery,
> Whose white leaves
> Lattice deep blue night,
> The unknown craftsman
> Who carved in stone
> The sky.

(p. 16)

The real attraction of this book, however, lies in its shorter pieces like "Cricket," "Paean," "Mood," "Shoes," and "School Uniform," wherein we have a glimpse of aspects of life sustained by experience and woven into a fine web of artistry.

The best of all that Margaret Chatterjee has written so long has been put together in *The Sound of Wings*, her fourth and last book of verse. Containing four pieces each of her previous volumes and forty-one fresh ones and dedicated to Amala, this book is cast in a shining get up and serves as a charming specimen of the blending of the poet's western mind and eastern experience. It offers a rich evidence of her skill in condensing complex ideas into memorable images, of her control over the poetic tools, and of her concern for the human predicament in this war-torn age of ours. There is much in it to appeal both to the heart and to the head. The themes of her poetry here remain almost the same as in the other three volumes, but it allows for more space to accommodate certain well-known artists and lay bare some deep speculations of philosophy for the pleasure and profit of the general reader. The poet speaks highly of Pablo Neruda, Henry Moore, Robert Frost, and a sculptor friend, gives us glosses on the Hindu texts like the *Brhadaranyaka Upanishad* (IV, 4) and the *Bhagavadgita* (VI, 21), and talks freely about the body, the mind, the wind ("Vayu"), *Karma*, and a Carvaka philosopher. The title-piece, "The Sound of Wings," carries a peculiar simile between 'the bird' and 'you,' — 'peculiar' in the sense that it is a little far-fetched and unconvincing. "Of Language," a good poem no doubt, unravels the mystery and energy of unspoken words, prompting the lover to take her beyond the seen. And last of all comes "Ciphers," which must be mentioned here because it is a string of some eleven small haiku-like poems and because it is pleasing enough for its simple diction and direct utterance :

> No one could understand
> Why I punished myself
> By fasting, forgetting that
> The camel in the desert
> Who has once tasted
> The leaves of the
> Sandalwood tree
> Desires nothing else.
>
> (p. 42)

Evidently, a good deal of planning and logical argument has gone into its making. The undertone of love is unmistakable in it, and, significantly, the last line ends with 'To love again.'

It is in place to speak a little about Margaret's diction and imagery here. Generally, her diction is vigorous and communicative, and does not indulge in unnecessary word-jugglery or punning. Occasionally, it becomes simple, lucid, straightforward, as may be seen in the following from "Vayu" :

> Breath belongs
> To the sky.
> And the waters know
> For somewhere
> A small breeze
> Moves the waters
> And healing begins.
>
> (*The Sound of Wings*, p. 64)

The air is associated here with curative powers in a language that bespeaks itself to a common reader. For one thing, Margaret is free from the linguistic banality and distortions of many other Indo-

Anglian poets : Her first volume demonstrates her love of difficult and intricate words and phrases and lengthy and involved sentences, but her other volumes seem to have discarded this propensity for pedantry or Johnsonese. At times her diction tends to be very musical and rhythmical. Take the following extract from "Agni" as an illustration :

Here is the last leap
Of flame to flame,
Let me feed the fire
With my body.
Lick me with their tongue,
My limbs molten....

(*The Sandalwood Tree*, p. 41)

The recurrent use of 'f,' 'I', and 'm' sounds is to be specially marked herein. As an illustration of the fine use of alliteration and assonance, the poem "Flying Fox" may be taken up. Margaret has employed many other figures of speech, too, in her verse in a remarkable fashion.

The imagery in Margaret's poetry is explicitly striking and arresting. Basil Vitsaxis has taken note of her "original and impressive"[4] images. Some of the examples in this context are :

... Packed
As tight as a heady child's head
Is packed with mischief....

("The Spring," *The Sandalwood Tree*, p. 37)

and :

Her arms tight-packed
In her sleeves; tight-fitting
As coconut in its shell....

("Near Howrah Station," *The Sound of Wings*, p. 12)

and again :

Within this gentleness
Desire coils
Like spring....

("Gesture," *Towards the Sun*, p. 6)

These quoted excerpts put up a show not only of vibrant and captivating images, but also of her notable dexterity in poetic craft. Their vividness of details and immediacy of appeal are bound to capture the notice of the reader at once. They amply demonstrate that Margaret can sing and paint and sculpt with words. Though there are several philosophical poems in her four volumes, they do not bristle with the ambiguity or the foggy fancy of a philosopher. It is difficult to resist the temptation of quoting the following passage from "August 15" in the first volume in order to substantiate the statement :

> That was time
> When men saw visions
> And dreamed dreams
> Unrolling the future
> Like a golden carpet
> On which the youth of tomorrow
> Might walk
> With all the pride and certitude...
>
> (p. 7)

The image of 'golden carpet' is quite appropriately used here. It is highly suggestive; — suggestive of 'red carpet' and 'golden future' simultaneously.

By the foregoing account of Margaret's poetry, it becomes evident that an alert feminine sensibility is at work in it. The poet's subjects are far-ranging and her command of the English language is commendable. Beneath the hard surface of philosophy lies the kernel of humanism. Though she is not completely free of the charge of ambivalence and obscurity in her verse, humane critics like Prof. K.R.S. Iyengar have discovered in her "a trained sensibility" and "an individual note of her own;"[5] She also makes the mistake of frequently resorting to the device of repetition, some of the glaring examples of which are given below :

(1) In that grey grey glooming of yesterday...

(2) Turn, and a chill chill wind a-down your back...

(3) May deep deep longing for the north...

(4) In this flat flat land...

(5) His sharp sharp eyes...
(6) And the plough still moving still moving
    Plough this field.

No one can perhaps defend this poetic practice of hers, and yet Basil Vitsaxis claims for her an "established place as a great poetess."[6]

To conclude, Margaret Chatterjee's poetry has the charm of reconciling the twin pulls of poetry and philosophy, the conflicting claims of the 'materialistic' West and the 'spiritualistic' East. On the strength of this reconciliation, she occupies a distinct position in Indo-English verse being written today. As a poet, she is to be ranked with Lila Ray, an American lady married to a Bengali writer and now settled permanently in Calcutta, rather than with any India-born poet. This sort of ranking is inspired by considerations of their cultural and topographical ambivalence and their serious involvement in literary pursuits. As for Margaret, her poetry carries the brand of the interacting of the two intellectual disciplines chosen by her and of the two distinct climes and regions. For this reason, she is to be remembered as a typical child of the two worlds.

NOTES AND REFERENCES

1. K.R.S. Iyengar is wrong in mentioning that it is a collection of 'nine poems' only. See his *Indian Writing in English* (Bombay : Asia Publishing House, 1973), p. 682.
2. Margaret Chatterjee, "Note," *Towards the Sun* (Calcutta : Writers Workshop, 1970), no pagination.
3. T.S. Eliot, "The Metaphysical Poets," *Selected Essays* (London : Faber and Faber, 1946 ed.), p. 288.
4. Basil Vitsaxis, "Some Contemporary Indian Women Poets," *Commonwealth Quarterly,* 3, No. 9 (Dec. 1978), 36.

14

The Poetry of Syed Amanuddin : A Study in Diction and Versification*

I

Critics and scholar-poets have shown an unprecedented interest in Language and Versification during the 20th century. In truth, this is not an altogether new fashion and men of letters like Ben Jonson, John Dryden, Samuel Johnson, William Wordsworth, Samuel Taylor Coleridge, and Matthew Arnold were all, more or less, concerned with these linguistic and prosodistic considerations. Of the two, the problem of Language has assumed serious proportions. The poets have started using colloquial, slangy, and usually non-literary language as an acceptable thing for their practice. Surprisingly, the lead this time has been taken by American authors rather than by English poets, by such poets as E.E. Cummings, William Carlos Williams, Ezra Pound, and T.S. Eliot. In the process of standardisation, these poets and several others who followed them took recourse to an anti-sentimental stance and rendered their language quite current and colloquial, highly speech-like and occasionally vulgar, touching sometimes even the obscene and the forbidden, reaping immense advantage of *vers libre* and linguistic innovations, without bothering even a whit for traditional forms of verse or metre. As a result, they introduced in their poetry "new ways of expressing spiritual predicaments, ...new possibilities of feeling and subject-matter," and thereby renewed "the strength of

---

*Reprinted with permission of the editor of *JIWE* (Gulbarga).

poetry to affect the language of public affairs and of private intercourse."[1] This is, for instance, how T.S. Eliot writes in his poem "The Love Song of J. Alfred Prufrock" :

> Let us go then, you and I,
> when the evening is spread out against the sky
> like a patient etherized upon a table[2]...

and this is how E.E. Cummings, the greatest innovator in the American poetry of our day and the true inheritor of the celebrated poet Walt Whitman, writes in one of his poems :

> next to of course god america i
> love you land of the pilgrims and so forth oh
> say can you see by the dawn's early my
> country, tis of centuries come and go
> and are no more what of it we should worry
> in every language even deaf and dumb
> thy sons acclaim your glorious name by gorry
> by jingo by gee by gosh by gum
> ... ...
> then shall the voice of liberty be mute?[3]

If Eliot's language tends to be highly modernistic and technical keeping in tune with the Age of Science and Technology, that of Cummings smacks of an excessive liberty taken with the English language, having discarded the use of capitals, commas, full stops and having resorted to deliberated word-compounds as seen in 'deafanddumb.' And we may assure the latter that 'the voice of liberty,' so far as diction and versification are concerned will never be 'mute' in our age, because the tradition has become so firm-rooted in the poetic world of today.

And one such 'voice of liberty' in matters of diction and versification is that of Syed Amanuddin, the noted Indo-Anglian poet.[4] Syed has been a poet in whom the linguistic and poetic features pointed out above find their fulfilment. Syed's contemporaneity finds its full play in his verse and he comes out as a poet alive to the situation obtaining around. Now he is current and modern, now scientific and technological, now simple and lucid, now terse and compact. He actually adjusts himself according to his occasions and requirements, keeping his eye almost always on the overall effect of his poems on the minds and hearts of his readers. He is hardly ever led away by tempting slogans (*e.g.*, Surrealism and Naturalism) of foreign lands nor by slavish imitations of the giants of English or American poetry; he is rather true to his subject and grounded resolutely in his nation's cultural heritage he tackles his situations and characters (they are too many!) as per call of the hour and informs us about them in his characteristically individualistic fashion, without letting his grip over his poetic tools slip. As a poet, he is closer to Americans rather than to any English or Indo-Anglian poet. The question of paramount significance is not *where* one learns one's art and technique but *how* one absorbs and executes them. And Syed comes out with flying colours in this test.

Syed, who has had a long poetic career since 1967, has produced a number of poetical collections to this day : *The Forbidden Fruit* (1967), *Tiffin State Hospital* (1970), *Shoes of Tradition* (1970), *The Children of Hiroshima* (1970), *Poems of Protest* (1972), *Lightning & Love* (1973), *The Age of Female Eunuchs* (1974), *Adventures of Atman* (1977), and *Gems and Germs* (1978). Besides these, a few more volumes are likely to come out shortly.[5] In all these works, Syed appears as a sensitive poet of our times who is devoted to his cause with all sincerity and seriousness.

One of the distinguishing characteristics of Syed's poetic diction is its ingenuity and innovativeness. In his poem, "Gale of Uncertainty," the poet writes :

> yet life is an adventure
> waiting for the neverhappenedbefore
>
> (*The Children of Hiroshima*, p. 42)

Now, compare 'neverhappendbefore' with Cummings 'deafanddumb' and guess who of the two is more innovative, more experimental. And then, not only 'life' but also its reflection that is 'literature' is 'an adventure.' Syed has verily ventured beyond the commonplace complacence and traditional versification, and has made a bold and daring experiment with the language here. The same adventurous spirit is seen operating in the following extract too :

Sweetysunny hour
shotshotshot
haunhaunhaun

the tiger ran
dragging the man
haunhaunhaun

windanddust played with the papers
years of animal studies

(*Ibid.*, p. 20)

There are no pauses, no marks of punctuation, no capitalizations here, and still the passage has a musicality of its own and a deftness at synthesising sound and sense, especially in 'haunhaunhaun,' and a proneness towards the process of compounding, as seen in 'windanddust.' There is no dearth of such innovative passages in Syed's poetry, and the examples given above were picked up at random.

Syed introduces variety in diction, as may be deduced from his love poems, poems of protest, poems of science, and spiritual and mystical poems. Although these divisions may look to be content-oriented, they also indicate the variety of language in his poetry, as one level of language can't do the work of another level. For example, his love poems present a feast of tender feelings and lilting rhythms, whereas his poems of protest betray a rebellious spirit at the back of their compositions. This is a representative of the former type of language :

when Love touched me
beauty sparks unselfing the self

a touch of fire
the sparkler splits
splits into many many sparks
dancing in rhythms of loveliness

("The Sparkler," *The Forbidden Fruit*, p. 37)

and this is another of the latter category :

that purse that watch that ring
surrender man or die
my knife is bloodthirsty

there there stupidrogue
    well go fall into the water
    those who do'nt love life must be damned

        i row i row
        to the bay i go

("Calcutta," *Poems of Protest*, p. 5)

Similarly, Syed's science-inspired verse is utterly contrasted to that which searches into the soul and its relationship with God, the Ultimate Consciousness[6], as the poet himself puts it. To illustrate the point, two quotations from his verse are being given below :

DR ZZ3m8 is nice too
    but he is a bit cold
    more like those remote BIGSISTERS
yes shes very unlike DR XM99
    who reached me by a touch....

(*The Age of Female Eunuchs*, p. 14)

and :

this is the path of ultimate realization
where the extremes of white n black
    are blended into gray
for the outsider this is an unattractive
    path without sensual song
    n mortification of flesh
only a few wise persons ultimately
    arrive here
n only some of those few stay on

(*Adventures of Atman*, Canto 25, p. 39)

These two quotations are the specimens of two utterly different kinds of language, and both fit in their respective contexts.

Syed's diction tends to be figurative occasionally, especially so when he is writing about his spiritual and mystical longings and quests :

in the greengrass of my memory
    you are grasshoppers n daisies

flying n stopping
hiding n shining

(*Gems and Germs*, p. 40)

Here memory is presented as a 'green grass' where the beloved ever hops and haunts him. The diction has unmistakably become graphic and metaphorical at this juncture. But the truly figurative diction begins to operate in Syed's poems of spiritual adventures, *e.g.*, in the following passage :

Circumstance is beautiful i said
but i must reach the center
not yet not yet was the whisper
i must persist i said to myself
started running in the peripheral world of being
until i collapsed in sheer ecstasy

(*Adventures of Atman*, p. 19)

One has to get at its abstract meaning before one can really understand it. It is this type of language that is largely expected to be found in Syed's forthcoming work, *The Master*, too.

And there where the diction is not figurative and symbolical, it tends to be lucid and clear, musical and alliterative. This is an instance of the diction pure and crystal-clear, lucid and transparent :

my prison is in me
my fetters in my palm
i dont know who i am
i dont know why i am

(*The Children of Hiroshima*, p. 16)

and this is another of truly musical and cadenced diction :

she sat talking of this and that
little knew how her charms stirred my heart
as in moon's loving light we sat together

("My Love In Silks," *The Forbidden Fruit*, p. 17)

In the first instance the diction is reduced to monosyllables and a high-rated clarity is attained, and in the second, the first and third lines are quite soft, sweepy and rhythmical. Though the second one betrays a conversational tone, especially in 'she sat talking of this and that,' it does not produce any jarring effects on the ears of readers.

Another peculiar charm of Syed's diction is that it becomes, at times, very intense and dramatic. The lover's anxieties are very well reflected in the lines :

> My own Helen, Dearest, fly to my arms, away we will
> to Troy, far far away from the jealous Spartan eyes
> forever to live a life of love
>
> ("A Loveletter," *The Forbidden Fruit*, p. 8)

The 'strange fits of passion' known to the poet are beautifully enshrined in them. Syed's spiritual and mystical poems are also full of dramatic tensions, not unlike those of Robert Browning's dramatic monologues — like "My Last Duchess" and "Andrea Del Sarto," for instance — and here one feels one has to cross a series of hurdles before one reaches the divine domain. *In Adventures of Atman*, when the quester has walked the three paths — 'white black n gray' (p. 5) — bestrewn with baffling tortures and difficulties, he stands face to face with the reality, the life itself, which affirms the poet's faith in an existence that combines 'flesh and spirit' :

> one was your heartsdesire
> the other denial of the same
> both unrealities created by your mind
> who are you?
> i am life itself
> a manifestation of life in nature
> a blend of flesh n spirit
>
> (Canto 25, p. 38)

This passage obliquely raises the question : If man is surrounded by 'unrealities,' what is the reality? And it is this that the quester is out to seek.

A remarkable feature of Syed's diction is the abundant use of abbreviated words and phrases; *e.g.*, 'govt,' 'sab,' 'n,' 'blaze n ashes,' etc. He is also at home in the employment of slangs and jargons. And he resorts to colloquialism in the following :

> your beer sir said the barmaid
> thank you

eighty cents sir
keep the change
thank you sir

(*Adventures of Atman*, p. 11)

This is an exchange between the barmaid and the gentleman who has just taken his sip at the bar.

The observations made hitherto convince us that Syed is a conscious craftsman who handles his language with ease and command and who is quite alert to various situations and subjects.

II

Syed does not use rhymes and metres in his poetry; instead, he employs *vers libre* as the medium of his expression. And though T.S. Eliot and Ezra Pound were of the opinion that 'No *vers* is *libre* for the man who wants to do a good job,' they themselves wrote poems in it — "Ash Wednesday" and "Dance Figure...," for instance — and many more English and American poets like W.B. Yeats, D.H. Lawrence, E.E. Cummings have exploited it to the maximum advantage. What was the directing purpose behind *vers libre* is not certain, as the French practitioners who originally made use of it offer conflicting versions about it,[7] but the noted critic Graham Hough is of the view that it aims at "the free expression of the poet's individual sensibility"[8] and that in trying to achieve this objective it forsakes the unimportant divisions of verse and prose — "the phenomenon of free verse is simply an instance of the general fusion between verse and imaginative prose that has been characteristic of our century."[9]

In his poetic practice, Syed attempts to transcend the limitations of cumbersome metre or prosody and succeeds in this to a great extent. Without ever bothering for the rhymed verses of a bygone age when the nightingales and the skylarks sang joyously in an orchard, he keeps abreast of his time by writing in modern idiom and *vers libre*. Lest his verse be chaotic and disorderly, he arranges his poems in lines, stanzas and paragraphs. In *The Children of Hiroshima* alone, we have glimpses of these patterns. While "Subjugation" is a poem cast in free verse consisting of four verse paras (though they differ widely in the number of lines), "Time" is clearly structured in four symmetrical stanzas of five lines each. In this very volume, there is a poem called "Progress of Self" that invariably follows two-line stanzas, for instance :

> slow spreading
> to community country friends n foes
>
> (p. 43)

but they do not turn into the jingling couplets of John Dryden and Alexander Pope. The couplets of Dryden and Pope may still be valid for satires and feuds, but they are totally out of place for a serious poetry of the type that Syed wrote. In the matter of versification, Syed never loses sight of contemporaneity and current speech.

And there where the above divisions become difficult, Syed groups his poems into Cantos, such as in *Adventures of Atman*, on the pattern of Pound's Cantos. These Cantos, like verse paragraphs, can be both long and short (*Cf.* 1 and 25 in this connection).

Syed sometimes blends verse and prose in his art. This may be seen in his "Calcutta," a very powerful poem indeed :

> sootygrin of the moon
> in the sweaty waters
> siren hoots the midnight hour
> rats are out of the whole
> in the street
> on the bridge
> on the river
> i row i row
> to the bay i go
>
> (*Poems of Protest*, p. 5)

Here the passage beginning with 'sootygrin of the moon' is quite contrasted to the last two lines — "i row i row/to the bay i go'. And the overall impression created by this fusion of the prosaic and the poetic is almost Shakespearean.[10]

Occasionally, Syed concentrates on prose poems too, such as in "Musings on Consciousness" in *Lightning & Love*. They are a cluster of sixteen poems in all, and maintain a separate identity of their own. These prose poems are also longer or shorter. Though they are not so symmetrical or musical as those of Thakur Rabindranath Tagore, they breathe an air of verve and raciness, as may be gathered from the following : "Man is never free. Never free because he wasn't born all by himself in a vacuum. And he doesn't exist all by himself. He may be a cosmic experiment — but not the only one. He is a part of a huge (huge from man's point of view) conspiracy of elements, the geological forces, complex forces in the universe gathering elements for the conspiracy and creating of life on the earth" (*Lightning & Love*, p. 50).

Syed also neatly juxtaposes the modern and the colloquial in his poetry. This naturally introduces the quality of counter-balance or contrast in it. If the modernistic phraseology captivates our attention in *The Age of Female Eunuchs* and *Tiffin State Hospital*, such as in :

yes doctor i told the psychiatrist
    thats but natural she said
    stop worrying about it
maybe doctor the psychiatrist too has no idea
    of what happens to me

(*The Age of Female Eunuchs*, p. 20)

the colloquial rhythm bubbles up in *Lightning & Love*, such as in :

array shaitan
yahya khan
what are you up to man?
    stop this death of pakistan
    you cant rule a khabrastan

("Bangladesh Poems," p. 29)

Actually, in the latter the poet has used Hindustani to register his strong sense of protest against the tyrannical military rule of General Yahya Khan over Bangladesh in the living language of the people. The consequence is known to the world over : Bangladesh was liberated from Pak's clutches by the singular efforts of its most dynamic leader, Sheikh Mujibur Rahman. Sometimes Syed harnesses slangs and cants to a beautiful application, and this kind of speech is to be had in the conversations of the barmaids and the waitresses and the nurses (the Bigsisters of *The Age of Female Eunuchs*).

And what is more surprising than what we have observed above is the poet's refined taste for art as caught in glowing words. Syed has sensibly sketched fourteen poems in his work, *Shoes of Tradition*, and these he terms as 'Pictopoems,' where poetry becomes a graphic and visual art. Here it is evident that the poet is equally at home both with his pen and pencil.

III

Speaking of Poetry in general, Syed once remarked : "Poetry is essentially a verbal art — a result of contrived and controlled use of language. Language is an over-used medium, but the poet supplies it with vitality by adding freshness to words and creating new contexts for them. Through the medium of words — words which are emotionally charged, carefully chosen, and intellectually significant — the poet enriches the reader's experience of life and nature, enhances his perception, and provides him with new territories of human experience."[11] This remark makes it amply clear that Syed's own use of language is 'contrived and controlled,' vital and perceptive. No less evident is his skill in the execution of the art of versification. On both counts — diction and versification — he has taken advantage of his environment and has bettered himself and his poetic record through persistent endeavours and fresh experiments. His close contact with the native speakers of English, with Americans to be precise, has added a sharp edge to his poetic tools and practice. No doubt, his art is an ever-growing art that offers us a glimpse of his dynamism and inventiveness.

NOTES AND REFERENCES

1. David Ferry, "The Diction of American Poetry," *American Poetry* (London : Edward Arnold, 1965), p. 136.
2. T.S. Eliot, *Collected Poems* (London : Faber & Faber, 1963), p. 13.
3. E.E. Cummings, "next to of course god america i," *American Poetry of the Twentieth Century*, ed. Richard Gray (Cambridge : Cambridge University Press, 1976), p. 112.
4. Syed, however, does not like to be called so. *See* his poem "Don't Call Me Indo-Anglian" published in *Indian Verse*, 2 (1977), n.p.
5. In a Note Syed informs me : "I am working on another longer poem tentatively titled *The Master — Last Epic.*"

6. In his later poetry Syed has been busy evolving a theory of Ultimate Consciousness, and one may look up his poetical volumes like *Lightning & Love* and *Adventures of Atman* for this. The theory is likely to culminate in *The Master.*

7. Graham Hough tells us about it thus : "Gustave Kahn . . . said that he was seeking in his free verse *une musique plus complexe* ['a more complex music'], while his contemporary Laforgue was seeking an immediate psyschological spontaneity, a way of rendering the sensation as directly as possible. Mallarme in *Crise de Vers* suggested that the use of the Alexandrine should be reserved, *ainsi que celui du drapeau*, like the country's flag, for solemn and formal occasions; while for lesser and more personal affairs, free verse in all its variety would be more suitable. Still earlier Verlaine, who disliked the actual *vers libre*, had consciously sought in his own *vers libre* a slighter and more hesitant rhythm than that of official French verse. And these views have their analogues in English." — *See* his illuminating essay on "Free Verse" in *Twentieth Century Poetry*, eds. Graham Martin & P.N. Furbank (Walton Hall, Milton Keynes : The Open University Press, 1975), p. 109.

8. *Ibid.*, p. 112.

9. *Ibid.*, p. 123.

10. For a suitable comparison, one may see the following lines in *Macbeth*, Arden edition :

    All. Double, double toil and trouble;
    Fire burn, and cauldron bubble.

    (Act IV, Sc. I, II. 10-11)

11. Syed Amanuddin, "Why Do We Need Poetry?" *Indian Verse*, 4 (Winter 1976), 16.

15

K.N. Daruwalla : The Painter of Rural Landscape*

Keki N. Daruwalla is one of those gifted Indo-English poets of today who have earned recognition of their poetic worth and talent in the literary world. He has published four volumes of verse under the titles *Under Orion* (1970), *Apparition in April* (1971), *Crossing of Rivers* (1976), and *Winter Poems* (1980). Here in this brief paper, I want to dwell on his skill in painting the rural landscape of Northern India, its beautiful plains and pastures, its attractive hills and frightening rivers and seas, and demonstrate how, in this, he is essentially different from many other poets of India writing in English nowadays.

The vast landscape of this sprawling land comes alive in the pages of Daruwalla's poetry through his masterly touches. It gets its articulation in various forms and features, — as hills, rivers, valleys, trees, plains and pastures. It grips the poet's imagination inescapably, and he tackles it both in its wild and mild aspects. The poem "The Ghaghra in Spate" is an example of the wild aspect, unfolding "the terror of the villagers at night as they fought the river."[1] The change of the river's course every year and its colour at different times of a day is graphically depicted in the following :

> And every year
> the Ghaghra changes course
> turning over and over in her sleep.

*Reprinted with permission of the editor of *Rajasthan University Studies in English*, XVI (1984), pp. 86-95.

In afternoon she is a grey smudge
exploring a grey canvas.
When dusk reaches her
through an overhang of cloud
she is overstewed coffee.
At night under a red moon in menses
she is a red weal
across the spine of the land.

(*Under Orion*, p. 78)

A similar portrayal of the low-lying areas of the Tarai infected with malarial mosquitos and hard-core bandits is to be found in the poem "In the Tarai," which is addressed to his friend, Raju. But here instead of showing compassion and understanding as in "The Ghaghra in Spate," the poet becomes bitter and sarcastic. The following extract may be cited as an illustration of this biting tone :

It is not a bad district they all say
Over the Ghaghra you have a ferry
to carry your car
There's an ice factory in town
(ice that drips and sweats like flesh)
There's a dhobi in your compound
but take a tip, don't get your
bush shirts starched
they will hang limp all the same
and smell like an Insemination Centre........

(*Under Orion*, pp. 76-77)

In fact, the poet has written a whole cluster of such poems and put them together under a separate section called "Poems from the Tarai" in *Under Orion*. The other poems in this section are : "The Parijat Tree," "The Beggar," "Graft," "Death by Burial," "Ruminations I & II," and "Railroad Reveries." Of these, "The Parijat Tree" is an instance of the mild aspect of landscape, and the tree grows to be a symbol of greenery inspiring men to *yoga* and meditation :

And so they (the Pandavas) came to the Parijat tree
squatting in the shade of its fleshy branches

cross-legged and transverse-limbed
All *yoga* was here — all the *asans*
every fluent stance
in the arboreal jungle
of this single tree

(*Under Orion*, pp. 81-82)

The entire poem is structured around a legend about the Pandavas after the battle of Kurukshetra. Contrasted to this we find the scenes in "Death by Burial" and "Curfew — In a Riot-Torn City," which are really impressive in the whole range of Daruwalla's poetic universe. The poem "Railroad Reveries" is a nostalgic recollection of the charm of the distant landscape as experienced by the poet during a cold wave :

A landscape of distance
of meaningless milestones
crouching on the flanks
swallowed in the dust and the express-smoke
The sad-eyed bitch upon the platform
kicked about by urchins doesn't squeal
head drooping, eyes bored, she walks away.

(*Under Orion*, p. 72)

Towards its close, the poet is left with nothing to ponder over but his "bedbug" and "greasy doubt" (p. 93).

Daruwalla's second book, *Apparition in April*, though not as rich in landscape-painting as the first one, has nevertheless quite a few remarkable poems such as "The Snowman," "Pilgrimage to Badrinath," "To Writers Abroad," and "The Old Man of the Sea" (which is to be marked especially for its evocation of the dazzling yet devastating seascape). Some stray, sporadic forays into landscape-portrayal have been made here, but they are sufficient to show the poet's continued march along his chosen direction. As an illustration, the following excerpt from "Pilgrimage to Badrinath" is being quoted here :

Along the valley of the burning sun;
On flinty bridle-paths which centuries have trod
in penance and anonymous dust,
the caravan of pain proceeds towards the gods.

Stony eyes turn northward towards stone
and the grey austerity in the stance of hills;
the snow-hush under granite skies
and the wind biting like a dentist's drill,
whipping the mist into a horizon.

(p. 22)

Another illustration may be picked up from "To Writers Abroad," where the scene is laid in Delhi, precisely in the lanes around the Jama Masjid, crowded with poor Muslims and having spires and minarets :

Lanes around Jumma Masjid
welcome you to their coils
to spire and minaret
amulet and charm
the cry for baksheesh and the muezzin's call
and the dervish hawking potency drugs
Cave erotics call you to their glooms
where goddesses suffer from mastitis
Wounded statuary, one nostril
at Somnath, the other at Ghazni
The river calls : clay-lamp and libation
offered to the eclipse to release the sun
Ghats aflame with the dead;
Sorry we can't lay on these days
a suttee-display in the flesh for you

(p. 30)

In a cinematic, sudden shift of scene, the poet takes us from the heart of the metropolis to the river Yamuna and its *ghats* aflame with clay lamps and libations and burials of the dead.

The third book, *Crossing of Rivers*, contains a number of poems on landscape, the central metaphor being the "Ganga" here. About this metaphor, Vrinda Nabar, in an illuminating article on Daruwalla, writes thus : "The Ganga appears here with all its primal, religious, and emotive connotations. The river's rhythm is that of life and death, of birth and rebirth, of passion and rejection.... In and around it are all the signs of stagnancy, the tonsured heads, the fossilized anchorites, the tattooed harlots, and the dead who are brought to it shrouded in the anonymity of white."[2] Consisting of three parts — "The Waterfront", "Crossing of Rivers" and "In My Father's House" — and opening with "Boat-ride along the Ganga," this book makes an attempt to expose the age-old Hindu customs and rituals and their custodians. The tone grows highly bitter and biting here, as may be sensed in the following :

> Dante would have been confused here.
> Where would he place this city
> In Paradise or Purgatory, or lower down
> where fires smoulder beyond the reach of pity?
> The concept of the goddess baffles you—
> Ganga as mother, daughter, bride.
> What place of destiny have I arrived at
> where corpse-fires and cooking-fires
> burn side by side?
>
> ("Boat-ride along the Ganga," p. 12)

The book contains some charming snaps of landscape as well as those of "nightscape," "riverscape" and "ghostscape." In this context, the poem "Nightscape" may be particularly mentioned. Its pointed relevance tempts me to quote the whole of it :

> Votive lights are muzzled in the fog :
> bloodstains on a frosted window.
>
> As the night grows older
> as flesh turns to carbon on the ghats
> and the river keeps moving,
> dark as gangrene,
> temples have to strain their necks
> to rise above mist-scarves
> wrapped around their shoulders.
>
> The fog on the river is like
> a loaded raft
> which the current cannot move.
> Temple-lights
> are a splash of rhododendrons
> and temple-spires, cypress-dark,
> mark the waterfront ethereal.

Is this a ridge
black with pine
rising out of the mists
or a city of the dead
brooding over a ghostscape?

(p. 13)

Stationed in the holy city of the Hindus, Varanasi, and rowing over the river Ganga, the poet keenly observes the night, the dawn, the day and the dusk changing their faces. The bell-tower, the dip into the sacred waters, the wind beating on the outer bank, the river-silt arresting the flow of the river, the touching death of a bird, the fighting eagles, and the green snake are all depicted with an unerring brush of an artist who is out to capture the varying moods and forms of a culturally rich city and a legendary river."[3] The three "Vignettes" present striking images of death, disease and destruction, although "the Ganga flows swollen with hymns" (p. 16). The sad lot of humanity colours the poet's imagination "grey" and he notices a sort of vacuity in human lives :

The river is a voice
in this desert of human lives.

(p. 16)

and again :

Beggars hoist their deformities
as boatmen hoist their sails.

(p. 16)

The Ganga does not mitigate human miseries or sufferings : it only "shows" them, exhibits them to the public gaze. The second Vignette depicts the holy city as the repository of "kites" and "tonsured heads" where faith has dwindled considerably and where the people and the *pandas* have become ritualistic and superstitious. The poet's melancholy mood does not change and he watches with unblinking eyes the naked dance of confused mankind in the soiled hands of inexorable Fate and Chance. Such a mood may have a silver lining here and there, but on the whole it remains gloomy and despairing :

The light is greening —
despair turning to mould
in a pickle jar.

(p. 19)

And the poet does not try to conceal it at all; he rather makes it an integral part of the landscape itself and observes :

The landscape is so grey
they are milking the sun for fight.

(p. 19)

It is not that Daruwalla deliberately denigrates Varanasi : he rather discovers it to be no better than many other ancient cities of the Hindus despite the fact that it is taken to be the abode of gods and goddesses. His "seeing' eye enables him to grasp things as they really *are,* not as they *ought* to be. This is tacitly suggested by him in the lines :

Let thoughts fly away like a scatter of birds
to some other town. But where?

(p. 19)

To this question the poet himself offers a reply :

All cities are the same at night
when you walk barefoot
across their blistered backs.

(p. 20)

The last line here evokes a remarkable image of the macadamized roads and thoroughfares to be found in cities and towns.

Perhaps "death" is an essential part of life. This idea is beautifully articulated in the poem "Death Vignette." The city wakes to the reception of the dead who come here variously shrouded in white cover as the horizon is lit up :

They walk in time
outside time
walking with death on
their copper-shoulders
acid-etched
on the horizon

a part of the landscape
on which they are walking.

(p. 23)

Here a dip is bone-chilling (*see* "The Dip," p. 25) and the wind is unwholesome and lung-congesting (refer "The Wind on the Outer Bank," pp. 26-27).

But the ensuing poem "Mother" made up of two parts is really tender in sentiments towards the Mother Ganga. No halo or gloss is to be seen around her. Flowing through the ages she has grown old, brown, unglossy and has developed "a cataract" in her eyes. The poet feels her flow within himself :

Sleeping on your banks
as you flow by
I find you flowing within my body.

(p. 29)

She is associated with the past and "mudscapes" around her render her grey and monotonous. The muezzin's cry rising from a remote mosque snaps the reverie and reminds the poet that :

Heaven was built
under the feet of mothers.

(p. 30)

In this poem the long and labyrinthine course of the Ganga has been remarkably traced.

The poem "River-Silt" consisting of three parts evokes the image of death and dust in and around the Ganga — the dust having settled on the dead person's eye-floor and eye-pits :

The dregs upon the eye-floor speak
only of mudscapes of despair.

(p. 32)

In a swift transition of thought in the second part the poet recollects the Yangtze and the Amazon, the Amur and the Congo and the Atlantic receiving from its tributaries a million cubic feet of water per second. In the third the collective memories of years come alive before the poet's vision and the earth-brown river Ganga becomes linked up with the hoary history of the land. The poet is pained to see the river-silt, which will, he apprehends, cover up the whole of the river-bed one day and stifle it to death and devastation. Daruwalla is clearly hinting here at one of the impending disasters for the holy river to which no proper heed is paid. He is alarmed at the prospect because "the racial memory/of a nation (is) preserved here" (p. 34).

The second section of the book, "Crossing of Rivers," offers both unity and title to the collected poems here. Built on the subject of love between a young man and a fisher girl (later a mountain-girl) the symbolic narrative begins with a sudden plunge of the man into the undercurrents below the Ganga's placid waters and his rescue by the girl, moves through a budding sublimating love between the two after an elaborate ritual is performed on the banks of the river :

> Why installing a mistress
> is like installing a deity in the house!
>
> (p. 40)

and ends with the inevitable separation of the two according to the laws of our *dharma*. After fifteen years of surfeit of senses while living together, she begins to live the life of a nun. She whom he had "deified" and who had "descended from the hills" (p. 41) and mingled with the waters of the Ganga in her onward march (mark that her voyage becomes a symbol of eternal life) disappears from the scene in a most detached manner leaving behind her past and companion. In a season of river-crossing they had once met and now in another they must part company. The cycle of life-events thus keeps on and hence the repetitive use of "In every season comes a crossing of rivers" (pp. 37 & 44) at the beginning and the close of this long piece.

The third and last section of the book consisting of four loosely strung pieces[4] stands out as an example of Daruwalla's indulgence in rhetoric and artistic indiscipline bordering on sentimentalism as may be seen in the poem "Death of a Bird". But the poem "Haranag" is definitely an exception in this section. Running into three parts, it at once establishes Daruwalla as a poet of living landscape : the bamboo jungle growing about his house and haunted by "the porcupine and bamboo-viper" (p. 52), the superstition that after each serpent-dawn some disaster might strike and the appeasement of these crawling creatures by offering milk and grain in an earthen bowl and eventually the appearance of the dreaded serpent in the bathroom facing the forest twice where the poet's wife faints in great fear until he comes to her help and kills it with a stick in utter rage. But the drama of superstition does not stop here and the wife keeps on dreaming of the serpent at night when the poet is with her. She asks him for further appeasement of the ferocious serpent by offering milk and grain once again. Thus, we see that Daruwalla has created a memorable poem out of an ordinary incident. He doesn't simply tell us about the *Haranag* but recreates a proper background for its emergence and for superstition to have its full play. The bamboo jungle, the nearby house, the bathroom and the serpent and the wife's horror : all tend to create a living scene of lushgreen landscape. In its quality the poem stands beside Nissim Ezekiel's "Night of the Scorpion" which also recounts a similar domestic situation confronting the poet's family with utter confusion and consternation.

The fourth and last volume of Daruwalla, *Winter Poems*, does not contain too many poems of landscape, but the title piece is certainly an exception. Consisting of two sections — "suddenly the tree" and "the poppy," this poetic piece shows that the poet's capacity for drawing memorable pictures of landscape has not completely died out. In the winter season, the tree and its surroundings wear a deserted look, which the poet describes as follows :

> the tree is now all bark and bough.
> leafless twigs scratch
> against the glass
> like skeletal children
> scribbling on a slate,
> chalk-fingered.
> there is a smell of hail
> in the air and lightning-burns,
> the just-widowed wind
> beats her head against the glass-panes.

("suddenly the tree," *Winter Poems*, p. 13)

The same poem nicely sketches the unwanted disturbance created by the honey-thieves in the natural order of the universe in which the bees suffer inevitably, — the bees that slept so soundly, so quietly, in earlier times :

> as the afternoon wore on
> the honey-thieves came
> and smoked the bees out
> and carved out a honey-laden
> crescent for themselves
> and lcft a lump of pocked wax behind.
> the bees roamed the house
> too bewildered to sting the children.
> at night they slept, clinging
> to the tree fork, now scarred with bums.
>
> (*Winrer Poems*, p. 17)

Here the hapless condition of the bees has been compassionately brought out by the poet. In this volume, the only other moving pieces, from the viewpoint of our discussion, are : "curfew'' "and "lorca." While the former is remarkable for its artistic *finesse* and situational tension prevailing in a town, the latter is an appreciable piece of imagination abounding in striking images of time and space. The latter is quoted partly here for an illustration :

> Dawn will come as it always has,
> escorted with pearls,
> the earth-chalice
> spiked with frost.
> Sandwiched between your rivers
> "one lament and the other blood,"
> the land will flame like a tongue
> of fiery green
> threading the sierras.
> ... ...
> Nightscapes will still be the same :
> bars of flamenco carried by the wind
> gathered round a fire
> and sheep dogs barking
> at the rustle of dry oak-leaves.
>
> ("lorca," *Winter Poems*, p. 55)

In this extract, the lines "the land will flame like a tongue/of fiery green/threading the sierras" are of special significance for us.

In the end, Daruwalla has an unerring instinct for painting the landscape, the ever-flowing Ganga and the torrential Ghaghra, the mighty green, grey hills and mountains, the sprawling, mosquito-infected vales and valleys, the shaky yet pleasant boatrides and rowings, the countless trees and bamboos mating against the horizon, the darting rails, buses, trams and trucks speeding along the macadamized roads and dusty plains, the stinking burial grounds and the cracked *ghats*, and the rocky riverbeds and the gurgling rivulets. Since such spectacles are abundantly witnessed in the vast countryside, it may be safely said that Daruwalla is more a poet of rural surroundings than of urban ones, and in this he stands apart from most of our city-born and bred poets, — poets like Nissim Ezekiel, Shiv K. Kumar, P. Lal, Pritish Nandy, and a host of women poets. At one place, Daruwalla writes : "I am not an urban writer and my poems are rooted in the rural landscape. My poetry is earthy, which, while adding gloss, takes away from it the power to verse."[5] And Daruwalla must be complimented for his bold stance and original approach to the art of versification, for poetry need not be confined to the sophisticated boundaries of cities and towns (though this should not mislead one to believe that Daruwalla never writes about them); and when it emerges out of them on to the sunny landscape vibrating with pulse and power, it breathes in an air of freshness, originality and authenticity. This is precisely what we find in the poetry of Daruwalla.

NOTES AND REFERENCES

1. See R Parthasarathy, ed. *Ten Twentieth-Century Indian Poets* (New Delhi : Oxford University Press, 1979), p. 12.
2. Vrinda Nabar, "Keki N. Daruwalla : Poetry and a National Culture," *Osmania Journal of English Studies*, XIII, No. 1 (1977), p. 10.
3. The Ganga is called a "legendary" river because it has its own tell-tales about its origin in heaven and descent on earth.
4. Nabar, "After the unity found in the arrangement of the first two sections of the book, the four poems in the third section seem arbitrarily lumped together. It's a collage that does not work..." *Ibid.*, p. 13.
5. Cited from Parthasarathy, ed., *Ten Twentieth-Century Indian Poets*, p. 12.

16

Shiv K. Kumar's Poetry : A Thematic Study*

Shiv K. Kumar has contributed substantially to the expansion and enrichment of Indo-English verse during the last decade. Roger Iredele thinks that it is really rewarding to "turn to Indian poetry written in English and to find in it a freshness and variety that reflects the remarkable diversity and vigour of the culture from which it stems."[1] The last decade saw the emergence of K.N. Daruwalla, R. Parthasarathy, Jayanta Mahapatra, Shiv K. Kumar and a few others who seem to have realised in a large measure the hope expressed in William Walsh's remark that the future, the promise, of Indian writing in English lay in poetry.[2]

Shiv K. Kumar made his debut with his *Articulate Silences* (1970), and followed it up with *Cobwebs in the Sun* (1974), *Subterfuges* (1976), and *Woodpeckers* (1979).[3] The reviewer of *World Literature Written in English* finds that Kumar "has really succeeded in organizing his material into dramatic tensions of life's many contraries."[4] And that of *World Literature Today* comments on his poetry thus : "Today we seem to be poised for a breakthrough and something that may be truly Indian is being written."[5]

Critics have expressed admiration for the finished form, the tense diction and the arresting imagery of Kumar's poetry. It is poetry that rarely fails to fill his readers with joy and elation, and at once establishes him as a major presence on the Indian poetic scene.[6] It signals his authenticity, individuality and resourcefulness.

*Reprinted with permission of the editor of *Journal of English Studies* (Jan. 1984), 15, No. 1, 6-12.

Although some might sense the presence of certain irritants (the sensuality being one), most readers are struck by the irony and the wit of his poems, which also impress them by an original, a unique blend of the qualities of head and heart.

Kumar appears to favour a few themes. Their recurrence and his constant preoccupation with them might cause impatience at times. What redeems his work is the poise of mind and heart, the remarkably consistently sustained balance of outlook.

Love and sex, marriage, family relations, and cultural interaction are among the dominant themes of Kumar's poetry. Death — which at times figures as a secondary theme — seems to be viewed as an alternative to unrequited love and unfulfilled desire. Futility and frustration are more conspicuous than facile cheerfulness and optimism.

Marriage is the subject of "Married Too Long," "Cerebral Love," "Aftermath," "Back to Back," "My Mother's Lover," "My Correspondent," "Mission Beach," "A Dark Mood," and "Broken Columns." Rather like Robert Lowell's "To Speak of the Woe that is in Marriage," these poems of Kumar's highlight the dark side of marriage. They reflect the attitudes of a man, sensitive though a little ill-adjusted in his milieu, who seems to belong to a world far removed from that of Nissim Ezekiel's "Marriage," or Kamala Das's "The Winner." In Kumar's verses, marriage is viewed as "a semi-comic disaster, comedy being its saving grace."[7] The mood turns melancholy, and the tone bitter :

Not tonight —
not even if you creep foamfooted
into the bed
offering the salt-taste
of your flesh.

How can we exchange nudities tonight
when the shells on the ocean's bed
are wailing for the dead?

("A Dark Mood," *Cobwebs in the Sun*, p. 43)

In "A Dry River Bed," this attitude is ascribed to the lack of 'blood' in his veins. "Broken Columns," a long piece of twelve sections, partly deals with marriage.[8] There is a scathing irony and devastating wit in it :

> I look at my bride's crabbed fingers
> closing into a fist.

And again :

> I carry my bride home —
> a fungal seed to breed hydras.
>
> The first sunrise leaves at my door
> a dead cockroach
> in the milk-bottle,
> news of the porcupine's resurrection
> and a defaced horoscope.

(*Woodpeckers*, pp. 14-15)

The expression 'a fungal seed to breed hydras' well accords with the fury of the speaker's mood.

Love and sex are dealt with in a number of Kumar's poems, the tragic drama of inadequacy, infidelity or conflict being revealed generally through oblique suggestions. When marriage fails, love can lead one to no condition essentially more agreeable. Notable among these poems of love are "Parting," "Waiting," "The Face," "Genesis," "Before the Beginning" and "Before the End" (*Articulate Silences*), "Cerebral Love," "Kissing a Stranger in Alexandria" and "My Mother's Lover" (*Cobwebs in the Sun*), "Broken Columns" and "My Grandfather's Love Letters" (*Subterfuges*), "Young Maidservant," "Love Letter" and "Midnight Musings" (*Woodpeckers*). Usually love descends into sex and violence displaces softness. This applies to both love in marriage and love out of marriage. The tender, soothing aspect of love is to be found in the poem "The Face" :

> Let your face arch over mine
> so that my eyes
> outflanked by the wealth of your hair,
> may seek clues to
> an academician's *l'ides fixe.*
>
> ....

This is the face that launches
a thousand paper-boats
down my blood stream.

(*Articulate Silences*, p. 14)

Its exact opposite is apparent in :

....

we sank deflated into
some small talk of Zen
waiting to let detachment
claim our yet unborn
to spray napalm over
luscious paddy fields
or make dentures for spinsters.
She stirs again
but I see a cockroach
creeping up the bedpost.

("Aftermath," *Subterfuges*, p. 44)

H.B. Kulkani points out that sex breaks in even in Kumar's treatment of other subjects.[9] At times he dreams of a paradisal love of the past, but the reality shatters the dream. Love old and love new create a Hegelian dialectic — thesis and anti-thesis — the latter gaining the upper hand. "Sounds of Hunger," "Aftermath," "Cerebral Love" are beautiful specimens of love old. Kumar is quite frank in dealing with sex : His Lawrentian cult of this idolized god of the 20th century leaves the traditional Altar depleted. Irony grows savage occasionally, as in :

From every cornice
an owl hoots :
Do, do, do,
but my lady-bird is counting
calories before she slumps
beside me as a tombstone
while I wait for the breakers
to at least cleanse my feet.

("The Sun Temple, Konarak", *Subterfuges*, p. 28)

Among the various shades of sex in Kumar's verse, one shade

juxtaposes it against traditional morality and religion. It is here that he appears 'un-Indian,' as Nissim Ezekiel also seems to agree. While established ethical values seem to be rejected, a new deity called Sex is sought to be installed in their place. If the first volume of his poems expresses despair, the second reveals a sense of loss of love in wedlock, the third and the fourth repudiate religion. T.G. Vaidyanathan speaks of the "strange and disturbing marriage of religion and sex"[10] in Kumar's poetry. However, T.R.S. Sharma rejects this view on the ground that "there is hardly any religion as such in Kumar for any substantial marriage to take place," and that "there is the total absence of any regard for religion; ...of any 'irritable reaching after' any of the holy absolutes."[11] In "Kali," there is a heavy irony :

> Beyond the priest's monotone
> a lamb bleats for the knife-edge.
> A child clinging to famished
> nipples will die anyway,
> but your nectar is the blood
> that jets from fresh arteries.

(*Subterfuges*, p. 34)

And the same is to be had in "Lord Venkateswara's Temple" :

> Here the divine munificence is boundless —
> a devoted ruler's elephant was once blessed
> with a litter of nine —
> all male.

(*Woodpeckers*, p. 40)

The high priest of the temple is wryly commented on. In "At a Convent," the poet-speaker observes 'the insurgent breasts' of the nuns 'chained with silver crosses', which are enough to burn any man to 'ashes' (*Subterfuges*, p. 35).

Perhaps one does not find the ennobling effect of A.K. Ramanujan's poems in Kamar, whose dilemmas of sex and love remain unresolved. Kumar once said, "I seem to be constantly returning to the theme of cultural interaction.... With me, contrast is almost a mode of perception. It is this awareness that compels me to recapture my days in New York as a kind of life-in-death."[12] Kumar's "Cambridge Revisited," "New Year Eve," "Walking Down the Avenues of the Americas" and "A Letter from New York" reflect this aspect clearly. "Cambridge Revisited," notes change in the English city; the Cam is no Ganges with powers to work miracles. Kumar nostalgically recalls the scenes of Cambridge when he was there :

> Beyond the campus precints
> argent bulls chase mottled butterflies
> into the livid horizon.
> Freedom bares its sallow fangs
> for the primal assault.
>
> (*Woodpeckers*, p. 9)

In "A Letter from New York," Kumar grapples with the problem of identity.

> Are you a Puerto Rican?
> A Jamaican? A Red Indian?
> I look for the feathers on my skull,
> a band around my forehead.
> And mumble, 'No, a brown Indian ,
> from the land of Gandhi.'
>
> (*Subterfuges*, p. 18)

Kumar's association with the West has provided him with an essentially rational outlook and a critical approach to the human predicament. He, in the last analysis, comes out as a 'modern' poet of sharp sensibility, very much alive to his situation.

NOTES AND REFERENCES

1. Roger Iredele, "Indian Poetry in English", a talk broadcast over the All-India Radio on June 11, 1975.
2. William Walsh, "Introduction", *Readings in Commonwealth Literature* (Oxford : Clarendon Press, 1973), p. xviii.
3. The details about these four poetical collections of Prof. Kumar are : (1) *Articulate Silences* (Calcutta : Writers Workshop 1970), (2) *Cobwebs in the Sun* (New Delhi : Tata McGraw-Hill, 1974), (3) *Subterfuges* (New Delhi : Oxford University Press, 1976) and (4) *Woodpeckers* (London : Sidgwick & Jackson, 1979). Besides, Kumar also published a play, *The Last Wedding Anniversary* (1975) and a novel, *The Bone's Prayer* (1978), and a collection of short stories, *Beyond Love and Other Stories* (1979).

4. See H.B. Kulkarni's review of *Cobwebs in the Sun* in *World Literature Written in English*, 14, No. 2 (Rev. 1975), 413.

5. Cited from the back cover of *Woodpeckers* (1979).

6. T.R.S. Sharma, "Between the Confessional and the Rational : The Poetry of Shiv K. Kumar," *Tenor*, 4 (1980), 23.

7. *Ibid.*, p. 24.

8. (a) Sharma in his essay says that it is "about the failure of love or nerve in marriage" (p. 24). The truth seems to be that it is a record of the poet's growth through successive stages in life.

   (b) Shyam M. Asnani states that "Broken Columns" is the only poem taken from *Subterfuges*. — *See* his article "Mute Confessions and Voiceless Wailings : The Poetry of Shiv K. Kumar", *Indian Scholar*, III, No. I (Jan. 1981), 35-36. In fact, there is one more called "To a Prostitute" from the same volume.

9. Kulkarni's review of *Cobwebs*, p. 413.

10. T.G. Vaidyanathan, "Between Kali and Cordelia : The Poetry of Shiv K. Kumar," *Osmania Journal of English Studies*, XIII, No. 1 (1977), 73.

11. Sharma, *loc. cit.*, p. 28.

12. *See Ten Twentieth-Century Indian Poets*, ed. R Parthasarathy (New Delhi : O.U.P , 1979), p. 53.

17

The Poetry of Arun Kolatkar : A Study in Images and Symbols

Arun Kolatkar (born 1932) is one of those fortunate and gifted Indo-English poets who have earned recognition and reputation by a single volume. A graphic artist based in Bombay and a bilingual poet, Kolatkar has been publishing his poems both in English and Marathi since long, but his poetical collection in English entitled *Jejuri*[1] appeared as late as 1976 and became an immediate hit with the reading public. Before this collection, some of his verse had been published in such journals and anthologies as *Opinion*, *Literary Quarterly*, *Damn You*, *An Anthology of Marathi Poetry : 1945-65* (Nirmala Sadanand Publishers, 1967), *The Shell and the Rain* (George Allen & Unwin, 1973), and *New Writing in India* (Penguin Books, 1974). Beyond doubt, Kolatkar has written very little poetry — which may also be read as the desertion of the Muse — and often encomiums have been showered upon him for wrong things. I have not to object to his being called an "original" poet,[2] as R. Parathasarathy purports to say, but to brand him as 'a classic' is definitely questionable, since so long he has produced poetry largely as a dilettante and not as one constantly devoted to it (as, for instance, Nissim Ezekiel is). Obviously, I am not pleading for prolificacy or prodigality in versification, but for some sort of sustained and continued efforts directed towards it coupled with merit and excellence. Kolatkar has been praised for "a hypnotic stillness,"[3] for "the air of contemplativeness one notes in the poems,"[4] for his "laconic, deflating style,"[5] and for his "use of speech rhythms, without striving for some sort of 'international' (in place of universal) effects,"[6] but no one has taken pains so far to examine the use of images and symbols in his poetry and show the development of his poetic art in this direction, — a gap which the present paper aims at filling in.

Kolatkar's early verses, which were mainly translations of his Marathi poetry, do not employ any striking or startling images, let alone symbols. Of these, "Irani Restaurant Bombay," "Three Cups of Tea," and "The Hag," which first appeared in *An Anthology of Marathi Poetry* and which were later collected in Saleem Peeradina's anthology, *Contemporary Indian Poetry in English*, come to our mind immediately. The poem "Irani Restaurant Bombay" does attempt to evoke a picture of the Iranian hotel with all its royal pomp and show and modern amenities, but the utmost that the poet can offer us is 'the road neat/as a needle.' Now, the 'neatness' of the road makes him oblivious of the sharpness of the 'needle', and certainly the image does not click. More appropriate and arresting is the image of the thirsty loafer putting the match in the tea circle and beholding it rise :

> as when to identify a corpse one visits a morgue
> and politely the corpse rises from a block of ice.

and further :

> the burnt match with the tea circle makes a rude
> compass, the heretic needle jabs a black star.

Here 'the burnt match' becomes 'the heretic needle' that makes it way through the 'icy' and 'black' tea circle. The crackedness of the restaurant, particularly of its showcase, is supported by its gloominess, and the last lines ably conjure up this vision :

> tables, chairs, mirrors are night that needs to be sewed
> and cashier is where at seams it comes apart.

The picture seems to be of a place enveloped with darkness except where the cashier sits. The next poem, "Three Cups of Tea," is more an exercise in technical expertise than one in imagery or symbolism. In utter contrast to this piece is "The Hag," which brings out a perfectly graphic portrayal of the ugly old woman. Herein we have a string of images that delight us from the very beginning :

death pins his abstraction like a rare but ugly
butterfly on her brain. tells an off colour
joke.

The 'hag is stone deaf', but the curtain of her window is 'florid' and 'grimy'. Then follows a very vivid description of the hag in concrete terms and imagistic details :

entrenched behind it She devours oranges

in self-defence. She likes them baggy. She paws.
She claws. An orange isn't peeled. It's torn. Each
fruit a vapid debacle. An invalid pose

in tattered filigree. The hag incites her mandibles
to mob and maul a piece. Her entire face
converges in a featureless fury rushes to the battle's

toothless centre. Eyes. Like a dead horse
on a battlefield her eyes deny the avid farce.

Explicitly, the woman is old and ugly, wrinkled and toothless, off-colour and deaf, dirty and featureless; the details about her follow with consummate skill and great artistry.

There is one more poem written originally in English which deserves consideration before taking up *Jejuri* for a thorough investigation from the viewpoint of our discussion; and this is "the boat ride," which finds a berth in both *Contemporary Indian Poetry in English* and *Ten Twentieth Century Indian Poets*. This long poem has already secured wide critical attention for its "peculiar stillness"[7] and for its being "a series of perceptions."[8] Every verse is a vivid picture here, and the scene keeps shifting, as Daruwalla points out, from the pair of knees that shoot up and streak down the mast to the sail which spreads like an off-white miracle, the speed boat, the stony-faced woman, her child, and the two sisters looking past the boatman's facial profile. Speaking of this poem, Parthasarathy remarks : "The poem evokes a surreal world in which imagination and reality are fused, in which contradictions in logic are acceptable to the imagination, ordinary concepts of time and space do not operate, and everything is seen with an innocent eye."[9] As the boat is jockeyed away from the landing, the surge of the sea provides it with a rhythmic beat and the narrative gets underway presenting a series of snap shots. The very first verse offers us the following graphic picture :

after a pair of knees
has shot up and streaked
down the mast after
the confusion of hands about
the rigging

an off-white miracle

the sail
spreads

The seventh verse beautifully works up a series of similes and metaphors which render the whole description pointed and impressive. Mark a few lines from this section :

his wife has dismissed
the waves like a queen
a band of oiled
acrobats

winds
like the fingers
of an archaeologist
move across her stony face
and cross the worn
edict of a smile
cut thereon

While the first four lines quoted above illustrate the poet's use of simile, the remaining last lines bring before us both simile and metaphor in a striking manner. That the life of a boatman (to put it correctly, of a boatwoman) is none-too-happy and that it entails a lot of boredom and ennui, which is conveyed in the following extract from the eighth verse :

impatient with the surrounding gallons
of boredom spurning the rowdy
intangibles of waves
a two-year-old renounces
his mother's ear

The two expressions to be noticed above are 'the surrounding gallons/of boredom' and 'the rowdy intangibles of waves' which lay bare the dull, dismal surroundings of the life under review.

Through another sparkling simile employed in the tenth verse, the poet tries to trace the sad history of the Gateway of India :

> sad as a century
> the gateway of India
> struggles back to its feet
> wobbly but sober enough
> to account for itself

And in the eleventh, the boatride is rounded off : the boat returns to the landing, which is 'an expanse of/unswerving stone/encrusted coarsely/with shells.'

Metaphorically speaking, the whole journey by boat may be interpreted in terms of a man's journey of life. The frequently mentioned sea, its surges and waters, may thus denote the expanse of life itself; the boat may signify the small support that the man gets in his life journey; and its departure and arrival may symbolize the 'two shores' of life, namely birth and death. The mooring of the boat at the same landing is an indication that after his life journey the man will have to return to the same source whence he sprang.

We take up *Jejuri* now for our examination. As the book begins, the protagonist Manohar accompanied by Makarand has already boarded a State transport bus bound for Jejuri, an old town fifty kilometers from Pune where the sacred temple of Khandoba — an incarnation of Shiva — is situated. The bus takes him over the rough and uneven road — 'the bumpy ride', and the description tends to be chiefly matter-of-fact but for the following stanza of striking imagery :

> Your own face in a pair of glasses
> on an old man's nose
> is all the countryside you get to see.[10]

The last line of the first poem becomes somewhat mischievous and humorous —'You don't step inside the old man's head'. The second poem of *Jejuri*, "The Priest," pictures in glowing words and phrases the anxiety of the priest at the late arrival of the bus carrying pilgrims. It abounds in concrete and picturesque details. The priest in his utter dejection is a 'dew-drenched stone,' whose bleak prospect of earning is no less acute than 'the eventlessness/

of the fortune line on a dead man's palm' (p. 10). A memorable simile is to be had in the following :

> The sun takes up the priest's head
> and pats his cheek
> familiarly like the village barber.
>
> (p. 10)

And again in the depiction of the incoming bus which first appears a 'dot', then grows in size, and after a circle comes to a grinding halt inside the bus station :

> it begins to grow
> slowly like a wart upon his nose
>
> (p. 11)

And metaphors are beautifully employed in 'dew drenched stone,' 'under his lazy lizard stare,' and 'starts/purring softly,' and most effectively in —

> a catgrin on its face
> and a live, ready to eat pilgrim
> held between its teeth.
>
> (p. 11)

where the strong, shiny bus is likened to 'a catgrin' and its wheels that can crush anyone falling under them to 'its teeth.'

The next poem deserving consideration from our viewpoint is "Water Supply," which accentuates the aridity and sterility of Jejuri now reduced to ruins. This poem attempts a threadbare portrayal of the 'conduit pipe,' reminding us of the method of T.S. Eliot in depicting the London fog in the poem "The Love Song of J. Alfred Prufrock" :

> The yellow fog that rubs its back upon the window-panes,
> The yellow smoke that rubs its muzzle on the window-
>
> panes,
>
> Licked its tongue into the corners of the evening,
> Lingered upon the pools that stand in drains,
> Let fall upon its back the soot that falls from chimneys,
>
> Slipped by the terrace, made a sudden leap,
> And seeing that it was a soft October night,
> Curled once about the house, and fell asleep.[11]

Now, compare the above passage with the following lines of Arun Kolatkar :

> a conduit pipe
> runs with the plinth
> turns a corner of the house
> stops dead in its tracks
> shoots straight up
> keeps close to the wall
> doubles back
> twists around
> and comes to an abrupt halt
> a brass mouse with a broken neck
>
> (p. 14)

Whereas Eliot compares 'the yellow fog' to a sleepy cat, Kolatkar compares the 'pipe' to 'a brass mouse with a broken neck'. Another point of difference between the two is that Kolatkar has become more economical and condensed in his depiction than Eliot. And the last line of Kolatkar brings out clearly the broken condition of the tap as such.

The poem "The Door" is also quite grapahic in detail, and begins in a characteristically metaphorical fashion :

> A prophet half brought down
> from the cross.
> A dangling martyr.
>
> (p. 15)

The picture evoked in this poem is that the door of the ruined temple is completely worn out, that it is a heavy medieval door hanging on 'one hinge alone', that it is wholly covered with dust and stain, and yet its grain stands out on the wood —

> Like a memory that gets only sharper
> with the passage of time....
>
> (p. 15)

This 'dangling' mass would have collapsed but for a 'pair of shorts' that props it up. In this poetic piece, the first stanza (consisting of three lines only) makes use of Christian symbolism to point out the hanging of the door on its hinges and its sanctity.

The image of the door is unquestionably that of Jesus Christ hanging 'from the cross' and later becoming 'a prophet.' This symbolism is again resorted to by the poet in "A Kind of a Cross" (which will be examined later on).

The three "Chaitanya" pieces in *Jejuri* are highly relevant to understand the Pilgrim's Progress, as detailed here, and his religious attitudes. They, in fact, occupy the very core of the text, and are crucial towards a proper analysis and interpretation of *Jejuri*. They come at serial numbers 7, 13 and 29, and takc us back to thc 16th century, when the well-known Vaishnavite saint, Chaitnaya Mahaprabhu (1485-1533), had visited Jejuri (to be precise, around 1510) and exhorted the traditional worshippers of Khandoba called Vaghya-Muralis to mend their manners of living. The first piece underlines the truth that the stones of Jejuri are mere stones; the second one points out that these stones, 'sweet as grapes,' become godlike with the traditional red paint; and the third and last one signifies that the saint's visit to the place has made no impact on the superstitious people of Jejuri, who have been aptly described as 'a herd of legends/on a hill slope' (p. 49) that continued its grazing during and after the saint's appearance on the scene. Through a very appropriate image of grazing animals the poet has carried home his point.

Undeniably, the poems before the first "Chaitanya" actually lack the power of suggestiveness, but we witness it abundantly in the short piece "The Pattern," wherein imagery and symbolism blend to paint a sad picture of the surroundings. The 'checkerboard pattern' drawn with a piece of chalk on the back of the twenty foot tortoise signifies 'the traditional pattern of worship.' Trying to interpret this symbol, M.R. Satyanarayana observes : "The meaning of the worship is not understood by present day men (the children) and soon the meaning will be wiped away."[12] The predicament of modern men is that they lack a mystic understanding' of the divinity of God.

The next poem in the volume, "The Horseshoe Shrine," mingles memory and desire, myth and reality, in its texture, and is rich enough in imagery. It offers us such details as 'a hoof/struck/like a thunderbolt,' 'and the three/went on from there like one/spark/ fleeing from flint,' and 'a home...like a hay/stack' (p. 19).

The poem "An Old Woman" is more remarkable for its sweeping rhythm and masterly composition than for its imagery, but it is not totally devoid of images. For instance, in the following :

> She won't let you go.
> You know how old women are.
> They stick to you like a burr.
>
> (p. 21)

The comparison here is made between an old, irresistible woman and the sticking 'burr.' And the deep hollow eyes of hers are precisely captured in the expression 'the bullet holes' (p. 22); they are so piercing and so horrible.

Another highly evocative poem is "Hills," which is so economical and tense in diction and so forceful and animating in the handling of metaphors. Words and phrases have that rudimentary vivacity in them which can create living pictures with the slightest brushwork — 'sand blasted shoulders/bladed with shale,' 'through ribs of rock,' 'limestone loins,' 'cactus fang in sky meat,' 'thighs of sand stone,' 'pelvic granite,' etc. The grating music in the poem produces the impression of the aridity and roughness of the rocky hills which are a suitable abode for the demons rather than for the gods.

"The Butterfly" is actually intended as a contrast to the general chaotic situation obtaining in Jejuri. Though it is fragile and split 'like a second' — what a beautiful use of simile here! — it has mapped the whole of the surroundings. As it is full of life, beauty, and energy, it is taken as a symbol of the Life-Principle, as Prof. Naik suggests.[13]

While "A Scratch" is not important from the angle of our discussion, "Ajamil and the Tigers", an invented story indeed, is to some extent. Ajamil, a shepherd, keeps a vigilant dog which does not allow the tigers to come anywhere near his sheep. In moments of victory, Ajamil signs a bond of friendship with the tigers and their king, for he knows well that 'even tigers have got to some time' (p. 32). Prof. Naik considers this poem, too, as an expression of a "significant aspect of the Life-Principle in Nature."[14] To me, it is a vigorous plea for a state of existence free from starvation and exploitation, in which all creatures, strong as well as weak, should get enough to eat and live as friends — 'with a full stomach for a common bond' (p. 32). The narrative moves through a conversational pattern and a colloquial speech, and becomes very impressive in such lines as :

> Quick as lightning
> the sheep dog was.
>
> (p. 30)

Mark the naturalness of the imagery here.

Then follow the two songs devoted to the worshippers of Khandoba — "A Song for a Vaghya" and "A Song for a Murli." Whereas Vaghya is a male, Murali is a female. The first song is set in daylight, but the second in moonlit night. As Vaghya's dedication to his god is total, he carries a one-string instrument which signifies his single-minded devotion to his pious calling. The last stanza in the first song makes a fine application of similes and metaphors :

> God is the word
> and I know it backwards.
> I know it as fangs
> inside my flanks.
> But I also know it
> as a lamb
> between my teeth,
> as a taste of blood
> upon my tongue.
>
> (p. 34)

The ironic intent is so clear here, but no less efficacious is the use of metaphorical language. In the second song, the 'moon' is visualised as an animal out to 'graze along the hill top' (p. 35).

The small poem "The Reservoir," like "Water Supply," is without water and with huge deposits of 'silt.' The waterlessness of the place reminds one of a similar situation painted by Eliot in *The Waste Land* (1922), and this may serve as "a possible symbol of a permanent drought."[15] In other words, the spiritual resources of Jejuri are now completely dried up. The next poem, "A Little Pile of Stones," is meaningful only when it is approached with a knowledge of the waterless locale. And the fifth stanza in it must be marked for the aptness of its simile — 'may you be/just as lucky/as you are smart' (p. 38).

"Makarand", like its companion piece "Manohar" earlier, is devoid of imagery, but "The Temple Rat," which brings us face to face with 'the warrior god' (p. 40), *i.e.*, Khandoba who is variously known as Malhari Martand, Mallari, Mhalsakant, Mailar, and Mairal, makes some good moves towards image-building. Mark the following passage in the latter :

> The temple rat uncurls its tail,
> ... ...
> Oozes halfway down the trident
> like a thick gob of black blood.

(p. 40)

Here we can see a simile that works in a way. The sixth stanza in this poem is highly visualised and sensuous :

> bangles massed in the hands
> of the teen age bride on her knees,
> crushing bananas on the top
> of the stone linga.

(p. 41)

In its brilliance and suggestiveness, the above extract at once recalls Keats to our minds, especially his line — 'Thou still unravish'd bride of quietness' — in the poem "Ode on a Grecian Urn."

The irreligious, irreverent attitude of the protagonist which we have been watching throughout this volume to this stage continues even in "A Kind of a Cross," where the poet concentrates on the metal-plated body of the holy bull calf in the temple courtyard. The poem is a fine piece of artistry and paints before us a living picture of the calf along with its horn, hump, 'strange instrument of torture,' tail, and the two cross bars for its resting. As the poem progresses, the religious overtones disappear completely, but not without leaving an indelible mark of Christian symbolism in it.[16] The first half of the poem is actually structured around the symbol of the 'cross,' and the protagonist imagines himself swinging round this cross. The poem "tends towards a surrealistic image"[17] as it slowly builds up 'crescendo of a cosmic dance' :

Hills and temples dance around.
Bull calfs and tortoises swim around.
Constellations wheel overhead like vultures
in one mad carousel.

(p. 43)

This 'cosmic dance' passage immediately recalls a similar passage in Eliot's *Four Quartets* :

The dance along the artery
The circulation of the lymph
Are figured in the drift of stars....[18]

The 'cosmic dance' might denote the perfect harmony in the universe, but soon it is disturbed by the assailing doubts and agnosticism in the protagonist's mind and heart.

The succeeding poem, "The Cupboard," contains not merely an incisive irony but also the modernity of imagery; for example, in the following :

you see a hand of gold
behind opinion
still with starch

(p. 44)

What is being suggested here is the mercenary attitude of the modern human world, — an attitude that has not spared even the divine domain.

The two pieces that follow — "Yeshwant Rao" and "The Blue Horse" — do not have any flashes of imagery or symbolism in them. But the poem "Between Jejuri and the Railway Station" is definitely full of meaning and significance. The protagonist leaves behind Jejuri with a none-too-happy experience (as the statistical details verging on boredom will bear out in the first part of this poetic piece), but stops enraptured on his way to the station on seeing 'a dozen cocks and hens in a field of jowar' (p. 51) performing 'a kind of a harvest dance.' This charming vision is so ecstatical that he watches the birds intently as they go up and down — 'up and down and up & d' (p. 51). The entire scene signifies, as Prof. Naik maintains, "the Life-Principle which predates all civilization and tradition."[19] The absorption of the protagonist is remarkably caught up in a concretely visualised image which we have in the lines —

> You stop dead
> and stand still *like a needle in a trance.*
> Like a needle that has struck a perfect balance between equal scales
> with nothing left to add or shed.
>
> (p. 50, Italics mine)

In this citation, the words 'needle' and 'trance' are highly significant in that they indicate the protagonist's condition unmistakably. 'Needle' stands for a perfect poise and balance between the forces of faith and scepticism, between Jejuri and the Railway Station, between the sense of gain and that of loss, and 'trance' shows the total absorption of the protagonist in the delightful scene before his vision.

The last poem (31st in *Jejuri*), "The Railway Station," consisting of six sections altogether, comes as an ironic parallel to the previous poems depicting Jejuri and its surroundings, as one may deduce from the continued application of 'religious imagery' in it. Everyone knows that a railway station is not the place of worship, and yet the poet presents the worn-out 'indicator' as 'a wooden saint/in need of paint' (p. 52). The station dog has a 'mangy body' and has been doing 'penance for the last three hundred years under/the tree of arrivals and departures' (p. 53). The railway timetable is 'eight armed' like the goddess at Jejuri (*see* "A Low Temple"). The young tea-stall waiter has taken 'a vow of silence,' and he 'continues with his ablutions in the sink/and certain ceremonies connected/with the washing of cups and saucers' (p. 54). The booking-clerk, a dullard indeed, believes in 'the doctrine/of the next train' (p. 55), and the two-headed station master 'belongs to a sect/that rejects every timetable/.../as apocryphal' (p. 55), and he 'keeps looking anxiously at the setting sun/as if the sunset were a part of a secret ritual' (p. 56). The fourth section, "the station master," makes use of a fine simile in the lines :

> finally he nods like a stroke
> between a yes and a no
>
> (p. 56)

And the fifth section informs us elaborately about the rituals to be performed by a man curious to know when the next train is due :

> slaughter a goat before the clock
> smash a coconut on the railway track
> smear the indicator with the blood of a cock
> bathe the station master in milk
> and promise you will give
> a solid gold toy train to the booking clerk

(p. 57)

And the sixth and last section, "the setting sun," immediately evokes the picture of 'the parallels of a prophecy' as well as that of 'a wheel' (p. 58) in its largeness. It is, thus, evident that the poet keeps his eye not only on the accuracy of the details observed but also on their religious connotations.

Finally, Kolatkar, who has "a crystallographer's eye for the particularities of a scene — a boatride, a bus journey,"[20] succeeds admirably in the handling of his images and symbols, but they are not so dazzling or sensuous as those of R. Parthasarathy and not so shocking or startling as those of A.K. Ramanujan. One conspicuous failure of his is that he has not been able to transmute his images into symbols, and in the whole length and breadth of his poetry he has employed only a few symbols at all — a dry water pipe, a cross, and a sun. Prof. S.K. Desai thinks that, of all the symbols used by Kolatkar, the sun is a "central symbol in the poem" because "Khandoba is associated with the sun."[21] Obviously, there is the 'rising sun' at the beginning of *Jejuri* and there is the 'setting sun' at its close, and the 'sun' is undeniably associated with power and glory. It would, therefore, be improper to assert, as K.N. Daruwalla does, that "To look for any underlying symbol in the poem, to view it as a depiction of the modern predicament or the meaninglessness of all quests, is futile."[22] More appropriate is S.C. Harrex, though a foreigner — an Australian precisely, when he observes that *Jejuri* can be read "as a modern, slightly ironic version of *bhakti* poetry, a version especially appropriate to an age in which scientific rationality and religious faith are sceptical of each other."[23] Harrex at least could see the red thread of religious imagery running through the entire volume. To put the whole matter summarily,

Kolatkar has made a good beginning with *Jejuri*, but much more is required of him in the days to come to blossom forth into a great poetic artist.

NOTES AND REFERENCES

1. This was published by the Clearing House, Bombay, 1976, and won for the poet the Commonwealth Poetry Prize in 1977. Along with it was also published his first collection of Marathi poetry, *Arun Kolatkarchya Kavita*. Since then, however, he has published nothing worth the name.
2. R. Parthasarathy, "Arun Kolatkar," *Ten Twentieth-Century Indian Poets* (Delhi : Oxford Univ. Press, 1976), p. 40.
3. *Idem.*
4. M.G. Krishnamurthy, "Auun Kolatkar," *Contemporary Indian Poetry in English : An Assessment & Selection* ed. Saleem Peeradino (Delhi : The Macmillan Co. of India Ltd., 1977), p. 42.
5. K.N. Daruwalla, "Arun Kolatkar," *Two Decades Indian Poetry :1960-1980* (Sahibabad, Ghaziabad : Vikas Publishing House Pvt. Ltd., 1980), p. 98.
6. M.R. Satyanarayana, "Jejuri' : Arun Kolatkar's Waste Land," *Osmania Journal of English Studies* (Hyderabad : Deptt. of English, Osmania University, 1977), Special Issue, p. 216.
7. Krishnmurthy, *loc. cit.*, p. 41.
8. Daruwalla, *loc. cit.*, p. 97.
9. Parthasarathy, *loc. cit.*, p. 40.
10. *Jeuri*, p. 9. All the textual references to this volume are absorbed in the body of this essay.
11. T.S. Eliot, *Collected Poems* (London : Faber & Faber, 1963), p. 13.
12. Satynarayana, *loc. cit.*, p. 206.
13. M.K. Naik, "Arun Kolatkar and the Three Value-Systems," *Contemporary Indo-English Verse*, ed. A.N. Dwivedi, Vol. II (Bareilly : Prakash Book Depot. 1984), pp. 41-42.
14. *Ibid.*, p. 42.
15. Satyanarayana, *loc. cit.*, p. 208.
16. Daruwalla, *loc. cit.*, p. 98 : "The sight of a cross brings to mind the gamut of Christian symbolism."
17. Satyanarayana, *loc. cit.*, p. 210.
18. T.S. Eliot, "Burnt Norton," *Four Quartets, Collected Poems*, p. 191.
19. Naik, *loc. cit.*, p. 39.
20. See *British Book News* (April 1978); cited from Daruwalla's anthology, p. 99.

21. S.K. Desai, "Arun Kolatkar's *Jejuri* : A House of God," *The Literary Criterion*, XV, No. 1 (1980), 54.
22. Daruwalla, *loc. cit.*, p. 97.
23. S.C. Harrex, "Small-scale Reflections on Indian-English Language Poetry," *The Journal of Indian Writing in English*, Special Issue (Jan.-July 1980), p. 164.

18

Suniti Namjoshi — Art and Artifice in Her Work*

I

Having produced three volumes of verse, Suniti Namjoshi has come to be known through the academic world. Her three volumes are — *Poems* (1967), *Cyclone in Pakistan* (1971), and *More Poems* (1971). They are all Writers Workshop publications, but definitely very uneven in their quality. They demonstrate, at their best, the poet's promise rather than her fulfilment. Like her chequered career — from student life to teaching and finally to the I.A.S. cadre (which she joined in June 1964) — her verse also displays the ebb and flow of her imagination, the varying degree of attainment. There is certainly an evidence of her developing art in it, but it is not completely free of the sins of affectation and poetatory. The famous saying 'All that glitters is not gold' may be aptly applied to her verse that has come out in the glittering handloom bound Redbird editions. That it has met the approval of a poet-publisher (who is truly more of a publisher than a poet) does not guarantee it an abiding place in the annals of Indo-English poetry. Nowhere does it show an attempt at a sustained flight of fancy, and Namjoshi is more inclined towards smaller poems impregnated with witty statements. Occasionally, her art degenerates into artifice, and this is the focal point of the present paper. However, it has been planned in such a way as to highlight both the salient features of her art and the slipshod literary manipulations of her artifice here so

*Reprinted with permission of the publisher of *Studies in Contemporary Indo-English Verse*, Vol. I (Bareilly : P.B.D., 1984), pp. 227-239

that the reader is able to arrive at a reasonably balanced assessment of her work and worth.

II

One of the distinctive features of Namjoshi's verse is its exercise of "complete restraint"[1] in the matter of expression. This is corroborated by her understatements and subtle touches. When Monika Varma, another practising Indo-English poetess, picked her up for her critical evaluation and welcomed her first volume of verse, it was this artistic quality of hers that she had in her mind. This quality is abundantly reflected in such poems as "The Lesson," "Aphrodisiac," "Terra and the Spectator," "On Stage," "Courtship," "Beauty and the Beast," "Seeds," "In Three Tenses," "The Old Man and the Girl," "When Butterflies Die," "Sea-Gull," "Letter," "Grace," and "Call This A Forest." These poems have a great economy of words and an admirable control over the medium. They tend to be terse and disciplined, as may be witnessed in the example given below :

> There's sunshine in the garden,
> There are flowers in the hall.
> At your gate a lovesick beast
> Is breaking down the wall.

("Courtship")

Besides the economical language and rhythmical versification, the reader should also mark the rich suggestiveness of the poem. Another example to bear out the fact is the following :

> Why did you make a hole in the sky,
> Breaking the backdrop of placid blue days?
> The black crows are flapping wildly in my head
> While the blue air has closed about your absence.

("In Three Tenses")

This is the whole poem. Doesn't it recall Tennyson's "The Eagle" for its brevity and pictorial quality? Looking at these examples, one can safely state that Namjoshi's talent is best suited for shorter poems rather than for longer ones. The reason might be that she had possibly recongnized her limitations as a poet. She, therefore, confined herself to the chosen domain, without ever trying to overstep it. This may be attributed to her sincerity and candour in poetic expression.

Another salient characteristic of Namjoshi's verse is its singing quality. This is quite evident in her use of lyrical form, of alliteration, and of cadenced statement. The poems "Courtship," "Red Flower," "On Stage," "Grace," and "Call This A Forest" are all supremely lyrical. They may be sung to perfection in accompaniment with some musical instrument. Here is an instance of Namjoshi's lyrical rapture controlled by economy of wording and phrasing :

> My blind mouth
> talks too much.
> Cave-dweller hands
> grope for shapes.
> Eye sees nothing. Body
> whimpers a little,
> then swells up
> for apocalyptic farce.
> Wind shifts and cloud breaks :
> blue air burns in the sun's glance.[2]

This poetic passage is shorn of all embellishments and superfluities. In her attempt to be direct and precise, the poetess has discarded even the use of definite article herein. Moreover, there is a symmetry in the arrangement of words and lines, and the last two lines add force and support to the preceding ones. Another poem, "At Night," may be taken up to illustrate Namjoshi's sensitiveness towards alliteration and musical statement :

> Listen heart,
> The small sounds,
> Insect life.
> There's the resulting inside.
> The rustle of silk?
> My breath caught
> Till I shrugged
> And went back to sleep.

It seems, the night is besieged with small, rustling sounds. For alliteration, one must mark the second line in it. Added to this is the sibilant effect produced by the informal rhythm. The overall impact is that we have a sharp hissing sound in this short poem. Sometimes, the use of rhyme enhances the singing quality and overall beauty of a poem; for example, in the following :

> In a wine glass I float,
> Whoever I be,
> And the person who sits talking to them,
> In the person They see.

("On Stage")

A similar thing is also to be noticed in "Courtship" and "Beauty and the Beast."

A third distinct charm of Namjoshi's verse, as pointed out by Mrs. Varma, is its "rueful truth-telling"[3] Writing of this, she remarks : "It is this in particular that I find the most distinctive feature of her poetry."[4] The 'rueful musing' of the poetess comes from the wide expanse of her experience, — the experience that has provided her with a delicate texture and with thoughts recollected not in tranquillity but in the midst of 'the clatter of living.' The poems "Courtship" and "Beauty and the Beast" are really inspired by some secret thoughts but not out of the poet's reach. In them we witness an ironic perception of the kind we usually find in the poetry of Shiv K. Kumar, Jayanta Mahapatra, and Kamala Das. Mark its handling in "Beauty and the Beast" :

> Beauty loved the ugly beast
> And thinking 'twas a prince she'd wed,
> Waited for his shape to change,
> And found there were two beasts in bed.

The highly debunking irony leaps up from every line here, and the reader seems to be engulfed with a deep sense of horror and disgust in the matter of love and sex. But there is decidedly a certain amount of self-searching and truth-telling about it. This is to be discovered in many more poems contained in the three collections, *e.g.*, in "Terra and the Spectator," "Aphrodisiac." "The Lesson," and "Flawed" (in the first collection), in "Cyclone in Pakistan," "Perplexities," and "Small Point" (in the second one), in "In Three Tenses," "The Old Man and the Girl," "A Problem," and "Call This A Forest" (in the third one). This quality of Namjoshi qualifies her as an artist.

III

But that is only a side of the mirror, the other side of which is all wooden and cleverly framed. It is this other side which highlights Namjoshi's literary manoeuvrings and her open exultation at affectations in art. In truth, the second dark side eclipses the first bright side, and Namjoshi comes out as a pitiable poet in the long run, lisping in foreign tongue and alien numbers and breathing the Western air and showing unnecessary compassion for her motherhood. Definitely, after her first work, her art touches the lowest ebb, and she has to lash and whip the dull horse of her poetry to make it go ahead with uncharming gait and unsustaining vitality. It is Monika Varma complaining against *Cyclone in Pakistan* : "I wish I could say I was delighted [at reading] it but, I fear, it has been a matter of great regret to me that, instead of 'the head of a rose,' we are now handed what could practically be called literary doodles."[5]

In *Cyclone in Pakistan*, the degeneration of Namjoshi's art is quite evident. Here the singing voice of an emerging poet, the discerning vision of a true artist, disappears altogether. It appears that the rueful, unfortunate Philomela is silently singing the sad song of life here which nobody is inclined to hear or sympathise with. Who has the time and patience to fall in line of cynicism and disgust? And then, poetry has an ennobling purpose to serve. Even the immediate delight to be derived from poetry is badly missing in it.

Of her cynicism, there can be no two opinions about it. In this connection, therefore, it is pretty difficult for me to accept the verdict of Mrs. Varma when she remarks that "I...miss any trace of horror"[6] in such poems as "Death of Old Adam," "Beauty and the Beast" and "When I Die I Might Be Rich," and a host of others. It is a sure sign of her cynical attitude towards life when she dwells at length on and celebrates the aged and the dead, the ghastly and the appalling. If one were to accept her version of love, as indicated in "Beauty and the Beast," the whole human relationship between man and woman would flounder on the rocks of ruin. Her attitude to God is no better, and she says in "The Lesson"—

Truly, oh God, betwixt you both,
We have learnt *how to suffer.*

(Italics mine)

In another poem, "Aphrodisiac", she compares the human world with 'an ugly woman.' This harsh, inhumane attitude of hers is also reflected in poems like "Terra and the Spectator," "The Unicorn," "The Flea-Bitten Monkey," "The Old Man and the Girl," "My Aging Country," "The Old Country," "Dcaths Just a Shimmer," and "It's a Quality of the Gods." The poem "Death of Old Adam" might have originated in the feelings of pity and sympathy for the dead old man, but it eventually drifts towards Gerontionian whimper and tastelessness, especially in the lines—

Now dirt is dead and hurt is dead.
Not getting is dead.
There's nothing to get.
Let him lie, foul old man.
A little dirt and he'll be gone.

Here the poet is laughing in her sleeves at the poverty and foulness of the dead old guy, and apparently she is comparing him to 'dirt' which is unjust and undignified not only for him but for the entire humanity. Mere wit is not enough for the survival of man. What he should equip himself with is the feeling for others, — the feeling for which poets and philosophers have ever pleaded down the ages. It was actually the lack of this feeling that T.S. Eliot bewailed in *The Waste Land*— "...each in his prison/Thinking of the key."[7] Wordsworth in his famous sonnet "The world is too much with us" and Browning in his "The Lost Leader" and Arnold in his popular elegy "Thyrsis" also raised their strong voice against the debased money-mindedness and materialism of modern man which is keeping fellow-feeling at bay.

Namjoshi's propensity for the cruelty and tyranny of life is to be seen in poem after poem. In "Sea-Gull", we have the pithy, almost epigrammatic, statement of the poet—

Take a sea-gull
White, slender-boned,
Snap its back,

In order to prove
That life is cruel.

(Italics mine)

The short, pictorial poetic piece called "Laocoon" also underlines the hardness and cruelty of life :

Life crawls on you,
Like an affectionate snake
... ...
Circling your chest with steel.

The image aptly recalls the horrors of existence, and it does not matter whether the poet states them directly or indirectly. The phrase 'affectionate snake' is really awesome and terrifying. The fact is that poison is poison whether it is catered with sugar-coating or not. The poem relevantly recollects the wise Sanskrit saying — 'Payah panam bhujanganam kevalam visbardhanam.' In her quest for cruelty, Namjoshi does not spare even the gods. The poem "Rationale" brings out in unmistakable terms her spit and venom at the whole creation of God :

Perhaps creation is purely accidental?
Are the stars arranged in sets?
Do they come in a jewel box?
If God were a merchant I could deal with Him
And come away feeling pleasantly cheated.
My God is rock-faced. He does not move.
Perhaps if you push, He'd topple over.

Her chagrin is complete here. She is out to find fault not only with the creation but also with the Creator. I, for one, know several men of eminence who at an advanced age repented for such a malevolent attitude and corrected themselves at long last. Howsoever modernistic, Jungian or Lawrentian one might be, the ultimate resort for a man is the Supreme God. Let us hope, Namjoshi will also regret her ill-conceived and ill-digested notions of the universe, God and Man at a later stage when she retires from the active service and concentrates minutely on the vital issues of existence. She has, in fact, written another poem — "It's a Quality of the Gods" — which is simply horrible to think of. It is highly pessimistic, cast as it is in the vein and style of Hardy and Housman, and is irredeemably nihilistic in nature :

> It's a quality of the gods
> To see a creature with its back broken
> And be unmoved,
> ... ...
> The gods are unafraid,
> And the gods are unbroken,
> And cannot love and cannot grieve.

Now, this kind of assertion may be anything but Indian; it may be Greek or Roman in its concept and treatment of the gods as awe-inspiring and unfeeling, but not optimistically Indian at any cost. One simply wonders what made the young poetess so horribly pessimistic and bitingly ironical in her outlook upon life. Had her God died young? It is up to Namjoshi to answer it. But it adds a certain amount of dissonance and disharmony to the fibre of her poetic being.

On the artistic score, too, we find a touch of banality and gimmickry in her work. This is to be witnessed in her content, style and language. There are too many poems in her volumes which may be termed as mere "literary doodles."[8] Of such poems, mention may be made of "Apology," "Various Reasons," "On Stage," "Once I Saw," "In English," "Old Friend," and "Angler" (in the first volume), "Hiatus," "Altitudes," "Q.E.D," "Contemporary," and "Old Flame" (in the second volume), "Alwin Ailey," "Those Astonishing Anglo-Saxons," "The Old Man and the Girl," "How to Be a Foreigner," "Doubledate," "Gill and His Mermaid," "Past Matters," "Whittler," and "Sick in a Strange Country" (in the third volume). These 'literary doodles' have been beautifully compared with 'Tukbandi' in Hindi. They do not possess the qualities of poetry as such — no substantial subject-matter, no suggestiveness in style or treatment, no charm of language. Devoid of these qualities, they appear mostly as mere prose statements. Take the following as examples :

> (1) Brocade and silk, ambergis, attar and cloves,
> My Oriental princes listed to the sound of the exotic.
> A bullock cart trundled past the window.

An Oriental cock in russett, gold and blue
Is very male and doing nothing outside
You roll a heart-shaped *paan* for yourself.
More local colour. Oriental princess,
How can I make these foreigners understand you
are my mother?

("In English")

(2) When I am old and rich and gracious,
I shall have a little chapel in my garden,
And every morning I shall walk there,
Checking the red roses and white.
I shall always pray in a white sari —
White is so becoming to prayer.
In the mornings I shall pray,
In the evenings pour tea.

("The Little Chapel")

Such examples may be easily multiplied, but those that are given above are enough to show the sort of verse Namjoshi more often than not writes. Of the two poems quoted above, the first one suffers from verbosity and pomposity. There are obstruse and difficult words in it for the common reader, but the 'Oriental' colour and flavour that he comes across in it do not add to its poetic quality in any way. And the last line reminds one of the use of Alexandrine by Edmund Spenser where the line seems to drag itself on like 'a wounded snake' (as Alexander Pope would take it). It would have been better had the poetess stopped at 'make these foreigners understand you,' but that was not to be and the result is irretrievably bad poetry telling on the nerves of the reader. Even the purpose in writing the poem is lost in the mazes of its long-winded verbosity and vainglory. The second poem (only the first half is extracted here) is beyond doubt a glaring example of the poetry of statement, which can never be ranked as the poetry of high order. Added to this, it lacks imaginative fervour and deep thought of any kind, and hence one can very well visualize its artistic quality. The lines herein immediately recall those of Wordsworth — 'Cattle are grazing/Their heads never raising...' etc. — but even Wordsworth was assailed by his critics for writing trash verse. We know, he was hit hard by Coleridge in *Biographia Literaria* for this kind of composition, As for Namjoshi, neither she is a Wordsworth nor a Coleridge, as they were well established poets. And when the beginning of a poet is so badly made, what will happen to the verse of senile age? As an objective critic, I must hasten to add that either Namjoshi should learn her art properly or she should let it alone. There is no other alternative. Mere recounting of details or items is well in the known tradition of Walt Whitman, but that great American poet properly understood his poetic tool before he came to write something. This is what Namjoshi ought to have done before taking to versification.

Namjoshi's content is hardly ever valid from the Indian viewpoint. Those who seek for 'Indianness' in her verse will be disappointed. In this case, she is the opposite of Toru Dutt and Sarojini Naidu, of Kamala Das and Monika Varma. Very often she goes to the West for her poems, forgetting the variegated, picturesque landscape of India and her healthy, healing air. And when she becomes aware of her motherland, it is almost always to discover her disfigured face of twisted image. The India of her poetry is the India of poverty and pettiness, of old age and lost lustre. In *More Poems* we have two poems, at least, which bear out this fact : "The Old Country" and "My Aging Country." This attitude towards our country might perhaps become foreigners, but it does not behove Namjoshi crying aloud —

> You lie there,
> Smiling, lazy, wicked,
> Unashamed of yourself,
> Lazy in a blue sea.
> You really don't think
> You might smarten yourself?

("My Aging Country")

Even a cursory glance at lines 2,3 and 4 would convince the reader of her attitude towards her native land. Her earlier affectionate terms and her sense of pride (as seen in "The Old Country") : all go wasted in the face of these lines . And if I am to disclose my mind, there are numberless poems of Namjoshi which unmistakably demonstrate her fondness for the West, and this fondness increases with the passage of time. In *Poems* we do not have any trace of it, but within a span of four years when she published her second and third books of verse this becomes painfully repetitive. In *More Poems* alone, there are no fewer than thirteen poems showing her love of the Western places and customs; — the poems being "Alwin Ailey," "Those Astonishing Anglo-Saxons," "How to Be Foreigner," "Columbia," "America," "Doubledate," "Gill and His Mermaid," "New York Bird," "Sea-Gull," "Glaucus the Grass-Eater," "Theatre of the Absurd in Toronto," "After Ionesco," "Canadiana," and "Lord Randall." Obviously, there is nothing wrong in having cross-cultural contact, but the balance should not tilt in favour of foreign things. And this is precisely what we find in Namjoshi.

Even the style and language of this poet tend to be somewhat stale and unimpressive. In most cases, her poems display a propensity for prosaic, direct statements rather than for poetic, oblique expressions full of rich suggestiveness and moving evocativeness. We have already examined examples of dull, dreary prose statement. In *Cyclone in Pakistan*, we have a poem called "For E.P.," which is cast in the style of a Japanese haiku. The amount of success she achieves in handling it is certainly debatable. Namjoshi does not attempt fresh coinage of words or phrases, but occasionally she deviates from the beaten track of statement and displays her skill in using rhyme in her verse. For instance, in the poem "Doubledate" —

> Jo-Ann and Sally
> On a Friday afternoon,
> Combed their bright hair,
> Preparing for the moon.
> The moon was punctual.
> The pop-corn was salt.
> If there wasn't much else,
> It was nobody's fault.

The gingling metrical pattern is uniformly observed throughout here, producing a sort of nursery rhyme effect. The poem "Courtship" also creates such an impression. At times, the poetess tries to fall in line with the modernists employing speech-rhythm (prosaic, yes) and producing pyramid-like conal verses. Take the following as illustrations :

NOBODY COMMUNICATES ANYMORE

Here,
Here is
My vouchsafe.
Please,
Please,
Don't cry.

("After Ionesco")

and :

Or something
less
dramatic.

("Call This A Forest")

She is definitely not so innovative as Hopkins or Whitman, but she has her own share of it on a smaller scale. She employs big and difficult words, but this is not the usual trait. She can be economical with the help of simple and graspable vocabulary if she so wills. One can cite "At Night" as a pointed example in this matter. Another peculiar characteristic of her style is that she begins a good number of her poems with the word 'Listen;' for instance, such poems as "Cain," "At Night," and "Alwin Ailey." It is more of a trick to capture the attention of the reader than anything else, and sounds more like a fairytale than a lyrical poem.

The point of complaint against her diction is that it is more prosaic than poetic, more literary than realistic, that it is far removed from 'the language as really used by men' (Wordsworth). Here is being advanced just one example of the type of diction often used by Namjoshi :

Mourn Glaucus the Grass Eater, god of the sea.
The fishermen and sailors attend him daily,
By stray word or chance to *read his meaning*.
None save the sea-birds *read his meaning*.

(Italics mine)

This type of language might suit a pamphlet or treatise written in prose, but it definitely does not a poem. There is no fire, no force, no lyricism, no poeticism, in it, and it is this kind of language that has to be lamented. Her occasional metaphors and similes are often eclipsed by it.

There are, then, certain direct literary echoes in the verse of Namjoshi which create a poor impression on the minds of readers. They are so evident in such poems as "Various Reasons," "Aphrodisiac" (Congreve seems to be behind it), "Glaucus the Grass-Eater" (Arnold's "Merman" is reverberated), "Threatre of the Absurd in Toronto" (Shakespeare's shadow looms large over it), and "It's a Quality of the Gods" (Hardy-like). In her love poems we also notice the echo of Browning. What is surprising about these echoes is the fact that they have been introduced in her work without being fully digested. And this is unquestionably the hall-mark of Namjoshi's immaturity in the matter of art.

IV

Having observed the good and bad points of Namjoshi's verse, we can safely state that there is more of artifice than art in it, and that she ought to have learnt her tool first and then written her verses. The promise held out by the first collection has, indeed, remained unrealised in the later collections. As a result, the growth of art is arrested in her case, and she usually resorts to "a dry, ironic, cynical note"[9] in her verse. And for her sheer cynicism and literary manipulations, she can't be rated high as a poet.

REFERENCES

1. Monika Varrna, *Facing Four* (Calcutta : Writers Workshop, 1973), p. 3.
2. Suniti Namjoshi "The Eye," Section 4, cited from *Women Poets of India* (Calcutta : United Writers, 1977), p. 43.
3. M. Varma, *op. cit.*, p. 3.
4. *Idem.*
5. *Ibid.*, p. 8.
6. *Ibid.*, p. 3.
7. T.S. Eliot, *The Waste Land, Collected Poems* (London : Faber & Faber, 1963), II, 413-14.
8. M. Varma, *op. cit.*, p. 8.
9. K.R.S. Iyengar, *Indian Writing in English* (Bombay : Asia Publishing House, 1973), p

19

The Changing Pattern of Love : The Contemporary Scene*

Love is no more treated today as a social taboo as it was in the earlier times. Things are changing fast and events are shaping quickly in the present-day world, and so is the pattern or concept of love. It is no longer an inhibited subject, a thing to be talked about and practised in private. Possibly the movies, the theatre, the radio songs, the television shows, and the newspaper advertisements are some of the significant factors responsible for a shift in our attitude towards love and sex. Nothing is 'a forbidden fruit' for us. The idyllic Adam-Eve days in the charming garden of Eden are now over, and we approach love today in a more realistic and acceptable manner. The shift in our attitude is reflected in our literature, and we are particularly concerned with contemporary Indo-English poetry here. But before we plunge into a consideration of this brand of poetry, as being composed presently, we will have a backflash to take stock of the past situation.

In the 19th century Indo-English poetry, poets usually spoke of love in the glowing Romantic tradition. Love then was idealistic and romantic in essence. For example, Toru Dutt describes the newly sprouting love of Savitri for Satyavan thus :

> What was the meaning — was it love?
>
> Love at first sight, as poets sing,
>
> Is then no fiction? Heaven above

---

*Reprinted with permission of the publishers of *Love & Death in Indian Poetry in English* (Delhi : Doaba House, 1989), pp. 18-32.

Is witness, that the heart its king
Finds often like a lightning flash....

(*Ancient Ballads*, p. 40; Kitabistan edn.)

'*Was it love*?' carries the overtone of uncertainty, and then of divinity, of love born in the pure heart of a virgin for a loyal youth intent in sports. Tom's elder sister, Aru Dutt, who has not written much, speaks of love not much differently :

No longer sleep,
Oh, listen now!
I wait and weep,
But where art thou?

All look for thee, Love, Light, and Song;
Light, in the sky deep red above,
Song, in the lark of pinion strong,
And in my heart, true Love.

(*A Sheaf Gleaned in French Fields*, p. 30; 1876 edn.)

This is actually a translation from the original French, but one can very well read the feelings of the translator in it who took a lot of liberty in her task. Sarojini Naidu was another poetess of the Romantic school, and though she acts as a bridge between the 19th and 20th centuries, exactly like Thomas Hardy in English letters, she could not step out of her cosy bower while dealing with matters of love. Of course, she betrays varying moods and tones in her verse, but the predominant attitude in it is one of self-abnegation and self-surrender. Thus, in the poem "Devotion" forming the last string in "The Sanctuary" (*The Temple*), she says :

Take my flesh to feed your dogs if you choose,
Water your golden trees with my blood if you will,
Turn my heart into ashes, my dreams into dust
Am I not yours, O Love, to cherish or kill?

(*The Sceptred Flute*, p. 231; Kitabistan edn.)

There is a flash of conventionality about this poetic passage, and it creates the impression of having been written by a Classical or Medieval poet of India. The two most important poets, Rabindranath Tagore and Sri Aurobindo, mostly produce love poetry of spiritual-*cum*-mystical nature or with a pronounced message, which is something against which some modern poets, especially the Writers Workshop circle with P. Lal at the top, have risen in revolt, — at least in theory. Smitten by the pangs of love for his dead wife, Tagore writes :

> Bring beauty and order into my forlorn life, woman, as
> you brought them into my house when you lived.
> Sweep away the dusty fragments of the hours, fill the empty
> jars, and mend all that has been neglected,
> Then open the inner door of the shrine, light the candle,
> and let us meet there in silence before our God.

(Cited from *Indian Poetry in English*, ed. A.N. Dwivedi, 1980, p. 77)

And this is how Sri Aurobindo sings in honour of Love :

> It is God who is Love and a boy and a slave for our passion
> He was made to serve;
> It is God who is free and proud and the limitless tyrant
> Our souls deserve.

("Kamadeva," *Collected Poems*, p. 82)

Sri Aurobindo's elder brother, Manmohan Ghose, whose poetry has a genuine ring of passion, also wrote in the conventional mode though with a difference — he poured his 'bleeding heart' into it :

> I mind me how her smile was sweet
> And how her look was gay.
> O, she was laughter, joy complete,
> And can she now be clay?
> I see the roses on her grave,
> They make my sad heart bleed.
> I see the daisies shine like stars.
> And is she earth indeed?

("Can It Be?", *An Anthology of Indo-English Love Poetry*, 1976, ed. Subhas Saha, p. 41)

The theme here is the same as in the quoted poem of Tagore, but Ghose has succeeded in creating an aura of intensity of passion in his piece.

Now, the post-Independence scene. The poetry written during this period shakes itself off from the conservatism of the poets of the preceding age. Their utterances of love tend to be authentic and their approach to it sounds realistic. They speak about love and sex without any inhibitions and treat man and woman as creatures of flesh and blood. They know that India, which is mainly believed to be the land of austerity and asceticism, has had a rich tradition of eroticism, and that Vatsayan's *Kamasutra* (The Maxim of Love) and Kalidasa's *Megh-Doot* (The Cloud-Messenger) are the masterpieces of a wholesome relationship between the two sexes. The Tamil anthology of love poems, *Kurunthohai*, is the best representative of love poetry in early Indian literature, and some of our 'new' poets seek inspiration from it — the poets like A.K. Ramanujan and R. Parthasarathy.

Ramanujan creates an unforgettable situation in his verse to capture a moment of 'burning' passion in a remarkable fashion. Writing of his intense feeling of love for his beloved in his poem "Still Another View of Grace," he says :

> I burned and burned. But one day I turned
> and caught that thought
> by the screams of her hair and said : "Beware.
>
> Do not follow a gentleman's morals
> with that absurd determined air.
> Find a priest. Find any beast in the wind
>
> for a husband. He will give a houseful
> of legitimate sons. It is too late for sins..."

(*The Striders*, p. 43)

Though the entire drama of love-making is enacted here in thought only, the heat of passion is arrested in glowing words and phrases and striking animalistic images. No less impressive are some other love poems of Ramanujan, such poems as "Love Poem for a Wife 1," "Love Poem for a Wife 2" (*Relations*, 1971), "Two Styles in Love," and "Looking for a Cousin on a Swing" (*The Striders*, 1965). The second section of R. Parthasarathy's *Rough Passage* (1977), which is entitled "Trial," is also highly sensuous and romantic. The ninth poem in it partly runs as under :

> A knock on the door :
> you entered,
> Undressed quietly before the mirror

of my hands. Eyes
drowned in the skull
as flesh hardened to stone.
... ...
... ... The touch
of your breasts is ripe
in my arms. They obliterate my eyes
with their tight parabolas of gold.

(*Rough Passage*, p. 39)

One tastes a Keatsian flavour in these lines. Another poet of similar nature is Pritish Nandy, who nicely combines Love and Beauty in his poetry. In one of his poems, he writes thus :

wild Horses rage in your tresses on this savage
night of desire
when primal fire breaks through your loins
descend the dark mountain of sorrow tonight let a
black rain of
stars bath your limbs in blood
wild virgin of death teach me the fury of the night
teach me to bleed and not feel pain...

(*An Anthology of Indo-English Love Poetry*, 1976, p. 26)

Nandy has written a fairly good number of such poems, and he may truly be called the Poet of Love. A cluster of poems entitled *A Stanger Called I* records Nandy's pains and miseries as a lover. In one of them, he writes :

I have travelled all the lonely highways in the
autumn and watched all these lonesome cities pale at
duck. I have held all those tired strangers in my
waves, and whispered stranger secrets now forgotten.
This gypsy satchel carries all my sorrows, this
fatigued evening carries all my songs.

(*Tonight, This Savage Rite*, p. 47)

Another poet of repute, K.N. Daruwalla, has not written much about love and sex, but his poem "Love Among the Pines" is suffused with sensuous appeal :

what makes me whisper
destiny lies
in the parting of hair
in the parting of grasses
in the parting of thighs?
... ...
what is there in my hands that when it sidles into your
blouse
it prowls like an animal that makes you writhe?
turning your nipples into a black sprout of berries?

(*AIELP*, 1976, p. 30)

Such poems are beyond the range of prudish P. Lal, who is now more of a transcreator than a poet. A poem like "The Simplest Love," or "The Bee's Love" will make it amply clear that he cannot speak aloud what he feels within. In "The Bee's Love," we find the following :

This bee is sensible,
Loving fragrance, not flower;
Saint-like and stone-like
Limiting desire.
But lovers are wiser
Than saints or stones,
Loving rings round dark eyes
And brittle bones.
Love like a flower
Has roots that reach
Beyond fragrance, beyond power
Of loving speech.

(*Collected Poems*, p. 18)

Lal is evidently concerned here more with the abstraction of 'love' than with the faithful expression of 'love' as really found in life. As contrasted to this is the approach of Syed Amanuddin, who has composed a fairly good number of love poems. His poetical collections, *The Forbidden Fruit* (1967) and *Lightning and Love* (1973), vomit intense fire and flame of love. Speaking of his love, Syed jots down :

your beauty my love is a glimpse
to me into universal

loveliness, you are nature's
revelation to me Sweetheart
loving you I love the universe

(*The Forbidden Fruit*, p. 29)

Love is verily a self-consuming and self-fulfilling thing, and Syed is fully aware of the tragedy in love, such as in the poem "Tragedy of a Bangle," and of the divinity and unselfishness in it, such as in the following extract :

When Love touches me
beauty sparks unselfing the self

(*The Forbideen Fruit*, p. 37)

Lightning and Love has such remarkable love pieces in it as "Two Love Poems." Another poet of love is Subhas C. Saha, who has produced quite a few slender volumes of verse to date. His love poems abound in romantic yearnings and fitful images. His poem, "The Embrace," emits fire in a language of suggestiveness :

In Konark
I had seen
a man embracing a woman
with careless passion
on an intense stone.
Together,
they carelessly touch
each other's shoulders,
smile caressingly
to each other's
eyes and lips.

(*AIELP*, 1976, p. 8)

Although there is not the feverish tone of infatuation and sensuality of Pritish Nandy or R. Parathasarathy here, it does give us an idea of intense love-making by our forefathers as suggested by the Konark engravings. Another well-known poet of love and sex is Shiv K. Kumar who does not hesitate to offer the details about the ugly and the forbidden. His five volumes of verse have so many love poems in them. This is how he writes in one place :

I carry my bride home—
a fungal seed to breed hydras.

("Broken Columns," IX, *Woodpeckers*, p. 15)

The violence in sex is indicated in the poem "My Son," wherein we havc thc following :

Like a rhino
gored in the groin
I charged into my woman
nuzzling my head
into her supple breasts
like a young calf—
sucked blood from her navel
till the oyster's silver gullet
opened out to receive the drop.

(*Woodpeckers*, p. 22)

In the poem "Koval Beach", Kumar describes natural phenomena in terms of sexual details — "the vaginal creeks/lie open-thighed... .../miss an ovary" (*Cobwebs in the Sun*, p. 26). For him nothing is sacred and religious and in poems like "Goddess Kali," he combines a "pervasively secular attitude" with a "deliberately irreverent contemplation" (M. Sivaramakrishna, *WLWE*, XIV, No. 2, p. 374). His Western education enabled him to look at things and persons from a rational, even ironical, angle, and he laughed scornfully at the priests and the pundits alike. Another poet who frequently resorts to irony is O.P. Bhatnagar, who does not, however, burn in passion like Kumar. Bhatnagar's love poems are mostly sedate and tranquil in nature. His poem, "To my Nearea," lodges a strong protest against the beloved's tyranny and sternness, rendering the poet silent and stark and dashing his hopes to pieces. Many other love poems to be had in his poetic corpus are" : "The One I Loved Most," "Love in a Balance" (*Feeling Fossils*, 1977), "The Best Time To Love," "Adam and Eve," "Sex is Not a Baby Food" (*Angles of Retreat*, 1979), "Saint" and "Striptease" (*Oneiric Visions*, 1980). Bhatnagar's love poems are usually intellectual, whereas emotions are a must for a genuine love poetry which he, unfortunately, lacks. This is how he writes in "Adam and Eve" about the modern malaise of eve-teasing by our youths :

When Adam eved
He brought forth a race of men
Who frolicked with women
Even in their dreams.

(*Angles of Retreat*, p. 20)

In the poem "Saint," the satirical intent of Bhatnagar becomes quite obvious. Herein he speaks of a man who was exalted as a saint in his lifetime, but was, after his death, discovered to be a womangoer :

And when he died
More prostitutes came
To mourn the loss.

(*Oneiric Visions*, p. 49)

Bhatnagar is actually a poet who does not make a distinction between love and sex, and in this respect recalls Shiv K. Kumar and Kamala Das to our minds.

As a poet of love in marriage, Nissim Ezekiel, Kamala Das, and Dom Moraes stand out. It is not suggested that their experiences of marriage have been identical, but that this theme is a common factor for them. In this context, they resemble such Western poets as Anne Sexton, Judith Wright, and Robert Lowell. Mark how Ezekiel sings of 'marriage' :

Lovers, when they marry face
Eternity with touching grace.
Complacent at being fated
Never to be separated.
The bride is always pretty, the groom
A lucky man. The darkened room
Roars out the joy of flesh and blood.
The use of nakedness is good.
I went through this, believing all,
Our love denied the Primal Fall.
Wordless, we walked among the trees,
And felt immortal as the breeze.

(*AIELP*, p. 44).

Evidently, this poem smacks of the poet's contentment at his marriage with a supposedly charming woman, though there lurks beneath it a subtle touch of irony too. As opposed to this happiness is Kamala Das's deep despair and frustration at being wedded to an 'unfeeling' man. Writing of her husband in an article, "I Have Lived Beautifully," published in *Debonair*, III, No. 5 (May 15, 1975), 41, she observes thus : "My husband was immersed in his office-work, and after work there was the dinner, followed by sex. Where was there any time left for him to want to see the sea or the dark buffaloes of the slopes?" Her autobiography, *My Story*, is truly the story of her personal predicament right from the beginning of her life, and more so during her married days. This is how Mrs. Das writes in "A Relationship" :

> Betray me?
> Yes, he can, but never physically;
> Only with words ... . :. ...
> ... ... while
> My body's wisdom tells and tells again
> That I shall find my rest, my sleep, my peace
> And even death nowhere else but here in
> My betrayer's arms....

(*Summer in Calcutta*, p. 18)

She, therefore, wants freedom from this sort of thraldom, so that she should be able to assert her own individuality as a human being. And in utter despair, she flings herself to others' arms :

> After that love became a swivel-door,
> When one went out, another came in.

("Substitute," *The Descendants*, p. 7)

But Dom Moraes seems to be jubilant over his conjugal relationship. In the poem "Being Married," he says :

> I lost in night must hear you breathe in whispers,
> Your hater now for spendthrift of my breath :
> Lost in the night we fought; we rushed together
> At frontiers of our miles of loneliness
>   And lived, and parted at a gate
> Where the last touch of lips was meant to bless.

(*AIELP*, p. 53)

In the self-same tone and attitude, A.N. Dwivedi also writes in his poem "Conjugal Love" :

> It was sprightly April,
> and Spring was at hand;
> the moon shone high
> with her heavenly band.
> We, too, had our spring
> in the bloom of our love,
> until it was dawn
> when she left like a dove.

(*Rising Columns*, ed. O.P. Bhatnagar, 1981, p. 91)

One starts seeking love at others' doors, as Kamala Das does, when one is not fully satisfied with the legitimate source.

As a poet of love and sex, Kamala Das is outstanding among Indo-English women writers. She immediately recalls Sylvia Plath Anne Sexton, and Judith Wright to our minds as a poet of 'confessional' mode with sincerity of expression and urgency of purpose. All the above-mentioned poetesses write about love and sex both inside marriage and outside. What a candid voice one comes across in the poem "Substitute!"

> Yet, I was thinking, lying beside him,
> That I loved, and was much loved.
> This physical thing, he said suddenly,
> End it, I cried, end it, and let us be free.

(*The Descendants*, p. 7)

Repeatedly in her poetry Kamala Das speaks of her husband's physical contact, and not emotional one, with her. In "Convicts," she remarks :

> That was the only kind of love,
> This hacking of each others parts
> Like convicts hacking, breaking clods,
> At noon. We were earth under hot
> Sun. There was a burning in our
> Veins and the cool mountain nights did
> Nothing to lessen heat.

(*The Descendants*, p. 26)

But she does not relish this kind of love, and a pervasive gloom, loneliness haunts her day in and day out. The noted Indo-English poet, R. Parthasarathy, rightly remarks that in her poetry "the despair is infectious...." (*Ten Twentieth-Century Indian Poets*, p. 22). She does not like to be treated as a mere object of enjoyment, nor as a mere domesticated 'cat' looking after her man's kids and kitchen, but as an independent, vivacious individual. Hence, she protests vigorously against male domination and cruelty in many of her poems. In the poem "The Old Playhouse," she says :

> You called me wife.
> I was taught to break saccharine into your tea and
> To offer at the right moment the vitamins. Cowering
> Beneath your monstrous ego I ate the magic loaf and
> *Became a dwarf.* I lost my will and reason, to all your
> Questions I mumbled incoherent replies. The summer
> Begins to fall.
>
> (*The Old Playhouse & Other Poems*, p. 1 Italics mine)

In the presence of these heart-rending evidences, it is almost futile to suggest the prevalence of a Radha-Krishna myth in her love poetry, as some Indian scholars have attempted to do.

The only other woman poet who comes, close to Kamala Das in her love poetry is Gauri Deshpande, who, too, is very frank and honest in the articulation of her loveful emotions. She also accepts love and sex within the folds of marriage, but her miserable state is no less pronounced in her work. As an illustration of her frankness and honesty in love-making, we may cite her poem "On a Lost Love," wherein she states :

> I am earth.
> Vast deep and black
> and I receive
> the first rain
> sweet, generous,
> lashing, throbbing;
> its smell forever in my blood
> its imprint deep
> within my quick.
> Yellow daisies burst out

on my breast and thigh
at its very touch.

(*Lost Love*, p. 22)

But soon the mood deserts her, and she is found lamenting her loneliness and emptiness at the loss of her love :

I wanted to weep for you
And me
But I had already spent
All tears in useless mournings.
So now I watch arid eyed
As my fingers open slowly
And let you go.

("I Wanted to Weep," *Between Births*, p. 20)

It would be audacious to speak about the frankness and truthfulness of Margaret Chatterjee and Lila Ray, both being Westerners by birth though not by citizenship (they are now Indians), but there are other women poets like Suniti Namjoshi, Gauri Pant, Lakshmi Kannan, Sunita Jain, Lalitha Venkateswaran, and Meena Alexander, who deserve special mention as singers of love and sex. It may be observed here that women poets are more sincere and candid in the expression of their feelings than their male counterparts, keeping in mind that ours is a conservative society that ties them down to a life of restrictions. This is Suniti Namjoshi speaking :

There's sunshine in the garden.
There are flowers in the hall.
At your gate a love sick heart
Is breaking down the wall.

("Courtship," *Poems*, p. 11)

And this is Gauri Pant :

I walk towards the grave
With a handful of burnt seeds,
Seeds of my gangrened love.
There is a hole in my heart
Which life has dug,

I go the dark way
To find my lost soul.

("Spring," *Weeping Season*, p. 20)

And this is Lakshmi Kannan writing in a different tone from Pant's :

It is love for you
that makes you seem so
mortal to me, suddenly
so fragile
a breath could know you down?
As an object of hate
you stood deathless.

("Love Poem," *Impressions*, p. 10)

And this is Sunita Jain crying for love in despair :

My body bruised,
by your lust teeth marked;
the insatiable searing
of our last love
will it outlive
this despair?
Hold me love, hold me near.

("Hold Me Love," *Man of My Desires*, p. 14)

And this is Lalitha Venkateswaran beaming with love and laughter, beauty and delight, in the company of her lover :

Your love gives beauty back to me.
With you I am invincible.
My body learns a new delight
In its sweet curves and in the shape
Of fitting to your need and you.
I want no mirror now to speak,
Since all reflection's naught with you.

("Fired," *Tree-Bird*, p. 16)

And this is Meena Alexander writing in an erotic fashion :

She leads you
through the gate of salt,
to the foot of the golden thorn.

("Her Imageless Face," 15, *Without Place*, p. 31)

Clearly, love is the subject on which women can speak with emotion and authority. But we have a poetess in Monika Varma who stands apart from others in the celebration of Love. She is much more serious and sober than many other women poets. This should, however, not suggest that she is an inhibited writer, but that she thinks that a woman is more than a mere entity of "sighs and thighs" (*see* her *Facing Four*, p. 24). As a critic, she attacked Kamala Das and Gauri Deshpande on this ground. She has also written a large number of love poems, *e.g.*, "The Question," "The Essence of Living," "Gold-Mulched Hours," "My Loves" and "The Times of Green Leaves is Gold." In her "Gold-Mulched Hours," she notes down :

Gold-mulched hours
those days of rain,
I remember you, my love,
beside me,
held in your arms, loved,
but now the sombre clouds
hide
my gold-mulched hours.

(*Quartered Questions & Queries*, p. 40)

No doubt, the atmosphere of 'the sombre clouds' hangs over her poetry throughout, and thereby Monika succeeds in maintaining a happy, healthy climate in it.

Lastly, contemporary Indo-English poets mark a definite breakaway from the traditional practice of the 19th century poets with regard to the treatment of love. They deal with it without inhibitions or distortions, and do not put on masks in celebrating it, as the poets of the bygone days did. They do not treat it as something idealistic, divine, or idyllic, but as a hard physical reality and as an inevitable biological necessity. Subhas C. Saha, while writing about the 'entire corpus' of modem Indo-Anglian love poetry, rightly remarks that "The proliferation and progression shown in this area...is considerable" (*See* his *Modern Indo-Anglian Love Poetry*, p. 46). Love is a palatable dish, as 'music' was to the Duke in Shakespeare's *Twelfth Night*. The changing pattern of love has been from the romantic-idealists, through the inhibitionists, to the hardcore realists, as Syed Amanuddin points out in his scholarly work, *World Poetry in English* (1981, p. 77). And the common thread running through these three categories is 'romance' that is behind all genuine love poetry.

20

Irony as Technique in Some 'New' Indo-English Poets*

Irony has been a mode of poetic utterance down the ages. All the important Greek and Latin writers — Aeschylus, Sophocles, Euripides, Aristophanes, Plato, Cicero, Horace, Catullus, Tacitus, etc. — had been ironical in their vein and style. English and American writers have been no exception to this general assertion, and Chaucer, Shakespeare, Swift, Gibbon, Byron, Mark Twain, Henry James, and G. B. Shaw have prominently wielded this literary tool in their works. In fact, the list of writers can easily swell with some care and collection, and there is no point in approaching Irony sceptically, keeping in mind its long establishment in the world of letters. The noted scholar, D. C. Muecke, has rightly remarked that irony is "a phenomenon of very considerable cultural and literary importance", and that all representational art, including literature, resorts to "possibility of irony, very often rather than not". (*Irony*, 1970, pp. 1 & 4 respectively). Explicitly, non-representational arts like architecture and landscape gardening, and to a lesser extent music, can hardly afford to be ironical, but graphic arts like painting can definitely be.

From the foregoing observation it is obvious that 'language' is the most effective weapon of irony. But it does not imply that spoken words are the only means of irony. There are, in truth, certain well-marked and well-defined varieties of irony, of which the prominent ones are : Verbal Irony (of which we have just spoken), Dramatic Irony (such as we discover in Shakespeare's

*Reprinted with permission of the editor of *Journal of Literature & Aesthetics*, II, No. 4 (Oct. 1982), 83-94.

Twelfth Night, especially in the conversation of the Duke and Viola), and Irony of Situation (the shining example of which is Shakespeare's *Macbeth*, particularly when Duncan pays a visit to Macbeth's castle to meet his doom there). In Greek tragedies, sarcasm, impersonal irony, self-disparagement, self-betrayal, and simple incongruity are some of the constituent ingredients of irony.

Irony as technique has found favour with several 'new' Indo-English poets, of whom we have selected Shiv K. Kumar, Syed Amanuddin and K. N. Daruwalla for our discussion here. They are called 'new' because they started composing poetry mostly in the 'seventies' (with the exception of one volume of Syed's) and because they have made use of the most modern trends and techniques of English versification. These poets have largely employed Verbal Irony and very rarely Irony of Situation in their writings.

Shiv K. Kumar, a distinguished Professor of English holding a Ph. D. from Cambridge, entered the arena of creative writing in 1970 with his *Articulate Silences*, which was followed by *Cobwebs in the Sun* (1974), *Subterfuges* (1976), and *Woodpeckers* (1979). He has also published a collection of short stories and a novel, but it is as a poet that he is to survive in the creative world. Kumar is one who has assiduously cultivated the technique of irony as a mode of poetic perception. It helps him understand his complex situation as well as the modern man's predicament better. Explaining his position, he once observed : "In view of my extensive travelling in the West, I seem to be constantly returning to the theme of cultural interaction. I feel, unconsciously, I guess, that with me contrast is almost a mode of perception. It is this awareness that compels me to recapture my days in New York as a kind of life-in-death," (*Ten Twentieth-Century Indian Poets*, ed R. Parthasarathy, 1979, p. 53), The 'contrast' about which Prof. Kumar speaks here is nothing but 'irony,' wherein one thing is said but another is meant. Whether he is speaking of marriage, or of love and sex, or of religion and morality, or of family relations, or of cross-cultural contact, he often settles down at the 'contrastive' or 'ironic' technique, which decidedly offers him a unique position and a distinct individuality among the practising Indian poets in English.

Marriage, which forms the subject of a number of Kumar's

poems — "Married Too Long," "Cerebral Love," "Aftermath," "Back to Back,' "A Dark Mood," and "Broken Columns" (from section X on war), unmistakably evokes a dismal picture of horror and revulsion, not unlike Robert Lowell's poem "To Speak of the Woe That is in Marriage." Kumar usually views marriage as "a semi-comic disaster, comedy being its saving grace" (T.R.S. Sharma in an article published in *Tenor*, 4, 1980, p. 24). Throughout these poems, the mood remains melancholy and the tone highly ironical and satirical. "Broken Columns" (which appears in both *Subterfuges* and *Woodpeckers*) is a living example of the ironic attitude of the poet :

> I carry my bride home —
> a fungal seed to breed hydras,
>
> The first sunrise leaves at my door
> a dead cockroach
> in the milk-bottles
> news of the porcupine's resurrection
> and a defaced horoscope.

(*Woadpeckers*, pp. 14-15).

The expression 'a fungal seed to breed hydras' is really horrible and sickening, but well in accord with the fire and fury of the speaker's mood.

Kumar is also ironical in his poetic attitude when he writes about love and sex, which is the most recurrent theme with him. Very often, love degenerates into sex in his treatment, and violence erupts in his writings. He crucifies paradisal love to luxuriate in its perversion. The surfeit of love symbolized by 'a cockroach' in his verse pushes out charity and smoothness completely . If the utter exhaustion in love finds an outlet in the poem "To a Young Wife;"

> Ask me not to act,
> Deed is now my perdition.

(*Subterfuges*, p. 29)

the savage and nerve-breaking irony bubbles up in "The Sun Temple Konarak" :

From every cornice
an owl hoots :
Do, do, do,
but my lady-bird is counting
calories before she slumps
beside me as a tombstone
while I wait for the breakers
to at least cleanse my feet.

(*Subterfuges*, p. 28)

Some other poems of love and sex written by Kumar are : "Kovalam Beach," "My Son," "Young Maidservant," "Midnight Musings," "Before the Beginning," "A Mango Vendor," and "At a Convent."

Our traditional, tabooed society comes under fire in the poetry of Kumar. He hits hard at the established religion and ethical code of conduct. That's why he mingles it with sex and idolizes a prostitute as a goddess. In "To a Prostitute," he writes :

I have come to
join the congregation,
wash my hands at the same font
where others have dropped their fingers
and walked away.

(*Subterfuges*, p. 27)

The same ironic and irreligious attitude persists also in the poems "Kali," "At a Convent," "At the Ghats of Banaras," "Lord Venkateswara's Temple," and many others. The last-named gives us the following :

Here the divine munificence is boundless—
a devoted ruler's elephant was once blessed
with a litter of nine—
all male.

(*Woodpeckers*, p. 40)

And in this world-renowned temple of the Lord, the high priest remains, surprisingly enough, unholy and impure, and he steals occasions to peer at 'the woman's flanks — the length of a cushioned bed.' Similarly; in "At a Convent," the poet notices 'the insurgent breasts' of the nuns 'chained with silver crosses' — a thing that is enough to burn any man to 'ashes' in no time (*Subterfuges*, p. 35).

In handling family relations and cultural interactions, Kumar adopts the same ironic mode of expression. He has, thus, carved out for himself a characteristic technique of his own, which fully reflects the man, and it is the technique of irony without which Kumar will not be a representative voice in Indo-English verse abounding in wit and humour.

The second poet for our consideration here is Syed Amanuddin, who is again a Professor of English stationed in the U.S.A. since long. A prolific writer, Syed has produced some ten volumes of verse, two dramas, one novel, and two books of literary criticism. Not that all his poetical works are replete with irony, and so we will have to concentrate only on *The Children of Hiroshima* (1970), *Poems of Protest* (1972) and *The Age of Female Eunuchs* (1974), wherein ample ironical content is in witness.

The Children of Hiroshima, which concurrently moves on personal, social, and cosmic planes, opens with the title-piece that emphasizes the poet's bitter disillusionment at the happenings around him. In an Eliotian mood and tone, he ironically remarks :

> We are the junk
> no owner looking for us
> we are ashes n bones
> unmarked by tombstones.
>
> (p. 9)

In some of his social poems Syed seizes an opportunity to be satirical and ironical in his observations. Thus, in the poem "Meditations on the Ramazan," he writes :

> feasts for the poor
> fasts for the rich
>   should be the rule
> but the poor eat heavens of imagination
> passing through the hell here
> dreaming of honey and milk and lusty girls
> ... ...
> while the affluent are busy feasting here
>   and buying heavens
>
> (p. 26)

Here the poet unleashes his venom and vitriol against the rich and the affluent. In another poem, "India in Fifties," a very dark, dismal picture is painted of India, putting the messengers of peace, truth and salvation to flight :

> buddha sleeps in the stones of ellora
> gandhi's blood has hallowed the land
> more animals than men prowl the burning desert
>
> legends have reversed
> rama is slain
> multi-headed ravan reigns here
> with his gospel of hate strife bloodshed

(p. 34)

In the prevailing circumstances, only Ravans reign supreme here, perpetrating the evil forces of hate, conflict, and bloodbath.

Poems of Protest also contains a few poems of wit and irony such as "A Child on the BG Campus," "Interview for a Faculty Position at an Indian University," and "The Urinals of Hyderabad." In the first-named poem, we have :

> you need brains little one nobody wants heart
> here you must unlearn the nature that
> you are until you are trained n tested
> for the halls of the wise

(p. 7)

This comes in the form of advice to the child, on whom the poet imposes his own bitter, realisitic experiences of life. The poem "Interview for a Faculty Position" is really impressive for its ironic drive, which exposes the farce of an interview conducted in Indian colleges and universities. And the outcome of this interview is :

> no brothers i was not hired
> to teach composition and poetry
> because i laughed
> and did not summarize
> mourning becomes electra
> three weeks later the postman brought
> the printed rejection slip

thank you alma mater for conferring on me
    the highest academic degree

(p. 10)

It is a very bitter dig at the 'alma mater' whose rejection implies the rejection of its own degrees and testimonials. It is also a sad reflection on the method of appointment the Indian universities resort to. A similar fault-finding instinct is evident in the poem "The Urinals of Hydcrabad" :

the city fathers have built stinking urinals
    near busstops hospitals n railway stations
    you piss into piss standing in piss
when you rush to these aromatic attractions
    in the company of greedy flies
    your bladder about to burst
    and the urgency of emptying acting
    as automatic deodorizer
your innocence
    creates new hopes in me

(pp. 30-31)

The 'stinking urinals' are to be found not only in Hyderabad, but also in many other metropolitan Indian cities, but the case of Hyderabad is very poignant and deplorable, once being the capital of a magnificent ruler popularly known as 'Nizam.'

The Age of Female Eunuchs is ever to be cherished for its long, fine title-piece abounding in witty flashes and ironical remarks throughout. It envisages an age of liberation when women will be "completely free from any male influence leave alone male tyranny." ("Letters to a Reader," *The Age of Female Eunuchs*, p. 9). The dawn of such an age will inevitably bring about a new society and a fresh attitude towards man-woman relationship. Man will no longer be needed for the perpetration and propagation of human race, and womankind itself will manage such affairs. Mark the tone of the speaker (who is a woman) at the possible emergence of such a social order :

before we took over
before sanity prevailed

n earth was safe again
we have BIGSISTERS to think
    n plan for us
middle sisters to supervise
little sisters to work
never before was there such an order
    such a perfect society
adams only dreamed of perfection
but they spent all their time
    enslaving women
    n killing each other
we are the luckiest people on earth.
arent we doctors?

(p. 16)

Evidently, the poet does not like the idea of totally liberated womanhood, as may be gathered from his tone above. In their bid to 'make history' and introduce 'great revolution' against males, women are only trapped in greater chaos and anarchy. They are completely helpless when the 'animals and dragons of ancient stories' (p. 20) rush on them and attack them all over the body, especially between the legs. The poem is, on the whole, highly fantastic in its fabrics, and the poet's imaginative faculty is at its full display here. The irony helps him attain the fulfilment of his desire — that the women's lib movement should collapse, as it ultimately does in the poem.

The third and last poet to be examined now is K.N. Daruwalla, who has four collections of verse to his credit — *Under Orion* (1970), *Apparition in April* (1971), *Crossing of Rivers* (1976), and *Winter Poems* (1980). He has also published a collection of short stories and edited an anthology of Indian poetry in English. As Daruwalla is largely a poet of wider landscapes, spacious plains, lofty mountains, and deep seas and valleys, there is not much scope for irony in his poetry, but still it is not totally ruled out. Occasionally it does surface in his work, rendering it very lively and purposive.

There is a poem called "Pestilence" in Daruwalla's first volume which reveals his ironic bent of mind. Herein he says :

the hospital-floors are marble-white
black bodies dirty them
nurses in white habits
unicef jeeps with white bonnets
doctors with white faces receive them
"who says they have cholera?
they are down with diarrhoea
who says it is cholera?
it is gastro-enteritis
who says they have cholera?"

(*Under Orion*, p. 16)

This passage emphatically depicts the prevalence of the dreaded disease of cholera that nurses and doctors try hard to conceal for fear of public criticism. Another poem cast in ironic form is "Collage I" (1967), where we have :

Who says we have done nothing?
We have abolished zamindari
and liquor and English
and driven the prosses from the G.B. Road

What have we forbidden
veils in front of eyes
or eyes behind veils?
Freeing robbers and rapists
on Republic Day
amnesty adds
"We'll review with sympathy
the cases of the following
pimps, pederasts, poets"

and again :

We have inaugurated crematoriums
with an unclaimed corpse
a V.I.P. has opened
the sluice-gates of a drain
and given it an epithet
"the drain of hope"

It ends in a characteristic manner :

> If we had plague
> Camus-style
> and doctors searched for the virus
> there would be black-market in rats.

(*Ibid.*, pp. 52-53)

The poem "In the Tarai" (to friend Raju) takes a sarcastic turn in its portrayal of the life in the wide-stretching, boggy river-belt across North India. Here Daruwalla writes :

> Bandits of course are everywhere
> scraping the two-inch soil
> from the bone of the land
> burning thatch and chopping fingers
> — with gout or elephantiasis, there is
> no other way of taking a ring off.
> Perverse thought : how would a gold necklace
> be removed from a goitered neck?
> It is not a bad district they all say
> Over the Ghaghra you have a ferry
> to carry your car
> There's an ice factory in town
> (ice that drips and sweats like flesh)
> There's a dhobi in your compound
> but take a tip, don't get your
> bush shirts starched
> they will hang limp all the same
> and smell like an Insemination Centre

(*Ibid.*, pp. 76-77)

The evils of banditry and insanitaion are forcefully depicted in the above lines.

The second volume has made use of the technique of irony in the poems "To Writers Abroad" and "Maulvi Sahib." The poet wisely suggests, in "To Writers Abroad," certain subjects to his writer-brethren abroad to focus on. He says :

> The choice is wide, the space-clad sadhu
> the lunatic in hessian
> or the beggar with the running sore
> It sure feels good, Sir

discussing pus-pockets
with disinfected pen
on sterilized paper

(*Apparition in April*, p. 29)

This poetic extract is, on the one hand, a deplorable commentary on Indian society festerd with sadhus, saints, lunatics and beggars, and, on the other, a seething assault on the writers who write in a closed cello sitting in a distant land and shed crocodile tears on the miseries and grievances of fellow-creatures. The last few lines, in the poem "Maulvi Sahib," tend to be energetically vitriolic and sarcastic, where the poet attempts a penportrait of Maulvi Sahib :

He died with his circumcised
proteges around him
One couldn't help thinking
that had he excised the betel-leaf
with half the zeal he had the foreskin
he may have fared better

(*Apparition in April*, p. 53)

The physical appearance of this Maulvi is such that his skin is pasted to his bones, his pyjamas clinging to his legs, his deadly disease always attacking him, and yet he never gave up chewing betel-leaf mixed up with *zarda* (a kind of tobacco).

Crossing of Rivers, the third volume, also has certain ironic poems in it. "Boat-ride along the Ganga" is one which subtly exposes the age-old Hindu customs and rituals and their custodians living in the holy city of Banaras :

Dante would have been confused here.
Where would he place this city
In Paradise or Purgatory, or lower down
where fires smoulder beyond the reach of pity
The concept of the goddess baffles you —
Ganga as mother, daughter, bride.
What plane of destiny have I arrived at
where corpse-fires and cooking fires
burn side by side?

(*Crossing of Rivers*, p. 1)

The presence of the sacred and mighty Ganga does not mitigate the sufferings of the people. The second "Vignette" highlights the old Hindu city as the repository of 'kites' and 'tonsured heads' where faith has lost all force and where the people and the *pandas* have grown highly superstitious and ritualistic.

Winter Poems, the fourth and last volume, also displays the employment of irony here and there, esp. in "the professor condoles" and "Einstein explains to god the end of the world." In the latter towards the close, we find the following :

> We need someone acclimatized to hell-fires
> to survive the nuclear embers of the world
> someone who can eat
> what is available —
> baked fingers of children
> roasted female rumps
> and limbs charred to soft coke
> in the oven-earth.
>
> Don't tear your hair, Lord.
> If the angels were to see you doing this
> there would be a commotion!
> This is the age of science.
> We have no place for emotion.

(*Winter Poems,* p. 64)

Explicitly, the poet is very bitter and biting here at what he sees in the world happening around him.

To conclude, the three poets discussed here have resorted to the technique of irony for the sake of driving home their viewpoints or observations in an efficacious manner. But it is not that their use of it is quite identical. Prof. Kumar is almost obsessed with it, and at times he does not spare himself. Syed Amanuddin employs it on a rather social plane. And Daruwalla comes to it for the sake of emphasising or elaborating the social and religious evils. Put to the test of time, their apt handling of irony as technique is bound to prove an effective literary tool to further and reinforce the cause of Indian aesthetics.

INDEX

K

L

M

N

P

R